LEISURE ARTS PRESENTS

THE SPIRIT OF CHRISTMAS

CREATIVE HOLIDAY IDEAS
BOOK THREE

◆

More than a day or a season, Christmas is an experience of the heart — one that prompts us to give the very best of ourselves to those around us. Inspired by this understanding, we find that within each of us there lives a little bit of the kind old gentleman we've come to associate with the spirit of giving. Caught up in that same spirit, all our holiday preparations become an expression of the love and warmth that fills our hearts. This special book was written to help you fashion the best celebration ever. With its help, may you discover anew the joys of Christmas and create a memory to carry in your heart throughout the year!

◆

LEISURE ARTS, INC.
Little Rock, Arkansas

THE SPIRIT OF CHRISTMAS
BOOK THREE

EDITORIAL STAFF

Editor-in-Chief: Anne Van Wagner Young
Managing Editor: Sandra Graham Case
Senior Art Director: Gloria Hodgson
Assistant Editor: Susan Frantz Wiles
Production Director: Jane Kenner Prather
Production Assistants: Sherry Taylor O'Connor and
    Paula Henshaw Moyer
Food Editor: Micah McConnell
Test Kitchen Assistant: Johnnie Mac Henry
Editorial Director: Dorothy Latimer Johnson
Editorial Assistants: Linda Trimble and Marjorie
    Lacy Bishop
Art Director: Melinda Stout
Production Artist: Linda Lovette
Art Production Assistants: Sondra Harrison Daniel,
    Diane M. Hugo, Leslie Loring Krebs, Mike States,
    and Susan M. Vandiver
Photo Stylists: Karen Smart Hall and Jan Vinsant
Copy Assistants: Trisa L. Bakalekos, Eva Marie Delfos,
    Darla Burdette Kelsay, Julie Sowell Platt, Tena Kelley
    Vaughn, and Tammi Foress Williamson
Typesetters: Laura Glover Burris, Tracy Stanley Evans,
    and Vicky Fielder Johnson

BUSINESS STAFF

Publisher: Steve Patterson
Controller: Tom Siebenmorgen
Retail Sales Director: Richard Tignor
Retail Marketing Director: Pam Stebbins
Retail Customer Services Director: Margaret Sweetin
Marketing Manager: Russ Barnett
Circulation Manager: Guy A. Crossley
Print Production Manager: Chris Schaefer

*"...and it was always said of him, that he knew
how to keep Christmas well, if any man alive
possessed the knowledge. May that be truly said of
us, and all of us!"*

— From *A Christmas Carol* by Charles Dickens

International Standard Book Number 0-942237-04-8

TABLE OF CONTENTS

THE SIGHTS OF CHRISTMAS

Page 6

TABLE OF CONTENTS
(Continued)

THE SIGHTS OF CHRISTMAS

◆

There's no other time like Christmas. As the season draws near, the yuletide spirit beckons us to transform our homes with holiday magic. Out come cherished decorations, rich in memories of Christmases past. And with the familiar treasures, we're also stirred to create fresh, new tributes to the season, trimmings that are sure to become tomorrow's heirlooms. Caught up in the festive mood, we create a wonderful atmosphere that becomes our special gift to family and friends — a priceless endeavor that blesses us, too.

◆

W ith the last of the gifts wrapped and the tree trimmed and lighted, families everywhere settle in each year to enjoy their own special Christmas Eve customs. For many, it's a time to hear once again that enchanting poem, "The Night Before Christmas." As parents read this captivating tale of St. Nick's arrival, children sit with their eyes wide in hope and excitement. And for a few moments the story becomes real as listeners and storyteller alike lose themselves in the rhythm of the words. Written by Dr. Clement Clarke Moore in 1822 for his children, this beloved poem continues to bring wonder and delight to all generations.

In this collection, jolly decorations recreate St. Nick's nighttime visit, providing storybook charm all through the house. Colorful stockings hang from a mantel where antique clocks mark the approaching hour of his arrival. And a host of cheery ornaments brighten the tree as Santa climbs a ladder to deliver festive packages.

Instructions for the projects shown here and on the next three pages begin on page 13. Now you can enjoy the special enchantment of Christmas Eve throughout the holiday season.

The enchantment of **The Night Before Christmas Tree** *(page 13)* lies in its delightful array of ornaments. A summary of the trimmings is given on page 13, along with instructions for making the peppermint candy garland and the parchment strips with lines from the poem. Among the gaily wrapped packages and purchased decorations are handcrafted **Santa Ornaments** *(page 14)*, **Reindeer Ornaments** *(page 15)*, **Christmas Mice** *(page 18)*, **Ice Cream Ornaments** *(page 18)*, and **Stocking Ornaments** *(page 14)*.

Too excited to sleep, a family of **Christmas Mice** *(page 18)* scurry about on an antique clock. Their tiny stockings are 3″ long versions of the large **Stockings** *(page 13)* shown at bottom right. A verse from the poem and an assembly of miniature holiday decorations complete this charming centerpiece.

Hung by the chimney with care, these bright, roomy **Stockings** *(page 13)* are perfect for holding lots of surprises from St. Nick's pack. We opened the heel of one stocking to create a cozy home for a cheerful little mouse.

Continuing the cheery red and white emphasis of the tree decorations, this **Ruffled Tree Skirt** *(page 13)* makes the perfect finishing touch for **The Night Before Christmas Tree** *(page 13)*. A miniature ladder comes in handy as **Jolly St. Nick** *(page 16)* and a helpful little mouse deliver gaily wrapped packages.

Settling in for the night after their Christmas Eve journey, **Sleepy Santa** *(page 15)* and his adoring **Reindeer** *(page 19)* companion are ready for a long winter's nap. Joined by a nightcapped mouse, these precious pals make a delightful centerpiece.

Inviting all to join in the merriment of the season, **Jolly St. Nick** *(page 16)* and a **Reindeer** *(page 19)* wearing St. Nick's hat sit happily inside an evergreen wreath. A plaid bow, several sprays of jingle bells, and a greeting from the poem complete this easy-to-assemble wreath.

A **Reindeer Ornament** *(page 15)* sporting plaid antlers and a **Santa Ornament** *(page 14)* make lovable toppers for quick-to-sew fabric bags that will hold bundles of toys. These cheery bags also make an adorable grouping when arranged with cherished toys, books, and holiday decorations.

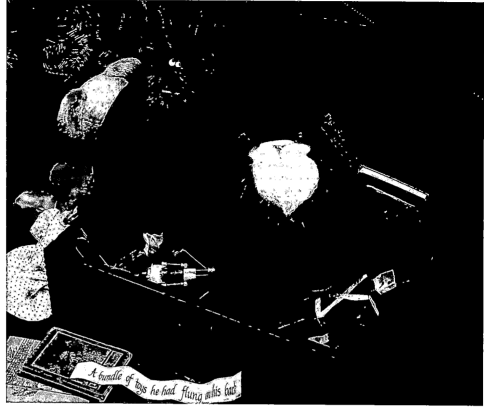

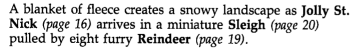

A blanket of fleece creates a snowy landscape as **Jolly St. Nick** *(page 16)* arrives in a miniature **Sleigh** *(page 20)* pulled by eight furry **Reindeer** *(page 19)*.

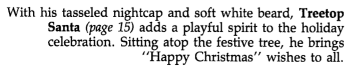

With his tasseled nightcap and soft white beard, **Treetop Santa** *(page 15)* adds a playful spirit to the holiday celebration. Sitting atop the festive tree, he brings "Happy Christmas" wishes to all.

THE NIGHT BEFORE CHRISTMAS TREE
(Shown on pages 8 and 9)

"Not a creature was stirring. . ." except mice, Santas, and reindeer galore on this very Christmasy. tree! Full of cheery red, white, and other traditional Christmas colors, the 7' tall Douglas fir brings to life the famous poem. The Santa perched atop the tree is made from a fabric cone so that he sits easily over the branches of the tree. Instructions are given for the treetop Santa, striped stockings, Santa and reindeer ornaments, ice cream cones, and the Christmas mice that scamper up the 4' long purchased wooden ladder and sit mischieviously on the tree. Also included are instructions for the ruffled tree skirt and jolly St. Nick who carries his pack of toys up the ladder.

Peppermint candies are strung on dental floss to form a garland sweet enough to eat, while packages wrapped in traditional paper and topped with purchased bows peek out from between the branches of the tree. Using a felt-tip calligraphy pen, lines from the poem are written on parchment paper. After cutting the paper into strips, the edges are scorched to give an old-fashioned look.

The finishing touches include purchased items such as the toy nutcrackers dressed in blue, large jingle bells, brass bugles hung from red cording, and strings of electric candle lights. Purchased sprays resembling bare tree branches tipped with tiny jingle bells add extra sparkle.

RUFFLED TREE SKIRT (Shown on page 11)

For an approx. 50" dia. tree skirt, you will need 1¼ yds of 44"w solid fabric, 2⅛ yds of 44"w striped fabric, thread to match fabric, thumbtack or pin, fabric marking pencil, and string.

1. Fold solid fabric in half from top to bottom and again from left to right.
2. To mark outer cutting line, tie one end of string to fabric marking pencil. Insert thumbtack through string 20" from fabric marking pencil. Insert thumbtack in fabric as shown in **Fig. 1** and mark one-fourth of a circle.

Fig. 1

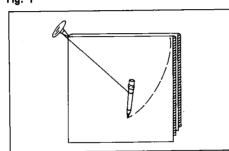

3. To mark inner cutting line, repeat Step 2, inserting thumbtack through string 2" from fabric marking pencil.
4. Following cutting lines and cutting through all thicknesses of fabric, cut out skirt. For opening in back of skirt, cut along one fold from outer to inner edge. Use straight pins to mark remaining folds along outer edge.

5. Fold inner edge of skirt ¼" to wrong side, clipping curve as necessary; press. Fold ¼" to wrong side again; press. Stitch in place.
6. Fold each straight edge of skirt ¼" to wrong side; press. Fold ¼" to wrong side again; press. Stitch in place.
7. (**Note:** Use a ½" seam allowance throughout unless otherwise stated.) For ruffle, cut six 12" x 44" pieces from striped fabric. With right sides facing and matching short edges, sew short edges of pieces together to form one strip.
8. With right sides together, fold strip in half lengthwise. Sew along each short edge. Cut corners diagonally; turn right side out. Matching raw edges, press ruffle flat.
9. (**Note:** For ease in gathering ruffle, break basting threads at seams and leave long thread ends.) Baste ¼" from raw edge of ruffle; baste ¼" from first stitching.
10. Matching short edges, fold ruffle in half; fold in half again. Use straight pins to mark folds along raw edge; unfold ruffle. With right sides together and matching pins, pin ruffle to skirt.
11. Pull basting threads, gathering ruffle to fit outer edge of skirt; pin in place. Using a ⅝" seam allowance, sew ruffle to skirt.
12. Press seam allowance toward skirt. Topstitch along skirt ¼" from ruffle.

STOCKINGS (Shown on page 10)

For each stocking, you will need two 12" x 18" pieces and one 1½" x 8" piece of fabric, two 12" x 22" pieces of artificial lamb fleece, thread to match fabric and fleece, tracing paper, fabric marking pencil, seam ripper (optional), hot glue gun, glue sticks, and desired items to decorate stocking (we used large Christmas Mice, page 18; one Santa Ornament, page 14; artificial greenery; peppermint candies; ⅞"w satin ribbon; and one ½" dia. jingle bell tied to ⅛"w satin ribbon).

1. Matching arrows to form one pattern, trace stocking pattern, page 45, onto tracing paper; cut out.
2. Leaving top edge open, use stocking pattern and follow **Sewing Shapes**, page 156, to make stocking from 12" x 18" fabric pieces.
3. For lining, use fleece pieces and repeat Step 2, extending top edge of pattern 4" (**Fig. 1**); do not turn right side out. Fold top edge of lining ½" to wrong side; whipstitch in place.

Fig. 1

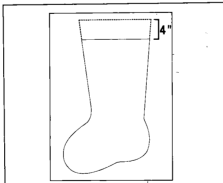

4. With wrong sides together, insert lining into stocking. Fold top edge of lining approximately 3¼" to outside of stocking and tack at side seams.
5. For hanger, fold long edges of 1½" x 8" fabric piece ¼" to wrong side; press. With wrong sides together, fold fabric in half lengthwise and sew close to folded edges.

Matching raw edges, fold hanger in half. Place ends of hanger in stocking at heel side with approximately 3¼" of loop extending above stocking; tack in place.
6. For open-heel stocking, use seam ripper to rip out approximately 5" of seam along heel of stocking. Repeat for lining. Turn raw edges of stocking and lining ¼" to wrong side; whipstitch folded edges together (**Fig. 2**). Fold one side of heel towards stocking; tack in place.

Fig. 2

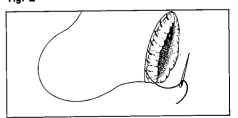

7. Referring to photo, glue desired items to stocking.

SANTA ORNAMENTS (Shown on pages 10 and 12)

For each ornament, you will need two 5" squares of unbleached muslin, two 3½" x 9¼" pieces of red knit fabric, wool roving, thread to match fabrics and roving, one ½" dia. jingle bell, two 4mm black round balls, one ¼" red pom-pom, 9" of 24-gauge gold wire, fabric marking pencil, tracing paper, small crochet hook (to turn fabric), craft glue, polyester fiberfill, cosmetic blush, electric hair crimper, and nylon line (for tree ornament hanger) or one 9" x 16" Fabric Bag (page 156; omit Step 5) and 18" of ⅛"w green satin ribbon (for gift bag).

1. Use Santa head pattern and follow **Transferring Patterns** and **Sewing Shapes,** page 156, to make one head from muslin squares. Stuff head slightly with fiberfill and sew final closure by hand.
2. For hat, place knit fabric pieces right sides together. Use fabric marking pencil to mark center on one short edge. On each long edge, mark 2" from marked short edge (**Fig. 1a**). Connect marks to form a point (**Fig. 1b**). Cutting through both thicknesses of fabric, cut on pencil lines.

Fig. 1a   **Fig. 1b**

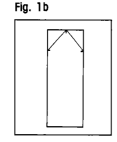

3. Using a ¼" seam allowance and leaving remaining short edge open for turning, sew hat pieces together. Trim seam allowance to ⅛" and cut corners diagonally. Turn hat right side out.

4. For hat cuff, fold raw edge of hat 2½" to wrong side. Fold cuff 1¼" to right side. Tack jingle bell to point of hat. Place hat 1" over straight edge of head; tack in place. Referring to photo, fold point of hat towards face; tack in place.
5. For face, refer to photo and glue balls (eyes) and pom-pom (nose) to head. Blush cheeks.
6. For glasses, bend wire as shown in **Fig. 2**, making each rim approximately ⅜" in diameter. Place glasses over eyes; adjust to fit. Bend ends of glasses around head to secure.

Fig. 2

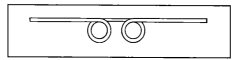

7. (**Note:** Pulling wool roving will create a more natural look than cutting it.) For beard, pull one 10" length of wool roving. Matching short edges, fold length in half. Referring to photo, shape roving as desired and glue fold to face. Use crimper to crimp beard. For mustache, pull one 6" length of roving. Use a small part of length and tie center with thread; knot thread and trim ends close to mustache. Glue mustache to face.
8. For tree ornament hanger, thread 8" of nylon line through fold of hat and knot ends of line together.
9. For gift bag, thread ribbon through center back of head. Tie ornament around top of fabric bag.

STOCKING ORNAMENTS
(Shown on page 10)

For each stocking, you will need two 5" x 8" pieces of fabric, one 1½" x 5" piece of artificial lamb fleece, thread to match fabric and fleece, tracing paper, fabric marking pencil, polyester fiberfill, and 8" of ⅛"w satin ribbon (for hanger).

1. Use stocking pattern and follow **Transferring Patterns** and **Sewing Shapes,** page 156, to make stocking. Fold raw edge of stocking ¼" to wrong side; press.
2. Fold long edges of fleece ¼" to wrong side and whipstitch in place. Referring to photo, whipstitch fleece to top of stocking.
3. For hanger, fold ribbon in half and place ends in stocking at heel side; tack in place.
4. Stuff stocking with fiberfill to within ½" of opening.

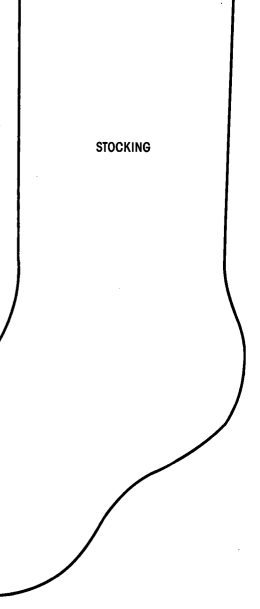

Leave Open

STOCKING

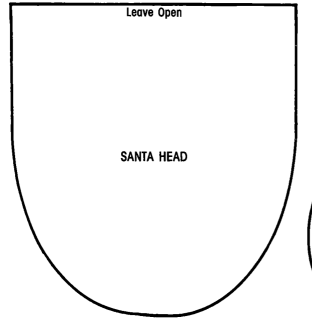

Leave Open

SANTA HEAD

REINDEER ORNAMENTS (Shown on pages 10 and 12)

For each reindeer, you will need two 6" squares and two 2½" squares of brown fake fur, two ¼" white pom-poms, two 5mm black round balls, polyester fiberfill, tracing paper, fabric marking pencil, craft glue, small crochet hook (to turn fabric), and thread to match fur and fabric.

For tree ornament, you will also need four 6" squares and two 2½" squares of light brown felt, one ¾" red pom-pom, 9" of ⅝"w white satin ribbon, 9" of ⅜"w red satin ribbon, and nylon line (for hanger).

For gift bag, you will also need four 6" squares and two 2½" squares of plaid fabric, one ¾" black pom-pom, 9" of ⅝"w red satin ribbon, one 9" length and one 18" length of ⅛"w green satin ribbon, and one 9" x 20" Fabric Bag (page 156; omit Step 5).

1. Use head pattern and follow **Transferring Patterns** and **Sewing Shapes**, page 156, to make head from 6" fur squares. Stuff head with fiberfill; sew final closure by hand.
2. Use antler pattern and follow **Transferring Patterns** and **Sewing Shapes**, page 156, to make two antlers from 6" felt or fabric squares. Stuff antlers with fiberfill to within ¼" of opening. Fold raw edges ¼" to wrong side; sew final closure by hand.

3. Use ear pattern and follow **Transferring Patterns** and **Sewing Shapes**, page 156, to make one ear from one 2½" felt or fabric square and one 2½" fur square. Repeat for remaining 2½" squares.
4. (**Note:** Refer to photo for Steps 4 – 9.) Securely tack ears and antlers to head at seam line.
5. For eyes, glue one ball to each white pom-pom. Glue pom-poms to head.
6. For nose, glue ¾" pom-pom to head.
7. Center 9" length of narrow ribbon on wide ribbon; glue in place. Wrap glued ribbon around head, overlapping ends at back; glue in place.
8. For tree ornament hanger, thread 8" of nylon line through top center of head and knot ends of line together.
9. For gift bag, thread 18" length of ribbon through center back of head. Tie ornament around top of fabric bag.

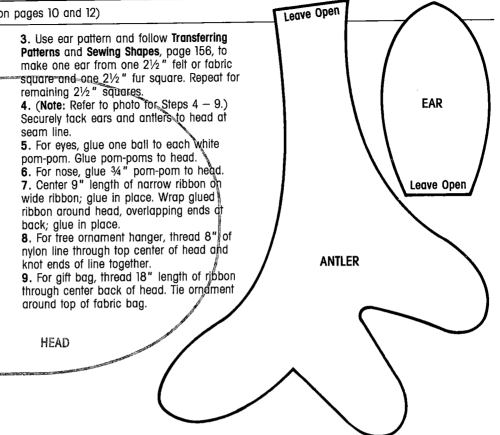

Leave Open

EAR

Leave Open

ANTLER

HEAD

TREETOP AND SLEEPY SANTAS (Shown on pages 11 and 12)

You will need one 22" square of heavyweight fusible interfacing, one 14" square and one 4" square of flesh-colored fabric, wool roving, black embroidery floss, one ⅜" dia. and one ¼" dia. dowel (or pencils of similar size), craft glue, spring-type clothespins, small crochet hook (to turn fabric), heavy thread (buttonhole twist), thread to match fabric, polyester fiberfill, tracing paper, fabric marking pencil, cosmetic blush, thumbtack or pin, string, and spray bottle filled with water.

For Treetop Santa, you will also need one 26" square of red felt (for body, arms, and legs); one 9" x 16" piece of red and white striped flannel (for hat); eight 5" squares of black felt (for hands and feet); one 4" x 28" piece of artificial lamb fleece (for trim); thread to match fleece; and 1 yd of red yarn.

For Sleepy Santa, you will also need one 26" square of red and white striped flannel (for body, arms, legs, and trim); eight 5" squares of flesh-colored fabric (for hands and feet); and one 8" square of red felt (for slippers).

1. For body, use interfacing and follow Steps 1 and 2 of **Ruffled Tree Skirt** instructions, page 13, inserting thumbtack 10½" from pencil; cut out. Cut circle in half.

Using one semicircle as a pattern, place pattern on wrong side of 26" fabric square. Use fabric marking pencil to draw around pattern; cut out body piece ¼" larger than pattern.
2. Following manufacturer's instructions, center and fuse one interfacing semicircle to wrong side of body piece. Fuse remaining semicircle to interfaced side of body piece. Fold raw edges of body piece ¼" to wrong side and glue in place.
3. Form body piece into a cone with an 8" dia. base. Glue overlapped edges (back) in place; use clothespins to hold cone in place while glue dries.
4. Use hand and foot patterns, page 17, and follow **Transferring Patterns** and **Sewing Shapes**, page 156, to make two hands and two feet from 5" squares of fabric.
5. (**Note:** Use a ¼" seam allowance throughout.) For arms, cut two 3½" x 12" pieces of fabric. For legs, cut two 5" x 12" pieces of fabric. With right sides facing, fold one arm piece in half lengthwise; sew long edges together. Repeat for remaining arm and leg pieces.
6. With right sides together and matching raw edges, insert hand into one end of arm. Easing in fullness, sew hand and arm together. Turn arm right side out. Repeat for remaining hand, arm, feet, and legs. Stuff hands and feet only with fiberfill.

7. (**Note:** For Treetop Santa, cut through backing of fleece only.) For trim, refer to photo and measure lengths of areas to be trimmed; add ½" to each measurement. Cut fleece or flannel pieces 1¼" wide by the determined lengths. Fold all edges of each piece ¼" to wrong side and whipstitch in place. Pin pieces in place; whipstitch along long edges.
8. To attach legs, position short edges of legs 1" inside cone at center front. Stitching through interfacing only, whipstitch legs to cone.
9. To attach arms, position short edge of each arm ½" from tip of cone and overlap edges (**Fig. 1**); whipstitch in place.

Fig. 1

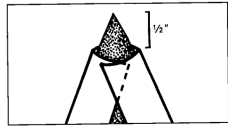

½"

10. For head, cut one 12" dia. circle from 14" square of flesh-colored fabric. Use heavy thread and baste ½" from edge of circle.

Continued on page 16

SANTAS (continued)

Pull ends of thread to slightly gather circle. Stuff circle with fiberfill. Leaving a 1" opening, pull ends of thread to gather circle (bottom of head); knot thread and trim ends.

11. For nose, cut one 2" dia. circle from 4" square of flesh-colored fabric and repeat Step 10, page 15, pulling ends of thread to close opening. Trim fabric ⅛" from basting.

12. (Note: Pulling wool roving will create a more natural look than cutting it.) For hair, pull one length of roving 3" wide and 20" long. Referring to photo, page 11, wrap roving around head; glue in place.

13. For curls, pull five 6" lengths of wool roving and separate each length lengthwise into four pieces. Using ⅜" dia. dowel, wrap one piece of roving around dowel (**Fig. 2**). Lightly mist curl with water and press with warm iron until dry. Without unwrapping curl, gently pull curl from dowel. Repeat to make seventeen beard curls. For mustache curls, use ¼" dowel and repeat to make two curls. Discard unused roving.

Fig. 2

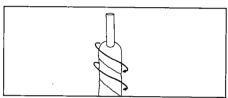

14. (Note: Use straight pins to hold curls in place while glue is drying. Remove pins before glue is completely dry.) Referring to photo, glue eight beard curls to head 1" below top edge of hair to form one layer. For second layer, glue remaining beard curls to head ½" below top edge of hair. Glue mustache curls in place.

15. Position nose above center of mustache; tack in place. Referring to photo, use 3 strands of embroidery floss and Satin Stitch to work ¼" dia. eyes. Blush nose and cheeks.

16. To attach head to body, insert tip of cone through opening in head. Securely whipstitch head to cone.

17. For Treetop Santa hat, use hat pattern, page 17, and follow Steps 9 and 10 of **Jolly St. Nick** instructions on this page (omit jingle bell). For hat tassel, cut six 4½" lengths of yarn. Tack center of lengths to point of hat. Place hat on head; tack in place.

18. For Sleepy Santa slippers, cut four 1½" x 3¼" oval pieces from red felt. Place two pieces together and zigzag stitch around edges. Repeat for remaining oval pieces.

19. Cut four 1" x 5½" pieces from red felt and repeat Step 18. Whipstitch short edges of each piece together to form a loop. Referring to photo, center one felt loop on each slipper; tack in place. Place slippers on Santa's feet.

JOLLY ST. NICK (Shown on pages 11 and 12)

You will need one 12" x 24" piece of flesh-colored fabric, one 18" x 22" piece of red wool fabric, one 5" x 16" piece of artificial lamb fleece, eight 4" x 7" pieces of black felt, heavy thread (buttonhole twist), polyester fiberfill, thread to match fabrics, one ½" dia. jingle bell, wool roving, black embroidery floss, craft glue, small crochet hook (to turn fabric), electric hair crimper, cosmetic blush, fabric marking pencil, tracing paper, and a 4" x 5½" Fabric Bag filled with desired items (page 156; optional).

1. (Note: Use a ¼" seam allowance throughout.) From flesh-colored fabric, cut one 9" x 14¼" piece for body, one 8" dia. circle for head, and one 2" dia. circle for nose. Set circles aside.

2. With right sides together and matching short edges, fold body piece in half. Sew short edges together to form a tube. Using a double strand of heavy thread, baste ½" from one raw edge of body. Pull ends of thread to close end of body. Knot thread and trim ends.

3. Turn body right side out. Using a double strand of heavy thread, baste ½" from raw edge of body (top). Firmly stuff body with fiberfill. Pull ends of thread to close end of body. Knot thread and trim ends.

4. Use arm and leg patterns, page 17, and follow **Transferring Patterns** and **Sewing Shapes**, page 156, to make two arms and two legs from felt pieces. Stuff each arm and leg with fiberfill to within 2" of opening (top).

5. Position top of one arm 1" from top center of body; whipstitch to body. Repeat to attach other arm to opposite side of body. Position tops of legs at bottom center of body with feet facing front; whipstitch to body.

6. From wool fabric, cut one 8" x 20" piece for coat, two 2¾" x 6" pieces for sleeves, and one 8" x 12" piece for hat.

7. For coat, fold one long edge of each sleeve piece ¼" to wrong side; stitch in place. On wrong side of coat piece, use fabric marking pencil to mark center on each long edge. Repeat to mark center on long raw edge of each sleeve piece. With right sides facing, match one center mark on coat piece to center mark on one sleeve piece; sew pieces together (**Fig. 1**). Repeat to attach other sleeve piece. Press seam allowances toward sleeves.

Fig. 1

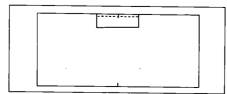

8. With right sides together and matching raw edges, fold fabric in half (**Fig. 2**). Sew where indicated by dashed lines in **Fig. 2**. Clip corners. Fold lower edge of coat ¼" to wrong side; stitch in place. Turn coat right side out.

Fig. 2

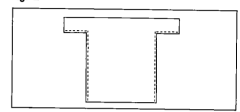

9. Use hat pattern, page 17, and follow **Transferring Patterns**, page 156. Matching short edges, fold 8" x 12" piece of wool fabric in half and place pattern on fold as indicated. Draw around pattern with fabric marking pencil and cut out.

10. Fold curved edge of hat piece ¼" to wrong side; stitch in place. With right sides together and matching straight edges, fold hat piece in half; sew along straight edge. Cut corner diagonally and turn right side out. Tack jingle bell to point of hat.

11. Cutting through backing of fleece only, cut one 1¼" x 16" piece of fleece for coat, two 1¼" x 7" pieces of fleece for sleeves, and one 1¼" x 10¾" piece for hat. Fold long edges of each fleece piece ¼" to wrong side and whipstitch in place. Referring to photo, pin fleece pieces to coat and hat; whipstitch fleece in place.

12. Place coat on body; tack to body at top center.

13. For head, use heavy thread and baste ½" from edge of 8" dia. circle. Pull ends of thread to slightly gather circle. Stuff circle with fiberfill. Pull ends of thread to tightly gather circle (bottom of head); knot thread and trim ends.

14. For nose, use 2" dia. circle and repeat Step 13. Trim fabric ⅛" from basting.

15. Referring to photo, position nose on face; tack in place. Referring to photo, use 3 strands of embroidery floss and Satin Stitch to work ⅛" dia. eyes. Blush nose and cheeks.

16. (Note: Pulling wool roving will create a more natural look than cutting it.) For hair, pull one 12" length of wool roving. Wrap roving around center of head below nose; glue in place. For beard, pull one 9" length of roving. Matching short edges, fold length in half. Gently shape wool roving until beard is approximately 5½" wide at fold. Use crimper to crimp beard. Referring to photo, glue fold of beard to face.

17. Center head on top of body; securely tack head to coat and body. Place hat on head; if desired, tack in place.

18. If desired, place sack over arm and tack in place.

SANTAS AND JOLLY ST. NICK PATTERNS

ST. NICK HAT
Place on fold of fabric
Leave Open
TREETOP SANTA HAT
Place on fold of fabric
ST. NICK LEG
TREETOP/SLEEPY SANTA HAND
Leave Open
Leave Open
TREETOP/SLEEPY SANTA FOOT
ST. NICK ARM
Leave Open

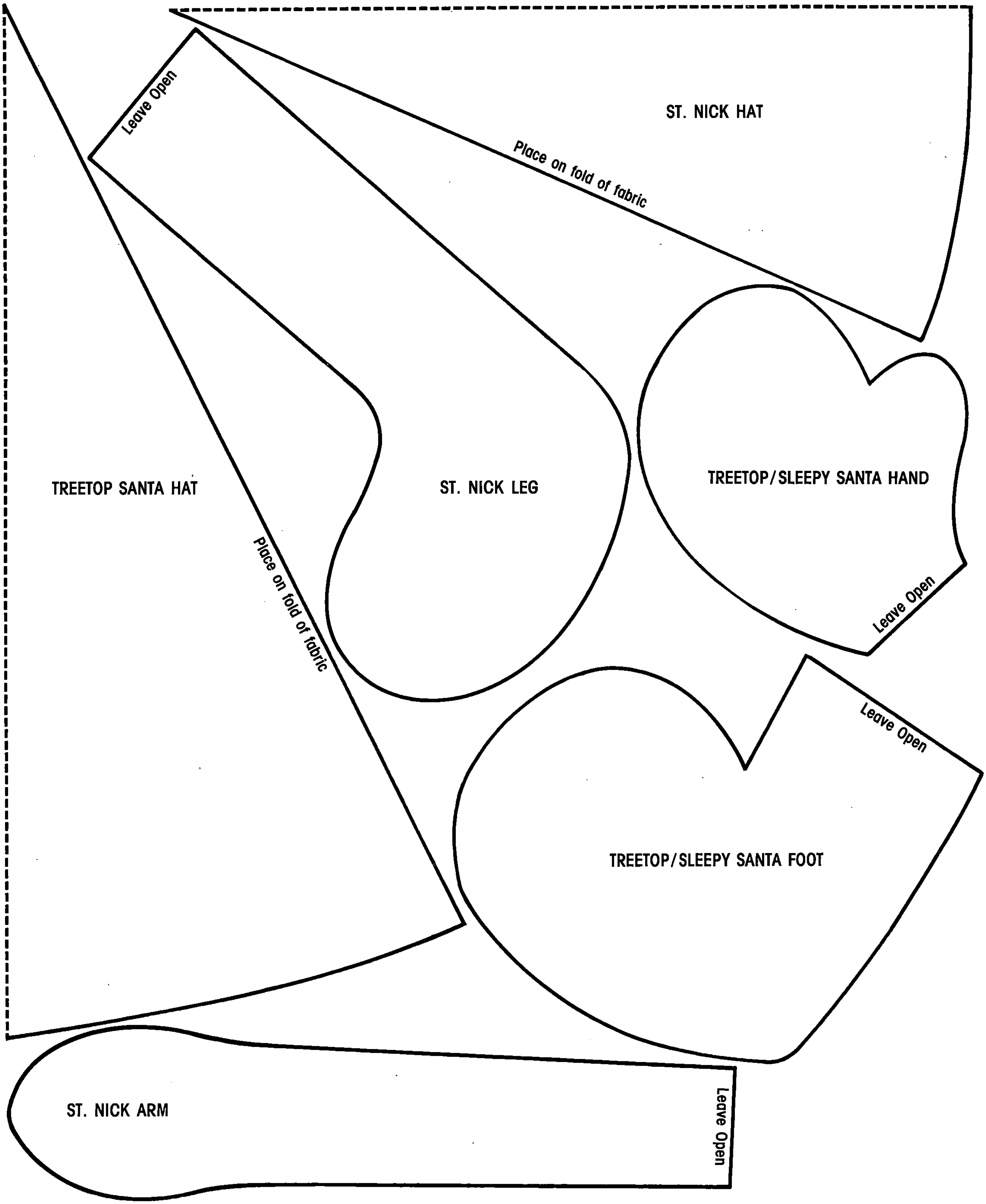

CHRISTMAS MICE (Shown on page 10)

Note: Instructions and supplies are written for the large mouse with sizes and amounts for the small mouse in parentheses.

For each mouse, you will need one 9" (7") square of grey felt, one 1" x 6" piece of black felt, small scrap of pink felt, 2½" (2") long Styrofoam® egg, 10" (8") of 20-gauge florist wire, three 5mm (4mm) black round balls, 9" (7") of black plastic whiskers, craft knife, tracing paper, fabric marking pencil, craft glue, and one floral pin to attach mouse to tree (this "U"-shape pin is available at craft stores).
For nightcap, you will need one 6" (5") square of red and white striped fabric, one ¼" (5mm) white pom-pom, and a small amount of polyester fiberfill.
For granny hat, you will need one 3" square of red fabric, red thread, 9" (7") of ¼"w lace trim, and a small amount of polyester fiberfill.

1. (**Note:** Use black lines for large mouse patterns and grey lines for small mouse patterns.) Trace body, ear, and ear lining patterns onto tracing paper and cut out.
2. Place body and ear patterns on grey felt and use fabric marking pencil to draw around patterns; cut out.
3. Using ear lining pattern and pink felt, repeat Step 2. Matching pointed ends, glue one ear lining to each ear.
4. For nose, refer to **Fig. 1** and use craft knife to trim small end of egg to a point.

Fig. 1

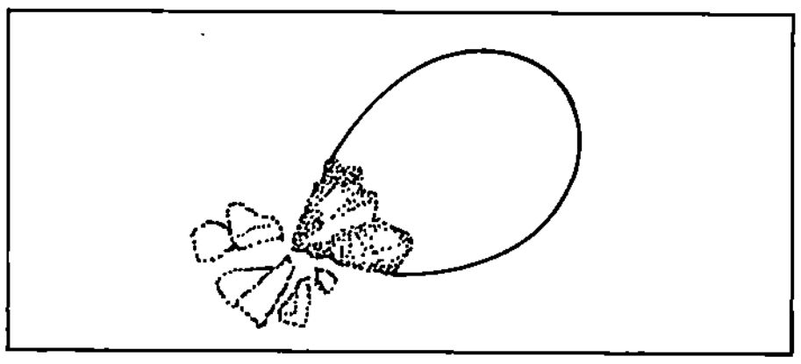

5. With pointed ends of body pieces on nose and with edges touching, glue body pieces to egg. Allow to dry.
6. To attach ears, use craft knife to cut small holes in egg at seam lines 1" (¾") from nose as shown in **Fig. 2**. Place a small amount of glue on pointed end of ears. With ear linings toward nose, use a dull pencil or small scissors to insert one ear in each hole.

Fig. 2

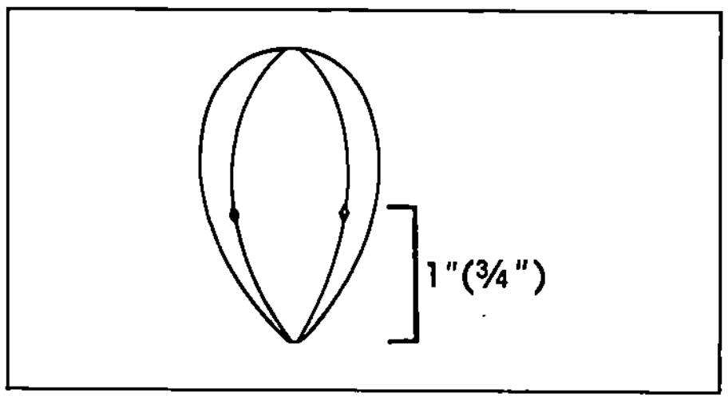
1"(¾")

7. For tail, cut a 4" (3") length of florist wire and a 1" x 5" piece of grey felt. Place a line of glue lengthwise in center of felt piece; place wire on glue. Matching long edges, fold felt over wire. Allow to dry. Trim felt close to wire.
8. To curl tail, wrap one end of tail twice around a pencil. Use craft knife to cut a small hole in the center of large end of egg. Place a small amount of glue on straight end of tail; insert tail in hole.
9. For feet, repeat Step 7 using black felt and a 4½" (4") piece of wire. Referring to **Fig. 3**, bend ends ½" and form felt-covered wire in a "U" shape. With bent ends facing front of mouse, center and glue feet to bottom of mouse; allow to dry.

Fig. 3

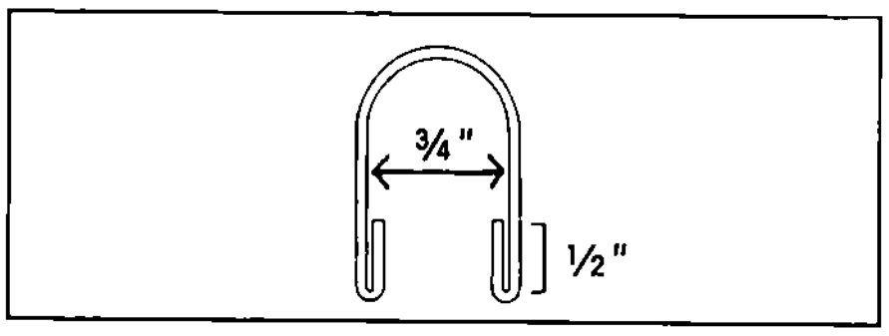
¾"
½"

10. For eyes and end of nose, refer to photo and glue balls to mouse.
11. Cut six 1¼" (1") long whiskers. Insert three whiskers in each side of nose.
12. For nightcap, trace pattern onto tracing paper and cut out. Fold striped fabric in half with right sides together. Place pattern on fold and draw around pattern with fabric marking pencil; cut out. On right side, overlap long edges ¼" to form a cone; glue edges together. Fold bottom edge ⅛" to wrong side and glue. Glue pom-pom to end of cap. Place fiberfill in cap; glue cap on mouse. Fold top of cap to one side; glue in place.
13. For granny hat, use fabric marking pencil to draw a 2½" (2") dia. circle on wrong side of red fabric; cut out. With right sides together and matching edges, sew lace trim to fabric. Press lace trim away from fabric. Baste approximately ¼" from lace trim. Pull basting threads to gather hat; knot thread and trim ends. Place fiberfill in center of hat. Glue hat on mouse.
14. To attach mouse to tree, place branch between prongs of floral pin and insert pin in bottom of mouse.

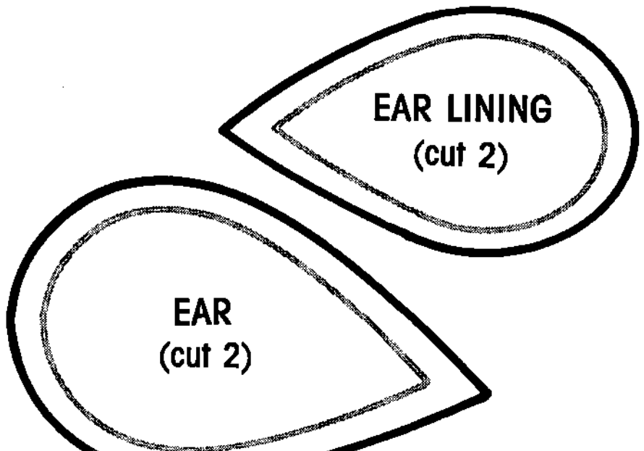
EAR LINING
(cut 2)
EAR
(cut 2)

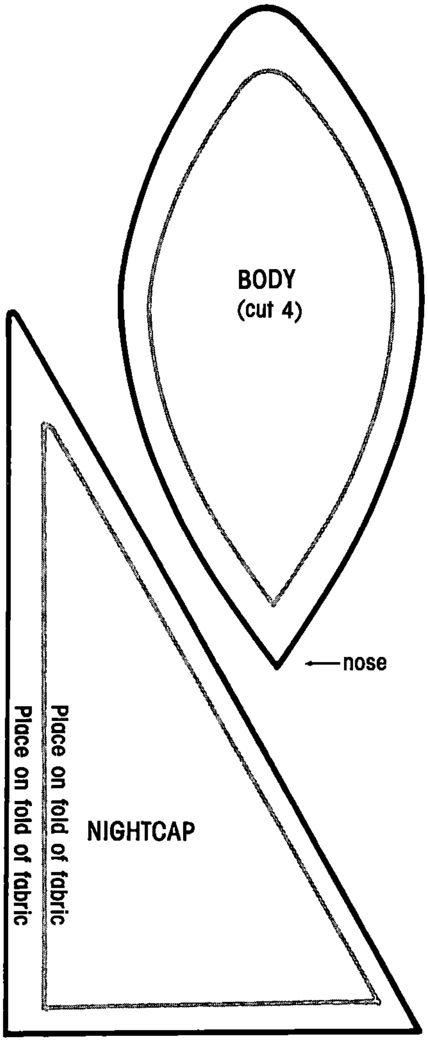
BODY
(cut 4)
nose
Place on fold of fabric
Place on fold of fabric
NIGHTCAP

ICE CREAM ORNAMENTS
(Shown on page 10)

For each ornament, you will need one 2½" dia. Styrofoam® ball, one 4½" long sugar cone, modeling paste (available at craft or art supply stores), candy sprinkles, table knife, one ½" dia. artificial cherry, craft glue, glossy clear acrylic spray, and straight pin and nylon line (for hanger).

1. Glue ball to top of cone; allow to dry.
2. (**Note:** Hanger and sprinkles are added before modeling paste dries.) Use knife to spread modeling paste over ball to resemble ice cream and to form drips down side of cone. For hanger, cut 8" of nylon line and knot ends of line together. Push straight pin through knot. Push pin through top of ball; cover top of pin with paste. If desired, decorate top of ball with sprinkles, lightly pressing them into paste. Allow to dry.
3. Glue cherry to top of ball.
4. Spray ice cream with acrylic spray.

For each reindeer, you will need two 12" squares, eight 7" squares, and two 3" squares of fake fur (draw arrows on wrong side of fur to mark direction of nap); two 3" squares of light brown felt; four 6" squares of dark brown felt; thread to match fur and felt; polyester fiberfill; tracing paper; small crochet hook (to turn fabric); fabric marking pencil; soft sculpture needle; heavy brown thread (buttonhole twist); two ½" white pom-poms; two 5mm black pom-poms; one ¾" red pom-pom (for nose; optional); hot glue gun; and glue sticks.
For harness, bridle, and reins, you will need one ¾" x 12½" piece and one ⅜" x 7½" piece of leather (scraps available at leather craft stores), one 17" length of leather lacing, and five ½" dia. jingle bells.

1. Use body and leg patterns and follow **Transferring Patterns** and **Sewing Shapes**, page 156, to make one body from 12" fur squares and four legs from 7" fur squares.
2. Use antler pattern, page 15, and repeat Step 1 to make two antlers from 6" felt squares.
3. Use ear pattern on this page and repeat Step 1 to make one ear from one 3" fur square and one 3" felt square. Repeat for remaining 3" squares.
4. Stuff body, legs, and antlers with fiberfill; sew final closures by hand. Sew final closures of ears by hand.
5. Referring to photo, tack ears and antlers to body.
6. To attach front legs to body, thread soft sculpture needle with a double strand of heavy thread and securely knot ends together. Referring to patterns and **Fig. 1,** insert needle through one leg at ●, through body at ●, and through second leg at ●. Pull thread until legs are tight against body; securely knot thread and trim ends. Repeat to attach legs to body at **X**.
7. Repeat Step 6 to attach back legs to body.

Fig. 1

8. **(Note:** Refer to photo for Steps 8 and 9.) For eyes, glue one black pom-pom to each white pom-pom; glue to body. If desired, glue red pom-pom to body.
9. For harness, glue ¾" x 12½" leather piece around center of body. Glue jingle bells to top of harness. For bridle, glue ⅜" x 7½" leather piece around head. For reins, knot each end of lacing and glue knots to opposite sides of bridle.

EAR

Direction of nap

Leave Open

BODY
Direction of nap

X ●

LEG

Direction of nap

Leave Open

Leave Open

SLEIGH (Shown on page 12)

You will need one 28" x 36" piece of solid fabric, one 10" x 14" piece of plaid fabric, mat board and poster board (available at art supply stores), craft batting, two skeins of green and one skein of red embroidery floss (for twisted cord trim), tracing paper, fabric marking pencil, craft knife, craft glue, hot glue gun, and glue sticks.

1. Matching arrows to form one pattern, trace sleigh pattern onto tracing paper. Trace side panel pattern onto tracing paper. Cut out patterns.
2. (**Note:** To reverse a pattern, turn pattern over and draw around it again. Mark right sides of all pieces.) Place sleigh pattern on poster board and draw around pattern; repeat for reversed pattern. Cut out. Repeat for mat board, using craft knife to cut out sleigh pieces.
3. Place side panel pattern on poster board and draw around pattern; repeat for reversed pattern. Cut out. Repeat to cut out two side panel pieces from batting.
4. From poster board, cut one 3¼" x 4½" piece (front), one 3¾" x 4½" piece (back), and one 4½" square piece (bottom). Repeat for mat board, using craft knife to cut out pieces.
5. Place solid fabric right side down. Leaving at least 1" between pieces, place sleigh, front, back, and bottom poster board and mat board pieces right sides down on solid fabric. Use fabric marking pencil to draw around each piece. Cut out pieces ½" larger on all sides than pencil lines.
6. Using poster board side panel pieces and plaid fabric, repeat Step 5.
7. For sleigh, place one fabric sleigh piece right side down. Center one poster board sleigh piece on fabric. At approximately ½" intervals, clip edges of fabric to within ⅛" of poster board edges (**Fig. 1**).

Fig. 1

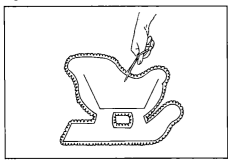

8. (**Note:** Leave corners unworked until Step 9.) Working along one side of sleigh piece, use craft glue to glue fabric to back of poster board (**Fig. 2**). Pulling fabric taut, glue opposite side. Repeat for remaining edges.

Fig. 2

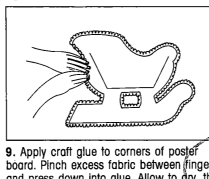

9. Apply craft glue to corners of poster board. Pinch excess fabric between fingers and press down into glue. Allow to dry, then trim excess fabric at corners.
10. Repeat Steps 7 – 9 for remaining poster board and mat board sleigh, front, back, and bottom pieces.
11. For side panel, place one fabric side panel piece right side down. Center one batting piece, then one poster board piece, on fabric. At approximately ½" intervals, clip edges of fabric to within ⅛" of poster board edges. To glue fabric to poster board, repeat Steps 8 and 9. Repeat for remaining side panel pieces.
12. Referring to photo, center side panel pieces on right sides of mat board sleigh pieces; use craft glue to glue in place.
13. To assemble sleigh, hot glue wrong sides of one poster board sleigh piece and one mat board sleigh piece together. Repeat for remaining sleigh pieces. Repeat for front, back, and bottom pieces.
14. Referring to placement lines on pattern, hot glue one edge of bottom piece to poster board side of one sleigh piece. Repeat to glue one short edge of front and back pieces to sleigh piece. Hot glue front and back pieces to bottom piece along adjoining edges.
15. Hot glue poster board side of remaining sleigh piece to back, front, and bottom pieces.
16. For twisted cord trim, unwind skeins of floss and cut each length in half. Align two lengths of green floss with one length of red floss and knot at one end. Fasten knotted end of floss to a stationary object. Pull floss taut and twist tightly. Matching ends, fold cord in half and let cord twist together; knot ends. Repeat for remaining lengths of floss.
17. Referring to photo, use craft glue to glue twisted cord around edges of sleigh.

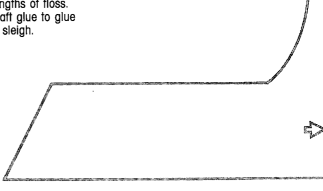

SLEIGH

Back

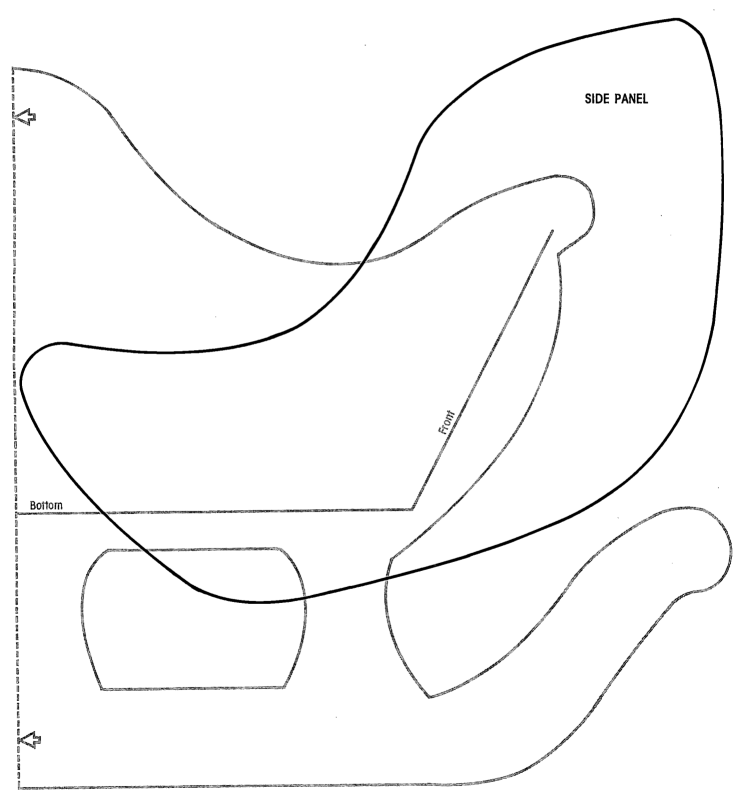

SIDE PANEL

Front

Bottom

Christmas is a time when our sense of neighborly goodwill is heightened by the spirit of the season. Cherished traditions link us to those long-ago times when closely knit communities marked the holidays with jubilant gatherings and cheerful trimmings throughout the house. To recapture the essence of those days, we've created a collection of decorations to fill your home with English Country charm.

At the heart of the collection are tidy little thatched-roof cottages with neatly groomed gardens. Crafted of twisted paper in soft colors, they bring a hint of Victorian romance to the holiday celebrations. A paper garland strewn with flowers winds through the lovely village on the tree, linking the little homes into one sleepy hamlet. Angel candles watch over the peaceful scene as Queen Anne's lace snowflakes bring a wintry look to the tree.

Instructions for the projects shown here and on the next four pages begin on page 28. This year, recapture the joy of Christmas in a peaceful English village — and create collectibles that you'll treasure forever.

A charming English village makes its home in the branches of our **Cottage Christmas Tree** *(page 28)*. A flower-strewn **Twisted Paper Garland** *(page 28)* outlines a path that passes each of the quaint **Christmas Cottages** *(page 29)*. A summary of the trimmings, plus instructions for the Queen Anne's lace snowflakes and plaid ruffle strips, is given on page 28. A plaid and floral **Gathered Tree Skirt** *(page 30)* finishes the tree with a touch of elegance.

An old-fashioned **Home Sweet Home** *(page 33)* design invites feelings of warmth and family love. This sentimental message is stitched on perforated paper, once popular with Victorian ladies.

Touched with romantic appeal, our **Duplicate Stitch Sweater** *(page 30)* makes a lovely gift — or nice attire for your holiday entertaining at home. The rose pattern is easy to add to any knit sweater by using a simple embroidery technique that covers the knitted stitches. A purchased lace collar enhances the feminine look.

Potpourri Sachets *(page 28)* make sweet remembrances for friends who drop by for a holiday cup of tea. To create your own special invitations or cards, pen your message on plain stationery and add a snowflake made of dried Queen Anne's lace.

A tailored cuff gives one of our **Corded Stockings** *(page 32)* a masculine look, while the ruffled floral cuff adds fancy femininity to the other. Paper flowers from the **Twisted Paper Garland** *(page 28),* miniature trees, a lacy scarf, and a watchful angel complete this charming mantel arrangement.

Twinkling with miniature lights, this charming **Cottage Wreath** *(page 28)* beckons family and friends to enjoy a season of peace and goodwill. Nestled among evergreens, the country cottage is ready for the holidays, its festive Christmas tree all alight. A pretty twisted paper bow tops the tranquil scene.

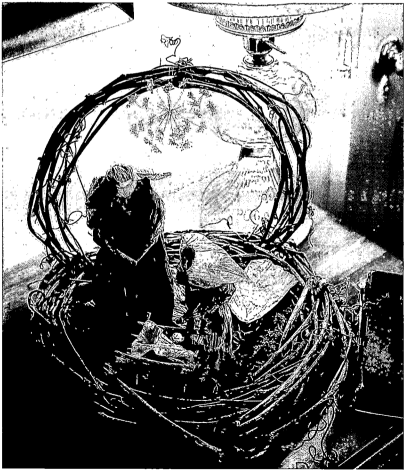

The simplicity of this **Twisted Paper Nativity** *(page 31)* reminds us of the humble circumstances surrounding the very first Christmas. In a rustic grapevine wreath "stable," Mary and Joseph watch over the newborn Baby Jesus.

(Page 27) Set on a backdrop of lacy "snow," this charming **Christmas Village** *(page 29)* brings life to the shelves of an old-fashioned desk. The buildings are crafted in two sizes using our basic patterns, but each is made unique by the different finishing details that you create. In our village, a tiny bell shines from the church tower, ready to herald Christmas Day's dawning. With windows aglow, the King George Inn is ready to comfort weary holiday travelers, and the baker's shop entices passersby to sample tasty goods. An apothecary shop, a tiny cottage, and 6" tall trees complete the village. After Christmas, these collectibles can be displayed for enjoyment all year long.

COTTAGE CHRISTMAS TREE

(Shown on page 22)

Softly colored and rich in detail, the charming cottages sitting in the 7 foot tall blue spruce tree are the star attraction. Made from cardboard forms and Paper Capers™ twisted paper, the two sizes of cottages are imaginatively decorated and landscaped using moss, dried flowers, and an assortment of other common materials. Instructions are given in this section for the cottages, the twisted paper garland decked with flowers, the plaid treetop bow, and the oversize tree skirt that features lots of gathers and poufs.

Dried Queen Anne's lace makes lovely snowflakes for the tree. Gathered in summer, these fresh-picked flowers are dried in a flower press or between the pages of a book. At Christmastime, small blossoms are glued to the centers of larger blossoms. The clusters are then lightly sprayed with white paint, and a loop of nylon line glued to the back of each snowflake forms a hanger.

Ruffle strips made from the same pretty plaid seen at the top and bottom of the tree create a garland of color among the branches. Made from a tightly woven fabric, 2½" x 40" strips are gathered by placing heavy thread along the center of each strip and zigzag stitching over the thread. The heavy thread is pulled to gather the fabric, and the ends are secured with a couple of quick stitches. It's not even necessary to finish the edges of the fabric!

Vanilla-scented angel candles are the last items added to the tree. The 3" high angels are purchased in joined pairs, but even when cut apart and hung singly, they make charming ornaments.

TWISTED PAPER GARLAND (Shown on page 24)

You will need pink, rose, and natural Paper Capers™ twisted paper, tracing paper, brown crepe florist tape, hot glue gun, and glue sticks.

1. Use petal pattern and follow Transferring Patterns, page 156.
2. For each flower cluster, cut a 12" length of pink paper and untwist. Matching arrow on pattern to grain of paper, place pattern on paper and cut out three petals. Place petals together. Referring to grey area on pattern, twist ends together and wrap with florist tape. Refer to photo to arrange petals, using thumb and index finger to roll curved edges of each petal away from flower center. Repeat for rose paper. Place taped areas of two flowers together and wrap with florist tape.
3. For garland, cut desired length of natural paper. Referring to photo, untwist paper, leaving 1" areas twisted between 5" untwisted areas. Place garland on tree and glue flower clusters to garland as desired.

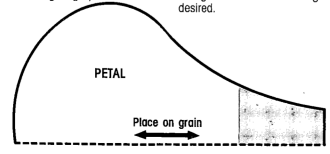

PETAL

Place on grain

COTTAGE WREATH

(Shown on page 26)

You will need one 18" dia. grapevine wreath, small Christmas Cottage with an approximately 5" x 6" decorated yard (page 29; omit grapevine wreath), sprigs of artificial greenery, dried natural baby's breath, one 6"h artificial Christmas tree, 44" of Paper Capers™ twisted paper (for bow), battery-powered miniature white lights, florist wire, hot glue gun, and glue sticks.

Note: For the following steps, refer to photo to assemble wreath.
1. Glue greenery to wreath. Glue cottage, baby's breath, and Christmas tree to wreath.
2. For bow, cut one 20" length of paper. Untwist paper and overlap short edges 1" to form a loop; glue to secure. For streamers, untwist remaining length of paper and tie around center of bow loop. Roll ends of streamers around a pencil to curl ends. Glue bow to wreath. Arrange streamers; glue to secure.
3. Use lights to decorate Christmas tree and wreath. Use pieces of florist wire to conceal wires and batteries behind wreath.

POTPOURRI SACHETS

(Shown on pages 23 and 25)

Sachets can be made from almost any piece of fabric that is at least two times longer than it is wide. We made sachets from 5" x 14", 7" x 20", and 9" x 25" pieces of fabric.

For potpourri, you will need two cups dried rose petals, 1 tablespoon sandalwood chips, 6 drops of rose essential oil, and a jar with a tight-fitting lid.
For each sachet, you will need fabric (see note above), thread to match fabric, lace trim (optional), and Paper Capers™ twisted paper or jute and acrylic paint (for tie).
For appliquéd sachet, you will also need desired fabric motif, lightweight fusible interfacing, fusible webbing, and thread to match motif.

1. For potpourri, mix ingredients together and place in jar. Secure lid on jar. Place jar in a cool, dark, dry place for two weeks. Every few days, shake jar to mix contents.
2. (Note: Follow Step 2 for appliquéd sachet only.) With wrong sides together and matching short edges, fold sachet fabric in half; finger press folded edge (bottom of sachet). Cut interfacing and fusible webbing slightly smaller than fabric motif. Following manufacturer's instructions, fuse interfacing to wrong side of motif. Following manufacturer's instructions, use fusible webbing to fuse motif to sachet fabric where desired; unfold fabric. Using a medium width zigzag stitch and a short stitch length, appliqué motif to sachet fabric.
3. With right sides together and matching short edges, fold sachet fabric in half. Using a ¼" seam allowance, sew sides of fabric together.
4. Fold top edge of sachet ¼" to wrong side; press. If desired, sew lace trim to top edge of sachet. If lace trim is not used, sew close to top edge of sachet. Turn sachet right side out.
5. Fill sachet approximately two-thirds full with potpourri.
6. For paper tie, cut desired length of twisted paper and untwist; cut untwisted paper desired width. Referring to photo, page 23, tie paper in a bow around sachet.
7. For jute tie, cut desired length of jute. Mix 3 parts paint with 1 part water in a small bowl. Dip jute in paint. Squeeze out excess paint; allow to dry. Referring to photo, page 25, tie jute in a bow around sachet; knot and trim ends.

CHRISTMAS COTTAGES

(Shown on pages 22 and 24)

Patterns are given for two sizes of cottages. However, no patterns are given for the details such as doors and windows. The differences in these details create unique cottages — no two are exactly alike.

For each cottage, you will need desired colors of Paper Capers™ twisted paper; tracing paper; poster board; cardboard; ruler; craft glue; craft knife; hot glue gun; glue sticks; sheet moss, dried flowers and weeds, bird gravel (paint grey if desired), sticks, and reindeer moss (for yard); pine needles (for optional roof); and 8" dia. grapevine wreath (for small cottage).

Note: When paper is used in instructions, it refers to untwisted paper.
1. Trace desired cottage pattern onto tracing paper and cut out. Use craft knife to cut out two cottage pieces from cardboard.
2. Use craft knife to cut out the following pieces from cardboard: one 5½" x 7" roof piece and one 4" x 4½" bottom piece for large cottage or one 4¾" x 6" roof piece and one 3⅜" x 3¾" bottom piece for small cottage.
3. (**Note:** To assist in folding cardboard, hold ruler firmly in place where fold is desired; fold cardboard over ruler.) Fold cottage pieces where indicated on pattern; hot glue pieces together to form a rectangle. Cover cottage with paper; use craft glue to secure. Hot glue bottom piece to cottage.
4. (**Note:** Refer to photos for Steps 4 — 8.) For roof, mark center on one long edge; repeat for other long edge. Draw a line connecting center marks; fold roof on line. For paper roof, cover roof piece with paper and use craft glue to secure. For pine needle roof, use craft glue to glue rows of pine needles to roof piece. Cover edges and folded area of roof with small pieces of pine needles. For shingle roof, use craft glue to glue rows of small, folded pieces of paper to roof piece. Hot glue roof to cottage.
5. For door and other details, cut out shapes from poster board. Fold as necessary and cover with paper; use craft glue to secure. Hot glue pieces to cottage.
6. For large cottage yard, draw yard on cardboard approximately 8" x 9" (ours were irregularly shaped); cut out yard. Hot glue cottage to yard. For small cottage yard, cut a piece of cardboard to fit inside grapevine wreath; hot glue to secure. Hot glue cottage to yard.
7. To decorate yard, use craft glue to glue the following items to cardboard: bird gravel for path, sheet moss for grass, reindeer moss for rocks, dried flowers and weeds for plants, and sticks for trees.
8. Use craft glue to glue pieces of sheet moss to cottage.

CHRISTMAS VILLAGE (Shown on page 27)

When adding the details (signs and other features) to the buildings, remember the more personal they are, the more special this village will be.

For each building, you will need supplies for Christmas Cottages (on this page; omit grapevine wreath) and black felt-tip pen with fine point.

1. Follow instructions for Christmas Cottages on this page to make building with an approximately 6" x 7" decorated yard (for large building) or 5" x 6" decorated yard (for small building). Refer to photo to decorate building (cakes and pies are drawn on poster board and displayed in the window of the bakery shop. A small bell is in the church steeple).
2. Use felt-tip pen to write name or address of building on poster board and use craft glue to glue sign to building.

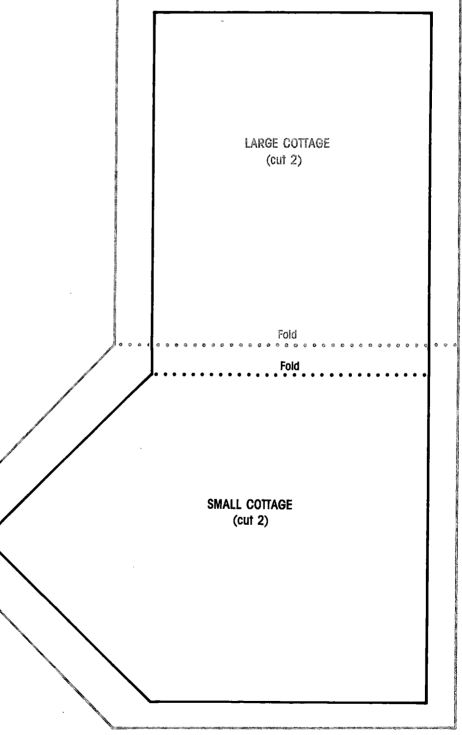

LARGE COTTAGE
(cut 2)

Fold

Fold

SMALL COTTAGE
(cut 2)

GATHERED TREE SKIRT (Shown on page 24)

For an approx. 68" dia. tree skirt, you will need two 54" squares and one 2" x 13" bias strip of fabric for skirt, 4⅔ yds of 1" dia. cord and 1 yd of 54"w fabric for cording, 4 yds of 54"w fabric for ruffle, heavy thread (buttonhole twist), thread to match fabric, fabric marking pencil, thumbtack or pin, and string.

1. For skirt sections, use one fabric square and follow Steps 1 and 2 of **Ruffled Tree Skirt** instructions, page 13, inserting thumbtack through string 25" from pencil. Repeat for remaining fabric square.
2. Follow Steps 3 and 4 of **Ruffled Tree Skirt** instructions, page 13, using both fabric squares.
3. **(Note:** Use a ½" seam allowance throughout unless otherwise stated.) With right sides facing and matching edges, place skirt section pieces together; sew along one straight edge. Press seam open.
4. Fold straight edges of skirt ½" to wrong side and press; fold ½" to wrong side again and press. Stitch in place.
5. To gather skirt, place heavy thread on

wrong side of skirt ½" from inner edge; zigzag stitch over heavy thread, being careful not to stitch into thread. Repeat for outer edge of skirt.
6. Fold all edges of bias strip ½" to wrong side and press. With wrong sides together, fold strip in half lengthwise and press.
7. Along inner edge of skirt, pull heavy thread to gather fabric to fit length of bias strip. Insert raw edge of skirt between folded edges of strip and pin in place. Stitch strip to skirt ⅜" from edge.
8. For cording, cut one 4" x 169" bias strip from cording fabric (piece as necessary). Fold short edges of strip ½" to wrong side; press. On wrong side of fabric, lay cord along center of strip. Matching long edges, fold strip over cord. Use zipper foot and machine baste along length of strip close to cord. At each end, whipstitch opening closed.
9. Use fabric marking pencil to mark 21" lengths along raw edge of cording. With right sides together and matching raw edges, match skirt seam to center mark on cording and pin in place. Match pins on skirt

to remaining marks on cording and pin in place. Pull heavy thread, gathering fabric to fit cording; baste skirt to cording.
10. For ruffle, cut seven 20" x 54" pieces from ruffle fabric. With right sides facing and matching short edges, sew short edges together to form one strip.
11. Fold short edges of strip ½" to wrong side and press; fold ½" to wrong side again and press. Stitch in place.
12. With wrong sides together, fold strip in half lengthwise. Do not press fold. Place heavy thread on fabric ½" from raw edge; zigzag stitch over heavy thread, being careful not to stitch into thread.
13. Fold ruffle into eight equal lengths and use fabric marking pencil to mark folds along raw edge. Matching raw edges and marks, pin ruffle to cording. Pull heavy thread, gathering ruffle fabric to fit cording; baste ruffle to cording through all thicknesses of fabric. Using zipper foot, sew ruffle to skirt as close to cording as possible.
14. Arrange skirt around tree. To pouf ruffle, refer to photo and pull layers of ruffle fabric apart.

DUPLICATE STITCH SWEATER (Shown on page 25)

You will need a sweater with a medium gauge stockinette stitch (5 or 6 stitches per inch works best), Persian yarn (see color key), and a #22 Tapestry needle.

1. Each color square on the chart indicates one Duplicate Stitch (**Fig. 1a** and **Fig. 1b**).
2. Use Persian yarn to work design in center of sweater with top of design approximately 2¼" below bottom edge of neck ribbing. The number of strands of yarn used will vary according to the gauge of the sweater; it may be necessary to increase or decrease the number of strands for adequate coverage.

Duplicate Stitch: To work Duplicate Stitch on sweater, separate strands and thread needle with desired strands of yarn. With right side facing, bring needle up from wrong side of sweater and pull yarn through bottom of stitch, leaving a short end at back to weave in later. Needle should always go between strands of yarn. Insert needle from right to left around knit stitch above, keeping yarn on top of knit stitch, and pull through (**Fig. 1a**). Insert needle back through bottom of same stitch where Duplicate Stitch began (**Fig. 1b**). Following chart, bring needle up

through next stitch and repeat for all charted stitches. Keep tension of stitches even with tension of knitted fabric to avoid puckering.

Fig. 1a 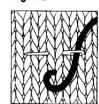　　　**Fig. 1b**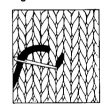

DUPLICATE STITCH SWEATER (43w x 37h)		
PATERNAYAN		**COLOR**
	661	dk green
	662	green
	902	vy dk pink
	905	dk pink
	906	pink
	915	lt pink

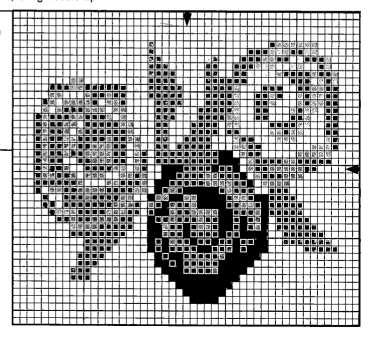

You will need the following colors of Paper Capers™ twisted paper: dk blue, sage green, cornhusk, lt blue, rose, natural, peach, and pink; craft glue; nylon line; jute; two 24mm wooden beads; one 12" dia. grapevine wreath; sheet moss; cardboard; and one Queen Anne's lace snowflake (see Cottage Christmas Tree, page 28).

JOSEPH

1. For head and body, cut one 12" length of cornhusk paper and untwist 3½" at one end of paper. Apply a thin coat of glue to one side of untwisted paper. Place one bead on glued side as shown in **Fig. 1a**. To form head, overlap side edges of paper over bead. Referring to **Fig. 1b**, fold top portion of paper over bead and wrap around bottom of bead (remainder of length is body).

Fig. 1a   **Fig. 1b**

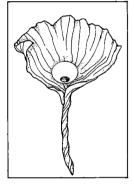

2. For arms, cut one 7" length of lt blue paper and untwist 6". Overlap long edges ½" to form a tube (**Fig. 2**); glue edges together. Allow to dry. Repeat for other arm.

Fig. 2

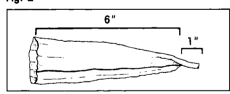

3. To attach arms to body, pinch one arm together 3" from twisted end and flatten remaining 4" (**Fig. 3a**). Apply a thin coat of glue to one side of flattened area. Place pinched area below head and wrap flattened area around body (**Fig. 3b**); allow to dry. Repeat to attach other arm to opposite side of body.

Fig. 3a

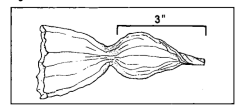

Fig. 3b

4. For tunic, cut two 9" lengths of lt blue paper and untwist. Place paper pieces together. Referring to **Fig. 4**, center base of head between pieces 2" from one short edge; gather paper at base of head and tie with nylon line. Fold pieces down over body. Below arms, overlap long edges ½" and glue edges together; allow to dry.

Fig. 4

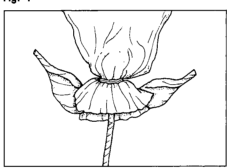

5. (**Note:** Refer to photo for Steps 5 – 8.) For robe, cut one 7" length of dk blue paper and untwist. From untwisted paper, cut one 2½" x 7" and two 1" x 7" pieces. Overlapping short edges ½", place 1" pieces on 2½" piece and glue in place (**Fig. 5**); allow to dry. Place robe on body.

Fig. 5

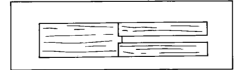

6. For headpiece, cut one 4" length of sage green paper and untwist. To form a triangle, match short edges and fold paper in half; cut a diagonal line from one corner to the opposite corner. Center and glue long edge of triangle piece to top center of head; allow to dry.
7. Cut one 8" length of jute and separate into plies. Tie 1 ply of jute around head; glue in place. Allow to dry. Trim jute ends.
8. Glue hands together; allow to dry.
9. Trim body even with tunic. Cut one 12" length of lt blue paper and untwist; crumple paper. Place paper inside tunic to stabilize figure.

MARY

1. Follow Steps 1 – 4 of Joseph instructions, using rose paper for arms and tunic.
2. (**Note:** Refer to photo for Steps 2 – 5.) For robe, cut one 7" length of pink paper and untwist. Cut paper into two 3" x 7" pieces. From one piece, cut a notch as shown in **Fig. 6**. Overlap notched edge and one short edge of other piece ½" and glue in place; allow to dry. Place robe over body with notched piece in front. Cut one 12" length of jute and separate into plies. Use 1 ply of jute to tie robe in place.

Fig. 6

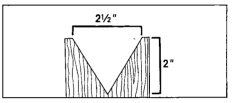

3. For headpiece, cut a 6" length of pink paper and untwist. To form a triangle, fold paper in half lengthwise; cut a diagonal line from one corner to the opposite corner. Center and glue short edge of triangle to top center of head. Glue corners of triangle together; allow to dry.
4. Glue hands together; allow to dry.
5. Trim body even with lower edge of tunic. Fold body 5½" from top of head into a kneeling position.

BABY

1. For baby, cut one 3½" length of cornhusk paper and untwist. From untwisted paper, cut one 4" x 3½" piece. Matching long edges, fold paper in half. Starting at one short edge, roll length loosely and glue in place; allow to dry.
2. For swaddling, cut one 5" length of peach paper and untwist. From untwisted paper, cut one 3½" x 5" piece. Matching short edges, fold paper in half. Center baby on folded paper. Fold paper over baby. Referring to **Fig. 7**, twist ends of paper together and glue in place; allow to dry. Pull folds away from center to reveal "face" (**Fig. 7**).

Fig. 7

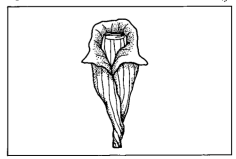

Continued on page 32

NATIVITY (continued)

MANGER

1. For legs, cut four 3" lengths of natural paper. For slats, cut six 3½" lengths of natural paper.
2. Referring to photo and **Fig. 8**, glue lengths together.

Fig. 8

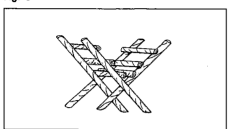

WREATH

1. Cut several semicircular vines from wreath. Twist vines together. Referring to photo, glue vines to wreath (back).
2. Cut cardboard to fit in bottom of wreath. Glue moss to cardboard. Referring to photo, arrange figures in wreath; glue in place. Hang snowflake in center of vines.

TREETOP BOW (Shown on page 22)

You will need ½ yd of 44"w fabric, 1¼ yds of 22"w lightweight fusible interfacing, thread to match fabric, fabric marking pencil, and 12" of florist wire (to attach bow to tree).

1. (**Note:** Use a ¼" seam allowance throughout.) For bow, cut one 10" x 33½" piece from fabric; cut one 9½" x 33" piece from interfacing. For streamers, cut one 8" x 44" piece from fabric; cut one 7½" x 43½" piece from interfacing. Following manufacturer's instructions, center and fuse interfacing pieces to wrong side of fabric pieces.
2. With right sides together, fold bow piece in half lengthwise. Leaving an opening for turning, sew edges together. Cut corners diagonally; turn right side out and press. Sew final closure by hand. Overlap short edges of bow piece 1" to form a loop; sew in place.
3. With right sides together, fold streamers piece in half lengthwise. Referring to **Fig. 1**,

use fabric marking pencil to draw a diagonal line at each short edge. Cutting through both thicknesses of fabric, cut along pencil lines. Leaving an opening for turning, sew edges together. Cut corners diagonally; turn right side out and press. Sew final closure by hand.

Fig. 1

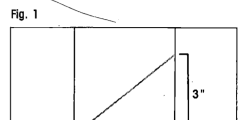

4. Tie streamers around center of bow; adjust streamers to hang down evenly from bow. Insert wire through center back of bow. Twist wire around top of tree to secure.

CORDED STOCKINGS (Shown on page 25)

You will need two 12" x 18" pieces of fabric for stocking, two 3½" x 14½" pieces of fabric for cuff, two 12" x 18" pieces of fabric for lining, one 2" x 5" piece of fabric for hanger, one 1½" x 60" bias strip of fabric (pieced as necessary) and 1⅔ yds of ⅛" dia. cord for cording, thread to match fabric, tracing paper, and fabric marking pencil.
For stocking with ruffled cuff, you will also need one 5" x 34" piece of fabric for ruffle and heavy thread (buttonhole twist).

1. Matching arrows to form one pattern, trace stocking pattern, page 45, onto tracing paper; cut out.
2. Place stocking fabric pieces right sides together and center stocking pattern on top. Use fabric marking pencil to draw around pattern; cut out stocking pieces. Repeat for lining fabric pieces.
3. For cording, lay cord along center on wrong side of bias strip. Matching long edges, fold strip over cord. Use zipper foot and machine baste along length of strip close to cord.
4. Matching raw edges, baste cording to side and bottom edges on right side of one stocking piece; clip seam allowance as needed along curves. Cut off remaining cording; set aside.
5. (**Note:** Use a ½" seam allowance throughout unless otherwise stated.) With right sides facing and leaving top edge

open, use zipper foot and sew stocking pieces together. Trim seam allowance and clip curves. Using regular presser foot, repeat for lining pieces.
6. Matching raw edges, baste remaining cording to one long edge (lower edge) on right side of one cuff piece; trim cording even with short edges of cuff piece.
7. (**Note:** Follow Step 7 for cuff with cording only.) Place cuff pieces right sides together. Using zipper foot, sew lower edges of cuff pieces together; finger press seam open. With right sides facing and matching short edges, fold cuff in half; sew short edges together to form a loop. With wrong sides together and matching raw edges, fold cuff in half so that cording shows at lower edge; press. Mark one side of cuff as wrong side.
8. (**Note:** Follow Steps 8 and 9 for ruffled cuff.) With wrong sides together, fold ruffle piece in half lengthwise; press. Place heavy thread on fabric ¼" from long raw edge; zigzag stitch over heavy thread, being careful not to stitch into thread. Pull heavy thread, gathering ruffle fabric to fit lower edge of cuff piece. With right sides together and matching raw edges, baste ruffle to lower edge of corded cuff piece.
9. Place cuff pieces right sides together. Using zipper foot, sew lower edges of cuff pieces together. Trim seam allowance. With wrong sides together and matching long edges, fold cuff in half so that cording and ruffle show at lower edge; press. With right

sides facing and matching short edges, fold cuff in half; sew short edges together to form a loop. Trim seam allowance.
10. To attach cuff to stocking, place cuff over stocking with right side of cuff facing wrong side of stocking; sew raw edges together. Trim seam allowance and turn stocking right side out. Fold cuff down over stocking.
11. With wrong sides together, insert lining into stocking. Fold top edge of lining ½" to wrong side and pin to stocking.
12. For hanger, fold long edges of hanger piece ½" to wrong side and press. With wrong sides together, fold hanger piece in half lengthwise and press. Sew long edges together. Fold hanger in half to form a loop. Place ends of hanger between lining and stocking at heel side with approximately 1½" of loop extending above stocking; pin in place.
13. Slipstitch lining to stocking and, at the same time, securely sew hanger in place.

HOME SWEET HOME (Shown on page 24)

You will need one 9" x 12" piece of brown perforated paper (14 ct), 9" x 12" piece of brown craft paper, embroidery floss (see color key), craft glue, and desired frame.

1. (**Note:** Perforated paper has a right and wrong side. The right side is smoother and stitching should be done on this side.) Center and stitch design on paper. Use 6 strands of floss for Satin Stitch (**Fig. 1**), 2 for Cross Stitch, and 2 for Backstitch.
2. Glue wrong side of stitched piece to craft paper. Frame as desired (design will fit an 8" x 10" frame without a mat; we used a custom frame).

Satin Stitch: Come up at 1 and down at 2; come up at 3 and down at 4. Repeat stitch as indicated on chart, varying length of stitch as necessary to complete design (**Fig. 1**).

Fig. 1

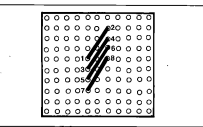

HOME SWEET HOME (103w x 77h)

X	DMC	Satin Stitch	B'ST	ANC.	COLOR	X	DMC	Satin Stitch	B'ST	ANC.	COLOR
△	319		◸	0218	green		931	◸		0921	blue
▨	335			041	pink		932	◸		0920	lt blue
▲	930	◸	◸	0922	dk blue						

Step back in time with us into a little farmhouse on the delta and find comfort and cheer in the simplicity of life long ago. You'll come to admire the hardworking people of those days for their resourcefulness. Their creativity in using the earth's bounty to bring beauty to their humble surroundings was often reflected best in their simple holiday trimmings.

Today our fondness for their homespun fabrics, primitive decorations, and salt-glazed pottery is captured in this nostalgic Old Times Not Forgotten collection. Taking our cue from antique crocks, we created pottery-look ornaments for the tree and the holiday table. Our muslin dolls, fashioned after those that creative mothers shaped from handkerchiefs or fabric scraps, look adorable with these pottery look-alikes. Touches of red, white, and blue mix with the natural and antique items to complete this sentimental scene.

Instructions for the projects shown here and on the next four pages begin on page 40. This year, recreate an old-time Christmas with these heartwarming decorations — and keep the charm alive!

Wearing their prettiest pinafores, these treetop **Muslin Rag Dolls** *(page 44)* play ring-around-the-rosy beneath a canopy of **Cotton Boll Twigs** *(page 43)*. A summary of all the trimmings on the **Old Times Tree** is given on page 40.

A butter crock overflows with lovable **Muslin Rag Dolls** *(page 44)* and easy-to-make **Homespun Hearts** *(page 43)*. These handmade ornaments add a playful touch to any corner or tabletop in the house.

Merry **Muslin Rag Dolls** *(page 44)* dance across the mantel in this cozy country kitchen while **Homespun Hearts** *(page 43)* add a bit of color here and there. These simple-to-make ornaments are clipped to a line of jute with old-fashioned clothespins. Matching fabric bows hold the festive clothesline in place.

Muslin Rag Dolls *(page 44)*, snowy **Cotton Bolls** *(page 42)*, and puffy **Homespun Hearts** *(page 43)* brighten our **Old Times Tree** *(page 40)*. A garland of whole peanuts and a ribbon of woven straw bring a touch of natural beauty to the tree, while **Pottery Balls** *(page 41)* and **Salt Dough Ornaments** *(page 40)*, accented in country blue, add homey appeal. Our cheerful **Tree Skirt** *(page 40)*, fashioned from fringed pillow ticking fabric and red homespun bows, is quick and easy to make. Below the tree, a gift wrapped in brown craft paper and trimmed with a fabric bow coordinates with the decorations.

Your guests will have to look closely to see that the natural-looking bolls on this **Cotton Boll Wreath** *(page 42)* are handcrafted from ordinary cotton and twisted paper. A puffy heart accents the cheery fabric bow. Grouped with a **Pottery Ball** *(page 41)* and salt-glazed crock, the grapevine wreath adds a down-home touch to the mantel.

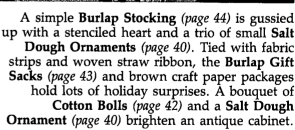

A simple **Burlap Stocking** *(page 44)* is gussied up with a stenciled heart and a trio of small **Salt Dough Ornaments** *(page 40)*. Tied with fabric strips and woven straw ribbon, the **Burlap Gift Sacks** *(page 43)* and brown craft paper packages hold lots of holiday surprises. A bouquet of **Cotton Bolls** *(page 42)* and a **Salt Dough Ornament** *(page 40)* brighten an antique cabinet.

Memories of old-time pillow ticking clothespin bags inspired this cottony **Door Bouquet** *(page 41)*. The **Cross Stitch Doormat** *(page 41)*, with its traditional heart design stitched with blue fabric, offers a cheery welcome to holiday visitors.

Pottery Animal Crackers *(page 40)* and homespun fabric strips transform a bundle of bare branches into an appealing twig tree. A pottery crock, filled to the brim with fresh whole peanuts, holds the delightful arrangement.

Hearty country foods become party fare when the table is dressed up with a **Simple Setting** *(page 40)* of fringed pillow ticking place mats and homespun napkins. Tiny place card muslin rag dolls await holiday diners with open arms. **Pottery Animal Crackers** *(page 40)* march around the bread basket, while **Salt Dough Ornaments** *(page 40)* hold the candles and secure the napkins.

OLD TIMES TREE
(Shown on page 37)

Enjoy decorating this tree that portrays an early period of American life and provides the opportunity to handcraft many of the decorations.

One of two garlands encircling the tree is created by using a long needle to string peanuts on buttonhole twist thread. After Christmas the peanuts could be roasted and enjoyed by a warm fire. The other garland is a purchased 1½" wide woven straw ribbon which is twisted and held to the branches with wooden clothespins.

The look of salt-glazed stoneware is reflected in the salt dough animal ornaments and the "pottery" glass ball ornaments. Complete instructions are given for these ornaments and the cotton bolls, small pillow ticking hearts, red and white plaid heartstrings, and the muslin rag doll ornaments. These dolls, which have a special charm all their own, were originally created when materials were scarce. Larger versions of the ornament dolls are used as a treetop decoration. The larger dolls have pinafores added to their dresses and look very much at home sitting among the cotton boll twigs.

At the bottom of the tree is one of the easiest tree skirts you will ever make. With strips of fabric tied at the corners and fringed edges, very little sewing is required to complete this skirt. Complete instructions explain just how simple it is!

SIMPLE SETTING
(Shown on page 39)

For each place setting, you will need one 13" x 18" piece of pillow ticking fabric for place mat; one 17" square of fabric for napkin; thread to match fabric; Salt Dough Ornament (tree ornament; on this page) and 14½" of jute for napkin ring; and 3½" x 5" piece of poster board, brown craft paper, Place Card Muslin Rag Doll (page 44), and craft glue for place card.

1. For place mat, sew ¾" from all edges of fabric. Unravel fabric to machine-stitched lines.
2. For napkin, fold all edges of fabric ¼" to wrong side; press. Fold edges ¼" to wrong side again; stitch in place.
3. For napkin ring, fold jute in half matching ends. Leaving a loop at back of ornament, thread ends of jute through hole in ornament. Referring to photo, insert napkin through loop and tie jute in a bow at front of ornament.
4. For place card, cover poster board with craft paper and glue in place. Fold poster board in half lengthwise. Referring to photo, glue doll to place card.

TREE SKIRT
(Shown on page 37)

For an approx. 60" square tree skirt, you will need 3⅓ yds of 32"w pillow ticking fabric, thread to match fabric, four 3" x 18" strips of coordinating fabric, fabric marking pencil, string, and thumbtack or pin.

1. Cut two 32" x 60" pieces of pillow ticking. With right sides together and matching long edges (selvages), use a ½" seam allowance and sew along one long edge. Press seam open.
2. Trim 1½" from each selvage so fabric measures 60" square.
3. Fold fabric in half diagonally to form a triangle; fold in half again.
4. To mark cutting line, tie one end of string to fabric marking pencil. Insert thumbtack through string 2" from pencil. Insert thumbtack in fabric as shown in **Fig. 1** and mark one-fourth of a circle.

Fig. 1

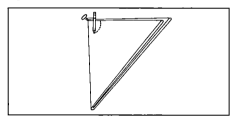

5. Following cutting line, cut through all thicknesses of fabric. For opening in skirt, cut fabric along one fold from one corner to inner edge.
6. Fold inner edge of skirt ½" to wrong side, clipping curve as necessary; press. Fold edges of skirt opening ½" to wrong side; press. Stitch close to folded edges.
7. To fringe skirt, sew ¾" from raw edges of fabric. Unravel fabric to machine-stitched lines.
8. Referring to photo, place tree skirt around tree. Using one fabric strip, tie opening closed at corner. Tie remaining fabric strips at each corner of tree skirt.

POTTERY ANIMAL CRACKERS (Shown on page 39)

Note: This is a decorative project and should not be eaten.

You will need animal crackers; the following colors of Folk Art™ acrylic paint: Platinum Gray, Butter Pecan, and Coffee Bean; Delta Dark Blue Fabric Dye®; small flat paintbrush; small stencil brush; small round paintbrush; toothbrush; small piece of screen wire; hot glue gun; glue sticks; glossy clear acrylic spray; and 4" of jute (for each hanger).

1. Using Platinum Gray and flat paintbrush, paint animal crackers; allow to dry.

SALT DOUGH ORNAMENTS
(Shown on pages 37 and 39)

Note: This is a decorative project and should not be eaten.

You will need 1¼ cups water; 1 cup salt; 1½ cups all-purpose flour; ½ cup whole wheat blend flour; 1 teaspoon Delta Hammered Iron acrylic paint; desired cookie cutters; waxed paper; aluminum foil; medium saucepan; large mixing bowl; two baking sheets; rolling pin; Delta Dark Blue Fabric Dye®; small round paintbrush; glossy clear acrylic spray; and 8" of jute (for each tree ornament) or 1"h wooden candle cup, hot glue gun, and glue sticks (for each candleholder).

1. In saucepan, bring water to a boil. Remove from heat and stir in salt.
2. Mix flours in mixing bowl. Stir in salt mixture and paint. Spread work surface with a light dusting of whole wheat blend flour; turn dough onto surface and knead until paint is evenly mixed and dough is smooth.
3. Cover baking sheets with aluminum foil (dull side up). Roll out dough to ¼" thickness between two layers of waxed paper; remove top layer of paper and cut out ornaments with cookie cutters. Place ornaments on baking sheets. Use a toothpick to make a hole at top center of each tree ornament.
4. Bake ornaments at 250 degrees for approximately two hours, turning ornaments over occasionally. Remove ornaments from oven and allow to cool.
5. Referring to photo, use fabric dye and paintbrush to paint desired details on each ornament; allow to dry. Spray ornaments with acrylic spray; allow to dry.
6. For tree ornament hanger, thread jute through hole in each ornament and knot ends of jute together.
7. For candleholder, glue candle cup to back of ornament.

2. Using an up-and-down stamping motion, use stencil brush to lightly apply Butter Pecan to crackers until most of the grey is covered and colors become mottled; allow to dry.
3. To spatter paint, follow Step 4 of **Pottery Balls** instructions, page 41.
4. Using fabric dye and round paintbrush, refer to photo and paint desired details on front of crackers; allow to dry.
5. Spray crackers with acrylic spray; allow to dry.
6. For each hanger, fold jute in half to form a loop; glue ends of loop to center back of cracker.

POTTERY BALLS (Shown on page 37)

You will need 2½" dia. glass ball ornaments; the following colors of Folk Art™ acrylic paint: Platinum Gray, Dove Gray, Butter Pecan, and Coffee Bean; Delta Dark Blue Fabric Dye®; gesso; small stencil brush; small round paintbrush; tracing paper; graphite transfer paper; removable tape; small piece of screen wire; toothbrush; glossy clear acrylic spray; and one 1" x 8" fabric strip (for each hanger).

1. **(Note:** To achieve the slightly rough texture of pottery, use stencil brush and an up-and-down stamping motion to apply gesso and paint in Steps 1 – 3.) Apply one coat of gesso to balls; allow to dry. Repeat to apply second coat.
2. Mix one part Platinum Gray with one part Dove Gray. Apply one coat of mixture to balls; allow to dry.
3. Lightly apply one coat of Butter Pecan to balls until most of the grey is covered and colors become mottled; allow to dry.
4. **(Note:** For fine, even paint spatters, practice spattering technique on paper before applying paint to balls.) Dip tip of toothbrush in Coffee Bean and brush downwards against edge of screen wire to lightly spatter balls.
5. For motif, trace desired pattern onto tracing paper; trim paper close to pattern.

Cut a piece of transfer paper approximately the same size as tracing paper. Center transfer paper, coated side down, on ball; tape in place. Position pattern on top of transfer paper; tape in place. Draw over lines to transfer pattern onto ball. Repeat to transfer motifs to remaining balls.
6. Referring to photo, use fabric dye and round paintbrush to paint motifs; allow to dry.
7. Spray balls with acrylic spray; allow to dry.
8. For each hanger, thread fabric strip through metal hanger of ball and tie strip to branch of tree.

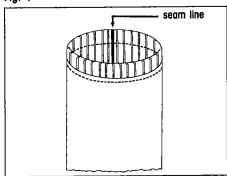

DOOR BOUQUET (Shown on page 38)

You will need one 9" x 5" oval wooden embroidery hoop, one 24½" x 11¾" piece of pillow ticking fabric for bag, one 24½" x 10½" piece of fabric for lining, one 24½" x 11¾" piece of craft batting, one 2" x 44" fabric strip for bow, thread to match fabric, wooden clothespins, small sawtooth hanger, Cotton Boll Twigs (page 43), artificial greenery, 1½"w woven straw ribbon, 7" x 7" x 3" Styrofoam® block, peanuts in shells, wire cutters, brown crepe florist tape, florist wire, hot glue gun, and glue sticks.

1. Baste batting to wrong side of pillow ticking. Treat pillow ticking and batting as a single piece of fabric throughout.
2. **(Note:** Use a ¼" seam allowance throughout.) With right sides facing, sew pillow ticking and lining pieces together along one long edge. Trim seam allowance and press seam open.
3. With right sides facing and matching short edges, fold fabric in half; sew short edges together to form a tube. Turn tube right side out.
4. With wrong sides together and matching raw edges, fold pillow ticking inside lining fabric.
5. Discard outer embroidery hoop (hoop with screw). Insert inner hoop between lining and pillow ticking and pull hoop snugly

against fold (seam should be at center back of hoop). Machine or hand sew below hoop as shown in **Fig. 1**.

Fig. 1

6. Matching seam at center back to center front of bag, flatten raw edges of bag. Sew raw edges together. Turn right side out. Remove basting threads.
7. Tack hanger to top center on back of bag.
8. For straw ribbon loops and peanuts, follow Steps 5 and 6 of Cotton Boll Wreath instructions, page 42.
9. Place Styrofoam® block in bag. Referring to photo, tie fabric strip in a bow around bag; pin clothespins to strip. Arrange sticks, greenery, ribbon loops, and peanuts in bag.

CROSS STITCH DOORMAT
(Shown on page 38)

You will need one approximately 14" x 24" sea grass doormat, 1 yd of 44"w cotton or cotton blend fabric, and one #16 Tapestry needle.

1. Wash and dry fabric. Cut or tear fabric from selvage to selvage into 1½" wide strips.
2. Each colored square on the chart represents one Cross Stitch. To center design (25 stitches wide and 13 stitches high) on mat, match center of mat to center of design (indicated by **X** on design). Using one fabric strip at a time, work design. Secure ends of strips on wrong side of mat by tying ends together or by weaving under previous stitching.
3. Referring to photo, use Running Stitch and fabric strips to work border.

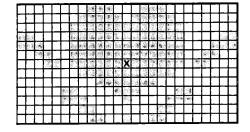

COTTON BOLLS (Shown on pages 36 and 38)

For each cotton boll, you will need sterile cotton (available at drug stores), two 7" lengths of 18-gauge florist wire, brown crepe florist tape, craft glue, 16" of natural Paper Capers™ twisted paper, wire cutters, tracing paper, and glossy wood tone spray (available at craft stores).

1. Beginning 1½" from one end, wrap two lengths of wire together with florist tape. Separate unwrapped sections of wires and cut off ½" from one wire. Pull short wire (branch) away from long wire (stem); wrap separated wires with tape.
2. Use pod pattern and follow **Transferring Patterns**, page 156.
3. Untwist twisted paper and place pod pattern on paper, matching arrow on pattern to grain of paper. Cut out two pod pieces. Insert 1" of stem through center of one pod piece. Pinch center of long edges of pod piece together at wire; glue to secure. Repeat for second pod piece, placing piece opposite first piece. Twist ends of paper ½" on each pod piece (**Fig. 1**).

Fig. 1

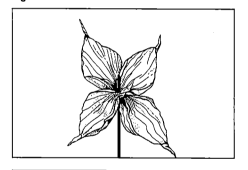

4. Unroll cotton and separate into ½" thick layers. From one layer, pull a small piece of cotton and glue around 1" at top of stem. Pull four pieces of cotton approximately 2" long and 1½" wide.
5. Pinch short ends of one piece of cotton to form points. Glue one pointed end of cotton to cotton-covered section of stem between pod pieces (**Fig. 2**). Roll remaining pointed end of cotton towards stem (**Fig. 3**); glue to secure. Repeat for remaining cotton pieces.

Fig. 2

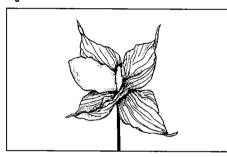

Fig. 3

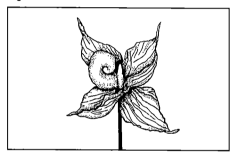

6. Referring to photo, shape each section of pod pieces by cupping lower half and bending upper half toward center of boll.
7. Lightly spray cotton with wood tone spray.

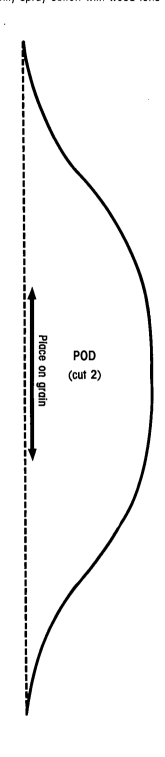

POD
(cut 2)

Place on grain

COTTON BOLL WREATH (Shown on page 38)

You will need one 18" dia. grapevine wreath; desired number of Cotton Bolls (on this page); 1½"w woven straw ribbon; two 3½" squares, one 3" x 20" strip, and one 3" x 24" strip of fabric; thread to match fabric; polyester fiberfill; tracing paper; fabric marking pencil; desired number of peanuts in shells; 18-gauge florist wire; wire cutters; brown crepe florist tape; dried natural baby's breath; hot glue gun; and glue sticks.

Note: For the following steps, refer to photo to assemble wreath.
1. Wrap a length of straw ribbon around wreath; glue ends to back of wreath to secure.
2. For bow, overlap short edges of 3" x 20" fabric strip to form a loop. Keeping overlapped area in center of loop, gather center to form a bow; use small piece of wire to secure. For streamers, gather center of 3" x 24" fabric strip; wire to back of bow. Wire bow to wreath. Arrange streamers; glue to secure.

3. Using small heart pattern, page 43, and fabric squares, follow **Transferring Patterns** and **Sewing Shapes**, page 156. Stuff heart with fiberfill; sew final closure by hand. Glue heart to center of bow.
4. Insert cotton bolls in wreath; trim wires and glue to secure.
5. For each straw ribbon loop, cut one 8" length of straw ribbon and one 4" length of wire. With wrong sides of ribbon together, match short edges to form a loop. Insert 1" of wire between short edges of ribbon and tightly gather ribbon around wire; secure with florist tape. Wrap wire with florist tape. Repeat for desired number of loops. Insert loops in wreath; trim wire and glue to secure.
6. For each peanut, cut one 4" length of wire. Insert ¼" of wire into one end of peanut; glue to secure. Wrap wire with florist tape. Repeat for desired number of peanuts. Insert peanuts in wreath; trim wire and glue to secure.
7. Glue clusters of baby's breath to wreath.

HOMESPUN HEARTS (Shown on pages 36 and 37)

For each clothesline heart, you will need two 6" squares of fabric.
For each pillow ticking ornament, you will need two 3½" squares of pillow ticking fabric.
For each heartstring ornament, you will need six 4½" squares of fabric, 18" of 1-ply jute (separate plies of 3-ply jute), large needle, and one ornament hanger.
You will also need thread to match fabric, polyester fiberfill, tracing paper, small crochet hook (to turn fabric), and fabric marking pencil.

1. For clothesline heart, use clothesline heart pattern and follow **Transferring Patterns** and **Sewing Shapes**, page 156. Stuff heart with fiberfill; sew final closure by hand.
2. For pillow ticking ornament, use small heart pattern and follow Step 1.
3. For heartstring ornament, use small, medium, and large heart patterns and follow Step 1 to make one heart from each pattern. Thread needle with jute. Refer to **Fig. 1** and thread jute through center of hearts, knotting jute above and below hearts. Tie ornament hanger to jute 1" above top of large heart. Trim jute close to knot.

Fig. 1

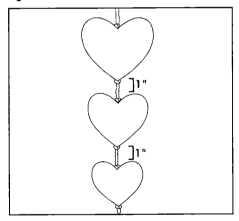

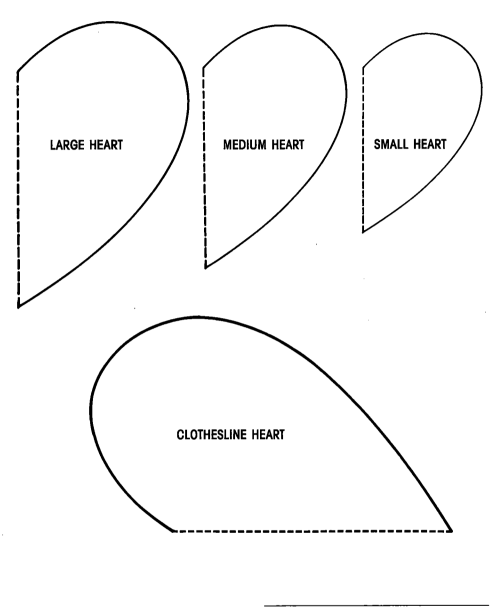

LARGE HEART

MEDIUM HEART

SMALL HEART

CLOTHESLINE HEART

COTTON BOLL TWIGS (Shown on pages 36 and 38)

For each twig, you will need sterile cotton (available at drug stores), one twig with several branches, brown craft paper, tracing paper, craft glue, glossy wood tone spray (available at craft stores), hot glue gun, and glue sticks.

1. Trace pod pattern onto tracing paper and cut out.
2. To cut out several pods at one time, cut a strip of craft paper 2½"w and 18" long. Leaving an area large enough for pattern, fanfold strip of paper. Draw around pattern on first folded area. Cutting through all thicknesses of paper, cut out pods.
3. Shape a small amount of cotton into a

½" to ¾" dia. ball; use craft glue to glue cotton to pod. To shape boll, place a small drop of craft glue in center of cotton and pinch sides of pod together.
4. Referring to photo, hot glue bolls to branches.
5. Lightly spray cotton with wood tone spray.

POD

BURLAP GIFT SACKS
(Shown on page 38)

For each sack, you will need one 15" x 38" piece of burlap, thread to match burlap, 2½" Roman lettering stencil, Delta Dark Blue Fabric Dye®, stencil brush, paper towels, and four 1¼" x 13" fabric strips (for ties).

1. Matching short edges, fold burlap in half. Using a ½" seam allowance, sew sides of sack together. Turn right side out.
2. Follow Step 5 of **Burlap Stocking** instructions, page 44, to center and stencil three **X**'s on one side of sack.
3. Place gift in sack. Fold top edge of sack 2" to wrong side. Referring to photo, tie one fabric strip around each corner of sack.

MUSLIN RAG DOLLS   (Shown on pages 36 and 39)

Note: Tearing fabric pieces will create a more natural look than cutting them.

For each treetop doll, you will need one 21" x 24" piece of unbleached muslin, one 10" x 18" piece of fabric for pinafore, 3" dia. ball of polyester fiberfill, and 5" of 1¼"w pre-gathered lace trim.

For each ornament doll, you will need one 10" x 11" piece of unbleached muslin, 2" dia. ball of polyester fiberfill, and 2½" of ½"w pre-gathered lace trim.

For each place card doll, you will need one 4½" x 6" piece of unbleached muslin, ¾" dia. ball of polyester fiberfill, 1¼" of ¼"w pre-gathered lace trim, and a crochet hook (to pull fabric through knot).

You will also need heavy thread to match muslin, one 2½" square of red fabric for heart, instant coffee, tracing paper, fabric marking pencil, and craft glue.

1. To give muslin an antique look, dissolve 1 tablespoon coffee in 1 cup hot water; allow to cool. Soak muslin in coffee several minutes; remove from coffee and allow to dry.

2. For head, fold one long edge of muslin the following amount to one side (wrong side): 5" for treetop doll, 2½" for ornament doll, or 1" for place card doll. Place fiberfill ball between layers of fabric at center (top). Tie thread tightly under fiberfill (**Fig. 1**); knot thread and trim ends.

Fig. 1

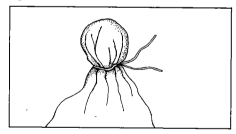

3. For arms, refer to **Fig. 2** and tie one corner at top of fabric into a knot close to head. Repeat for remaining corner at top of fabric.

Fig. 2

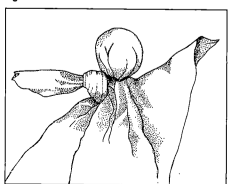

4. (**Note:** Follow Steps 4 and 5 for treetop doll pinafore only.) Referring to **Fig. 3** and spacing slits 2½" apart, cut a 3" slit for neck opening and 4" slits for arm openings on one short edge of fabric.

Fig. 3

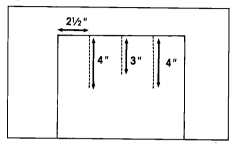

5. Referring to **Fig. 4**, place pinafore on doll. Tie edges of pinafore above each arm into a knot.

Fig. 4

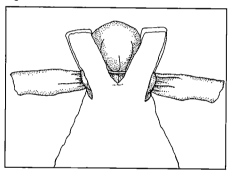

6. Referring to photo, tack lace trim around back of head.
7. Trace desired heart pattern onto tracing paper; cut out. Center pattern on red fabric and draw around pattern with fabric marking pencil; cut out. Referring to photo, glue heart to doll or pinafore.

BURLAP STOCKING
(Shown on page 38)

You will need two 12" x 26" pieces of burlap, one 4" square of tagboard (manila folder), tracing paper, fabric marking pencil, Delta Dark Blue Fabric Dye®, thread to match burlap, stencil brush, craft glue, paper towels, craft knife, jute, and three Salt Dough Ornaments (page 40; use 1" high cookie cutters).

1. Matching arrows to form one pattern, trace stocking pattern, page 45, onto tracing paper; cut out.
2. Place burlap pieces together and place pattern on top. Draw around pattern with fabric marking pencil, extending top edge of pattern 8" (**Fig. 1**). Leaving top edge open, sew fabric pieces together directly on pencil line. Leaving a ¼" seam allowance, cut out stocking; clip curves. Turn stocking right side out.

Fig. 1

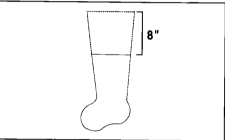

3. To fringe top edge of stocking, unravel burlap 1" along raw edge. For cuff, fold top edge approximately 4¼" to outside. With toe of stocking facing left, fold seam allowances to back of stocking; whipstitch in place.
4. For stencil, use small heart pattern, page 43, and follow **Transferring Patterns**, page 156. Center pattern on tagboard and draw around; use craft knife to cut out.
5. Place a layer of paper towels under front of cuff between layers of burlap. Referring to photo, position stencil on cuff. Dip stencil brush into fabric dye; remove excess dye by stroking brush on a paper towel (brush should be almost dry to produce a good stencil). Beginning at one edge of cut out area, apply dye with an up-and-down stamping motion. Remove stencil; allow to dry.
6. Cut 13", 15½", and 17" lengths of jute. Glue one end of each length to back of dough ornaments; allow to dry. Place lengths together with ends even. Fold ends to form a 2" loop.
7. Place ends of loop inside stocking at heel side with 1½" of loop extending above stocking; whipstitch loop to stocking.
8. From jute, make a 5" wide multi-loop bow with streamers; knot and trim ends. Referring to photo, tack bow to stocking.

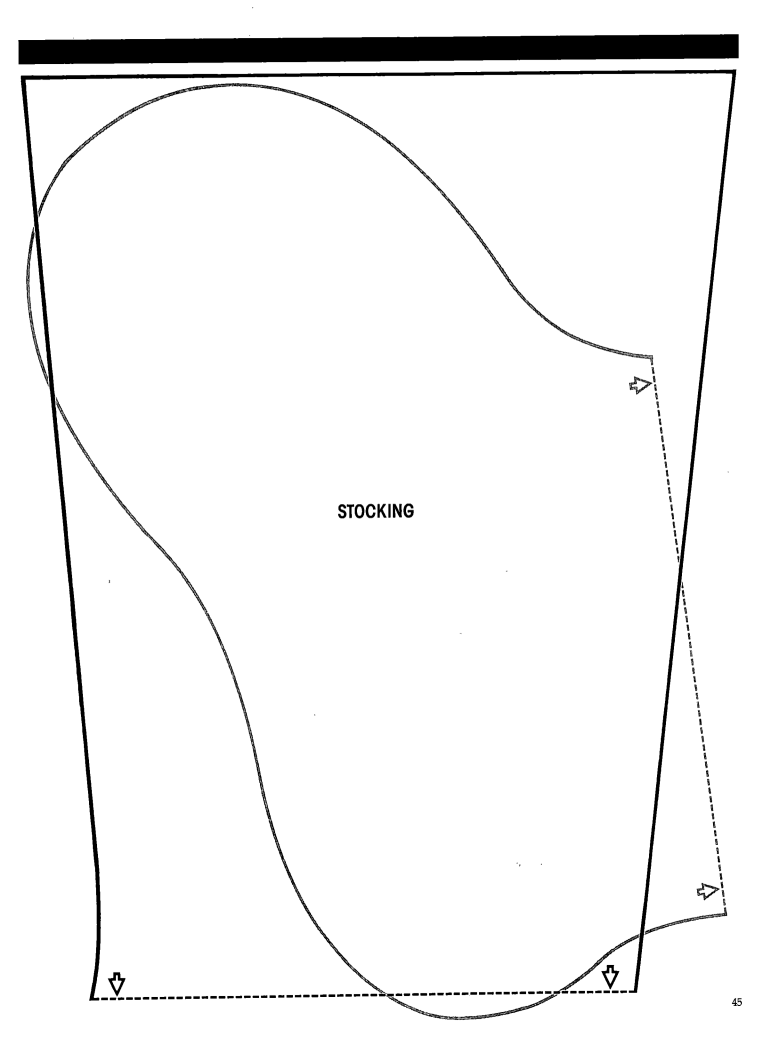

STOCKING

A SWEET NOEL

Back when the
hearth was the heart of the
home, preparations for the
Christmas celebration began in
the kitchen. It was a time
when mothers and
grandmothers worked for
weeks baking gingerbread and
making special candies and
cookies to fill the family's
stockings. Today, the aromas
of holiday baking bring to life
images of Christmases past
and inspire us to recapture
their old-fashioned charm.

Our Sweet Noel collection is
filled with good things from
the kitchen. Gingerbread
cutouts, tin punch stars,
garlands of shiny red apple
ornaments, and strings of
fresh popcorn and cranberries
adorn our tree with warmth
and cheerfulness. A time-worn
quilt surrounds the base of the
tree, making a very special
tree skirt. Apple and spice
potpourri, fresh evergreens,
and scented candles spread
holiday fragrances throughout
the house.

Instructions for the projects
shown here and on the next
six pages begin on page 54.
With these simple homemade
decorations, you can create
your own family traditions
and precious memories. Have
a sweet Noel!

Topping the **Sweet Noel Tree** *(page 54)*, a **Tin Punch Star** *(page 55)* looks like a treasured heirloom from generations past. To achieve the antique look, we used a simple technique that "ages" shiny aluminum flashing. We used smaller versions of the treetop star as ornaments to enhance the old-fashioned mood of the **Gingerbread People** *(page 57)* and other decorations.

Even on the chilliest winter day, this trio of friendly **Gingerbread People** *(page 57)* will warm your heart. For lighthearted cheer, we perched them on a shelf trimmed with hand-cut **Paper Lace** *(page 54)*.

Easily made from craft paper, these unusual gingerbread-colored **Paper Stockings** *(page 56)* are accented with perky paper bows. Fill them with evergreen and miniature kitchen utensils — or hang them to hold tiny treats from Santa.

As if watching for Santa, one of our large **Gingerbread People** *(page 57)* waits by a window hung with a gingerbread moon, heart, and stars. We used cookie cutters and our Gingerbread People recipe to make the hanging cookie ornaments. Before baking, we punched holes in the cookies with a plastic drinking straw so that we could attach the ribbon. These tasty decorations will look delightful in any window of your home.

This colorful arrangement will add a touch of cheer to any room. To make it, we attached apple ornaments to a rustic drying rack. Then we glued greenery, a raffia-tied bundle of cinnamon sticks, and one of our small **Gingerbread People** *(page 57)* to the center post of the rack.

With a trusty steed standing by to pull them through the town, this wagonload of **Paper Gingerboys** *(page 58)* is ready for an evening of caroling. Christmas gifts wrapped in brown paper and decorated with raffia and pleated paper bows await delivery.

Our **Sweet Noel Tree** *(page 54)* is filled with good things from the kitchen. **Gingerbread People** *(page 57)* dance among the branches and play peek-a-boo in muslin **Heart Pockets** *(page 56)*. Encircling the tree are a shiny red **Apple Garland** *(page 56)* and strings of popcorn and cranberries. Miniature kitchen utensils and red-checked paper bows add a homey touch. **Tin Punch Stars** *(page 55)* bring old-fashioned charm, while raffia bows make natural accents.

Nestled among evergreen branches in our **Sweet Noel Basket** *(page 54)*, this cheerful couple will charm visitors with their cross stitched holiday forecast. What a sweet welcoming committee for your front door or entryway!

Our old-fashioned **Tin Punch Star** candle ring *(page 55)* provides a festive base for a Christmas candle. Make several for your favorite scented candles and spread the season's warmth and fragrance all through the house.

Our **Simmering Potpourri** *(page 56)* is so pretty you'll want to put some on display as well as on the stove-top! When heated in water, it sends a heavenly aroma of apples, cranberries, cinnamon, and spice throughout the house. This delicious scent is sure to spark holiday appetites.

Rosy, fresh apples, sprigs of evergreen, and bright red and green holly create a pretty centerpiece that offers rich fragrance and color. For variety, we added more of nature's bounty — nuts, pinecones, and popcorn — and arranged everything in a wooden bowl. Cookies made from our **Gingerbread People** recipe *(page 57)* are a sweet finishing touch.

SWEET NOEL TREE

(Shown on page 46)

The spicy aroma of gingerbread filling the house signals the beginning of the holiday season — especially when the gingerbread goes straight from the oven to the Christmas tree! Plump gingerbread boys and girls hang merrily from the branches of the tree, while smaller figures are slipped into heart-shaped muslin pockets decorated with red stitching.

Topping the tree is an old-fashioned tin punch star made from aluminum flashing. Smaller versions of the star are also used as ornaments. In this section instructions are included for the gingerbread people, the treetop star, the star ornaments, the heart pockets, and the garland of apples which is easily crafted from purchased apple ornaments and jute.

Wispy raffia bows with long streamers and cheery paper bows are perfect companions for the other handmade decorations. To make the paper bows, 3½" x 6" pieces of wrapping paper are fanfolded and tied at the centers with raffia. A garland of popcorn and cranberries adds another bright accent to the branches.

Purchased miniature kitchen accessories make jaunty decorations for the tree — the utensils are painted cream and red and the 6½" long wooden rolling pins are hung from red ribbon. Instead of a tree skirt, a time-worn quilt draped around the base of the tree serves as the finishing touch for a very Sweet Noel tree.

SWEET NOEL BASKET - (Shown on page 52)

You will need desired wall basket (we used a 10" x 12" basket), two 7" x 10" pieces of Fiddler's Lite (14 ct), embroidery floss (see color key), embroidery hoop (optional), polyester fiberfill, large gingerbread boy and girl (see Gingerbread People, pages 57 and 58), 10" of ⅜"w red grosgrain ribbon, artificial greenery, raffia, hot glue gun, and glue sticks.

1. Center and stitch design on one piece of fabric. Use 2 strands of floss for Cross Stitch and 2 for Backstitch.
2. **(Note:** Use 2 strands of floss for Running Stitch.) For pillow, place fabric pieces wrong sides together. Leaving an opening for stuffing and stitching eight fabric threads from edges of design, work Running Stitch under one and over two fabric threads. Lightly stuff pillow with fiberfill. Use Running Stitch to stitch final closure. Trim pillow five fabric threads from Running Stitch. Unravel fabric to stitched line.
3. Cut ribbon in half. Referring to photo, glue one end of each ribbon to back of pillow. Fold remaining ends of ribbon pieces ½" to wrong side; glue in place.
4. Referring to photo, place gingerbread figures in basket and glue in place. Glue greenery in basket. Tie raffia in a bow and glue to basket. Glue folded ends of ribbon pieces to hands of gingerbread figures.

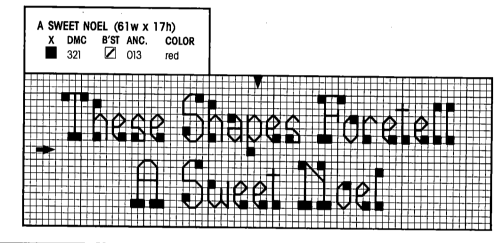

A SWEET NOEL (61w x 17h)

X	DMC	B'ST	ANC.	COLOR
■	321	◪	013	red

PAPER LACE (Shown on page 48)

You will need white butcher paper or banner paper (available at craft stores), craft knife and extra blades, tracing paper, graphite transfer paper, transparent tape, removable tape, and a cutting mat or thick layer of newspapers.

1. Trace paper lace pattern onto tracing paper.
2. Cut one 6" x 31½" length of butcher paper. Fold one short edge 3½" to one side. Using fold as guide, fanfold remaining length of paper. Use removable tape to tape edges of paper together so paper will not shift when cutting. Place folded paper on cutting mat.
3. With scalloped edge of pattern ½" from one short edge of folded paper, use transfer paper to transfer pattern to folded paper.
4. **(Note:** For ease in cutting through paper layers, change blade of craft knife often.) Use craft knife to cut out paper along solid lines only. Unfold paper and use a warm, dry iron to remove fold lines.

5. Repeat Steps 2 — 4 for desired number of lengths. Use transparent tape to tape lengths of paper together.
6. Fold paper where indicated by dashed line on pattern.

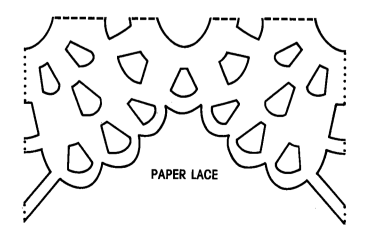

PAPER LACE

Note: Aluminum flashing and muriatic acid (20%) are available at hardware stores.

For treetop star, you will need one 10" square and one 30" x ½" strip cut from aluminum flashing.
For each ornament, you will need one 5" square and one 14½" x ½" strip cut from aluminum flashing.
For candle ring, you will need four 5" squares and one 16½" x ½" strip cut from aluminum flashing.
You will also need tracing paper, liquid solder, awl or ice pick, utility scissors, several pieces of cardboard, removable tape, muriatic acid (20%), two plastic buckets, tongs, rubber gloves, paper towels, permanent felt-tip pen with fine point, and spring-type clothespins.

1. Use desired pattern and follow **Transferring Patterns**, page 156. Place pattern on flashing square and use pen to draw around pattern; cut out with scissors. Repeat for remaining candle ring squares.
2. Place star on several layers of cardboard; tape in place. Position pattern over star and tape in place. Use awl to punch star where indicated by ●'s on pattern. Repeat for remaining candle ring stars.
3. (**Note:** Muriatic acid is used to remove the shiny surface from flashing. Caution should be used when using the acid; follow manufacturer's instructions and wear rubber gloves. Work in a well-ventilated area.) Pour acid into one bucket to a depth of approximately 2". Fill remaining bucket with water. Using tongs, place star in acid for several minutes; when surface of star begins to bubble, remove star from acid and rinse in water. Place on paper towels and pat dry. Repeat for strip and remaining candle ring stars.
4. For ornament or treetop star, refer to photo, page 48, and form strip into a ring around star, overlapping ends. Following manufacturer's instructions, solder overlapped ends of strip together; use a clothespin to secure. Solder points of star to inside of ring. Allow solder to dry; remove clothespin.
5. For candle ring, refer to photo, page 52, and form strip into a 4" square, overlapping ends. Following manufacturer's instructions, solder ends of strip together; use a clothespin to secure. Solder bottom points of one star to each side of square with smooth side of star facing outward. Solder side points of stars together. Allow solder to dry; remove clothespin.

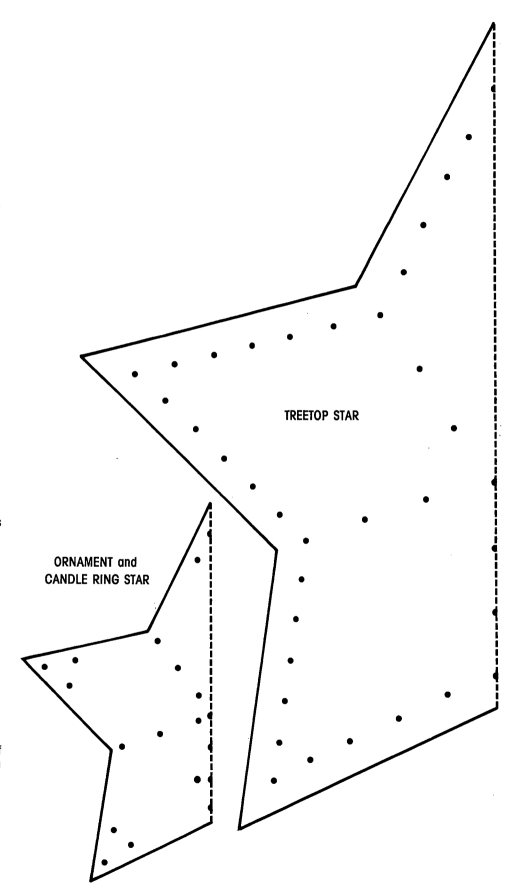

TREETOP STAR

ORNAMENT and
CANDLE RING STAR

HEART POCKETS (Shown on page 51)

For each pocket, you will need four 6" x 8" pieces of unbleached muslin, two 6" x 8" pieces of craft batting, red thread and thread to match fabric, washable fabric marking pen, tracing paper, instant coffee, small crochet hook (to turn fabric), raffia, and small gingerbread boy or girl (see Gingerbread People, pages 57 and 58).

1. Use heart pattern and follow **Transferring Patterns**, page 156.
2. Dissolve 1 tablespoon instant coffee in 1 cup hot water; allow to cool. To give muslin an antique look, soak muslin pieces in coffee several minutes; remove from coffee and allow to dry.
3. For each heart, place one batting piece on a flat surface and center two muslin pieces on top. Follow **Sewing Shapes**, page 156, trimming batting as close as possible to seam. Sew final closure by hand.
4. Referring to photo, use fabric marking pen to draw stitching lines on one side of one heart. Using a double strand of red thread and a long Running Stitch, stitch through all thicknesses of fabric. Follow manufacturer's instructions to remove pen lines.
5. To form pocket, place hearts together. Leaving area between ♦'s on pattern open, whipstitch edges of hearts together.
6. For hanger, cut several 12" lengths of raffia; twist strands together and knot ends. Place raffia knots inside pocket and whipstitch raffia to pocket.
7. Place gingerbread figure in pocket.

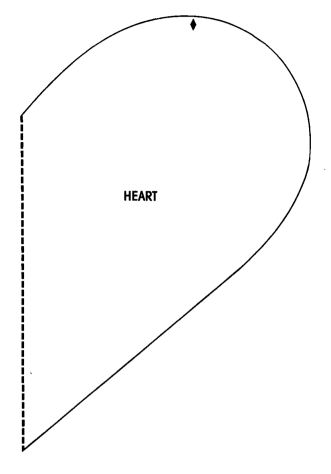

HEART

APPLE GARLAND
(Shown on page 51)

For an approx. 7 foot long garland, you will need eight 2"w artificial apple ornaments, nine 8" lengths of jute, hot glue gun, glue sticks, and glossy wood tone spray (available at craft stores).

1. Remove hangers from apples.
2. To give apples an antique look, spray apples with wood tone spray; allow to dry.
3. Knot each end of jute lengths. Referring to **Fig. 1**, glue the knots to the apples.

Fig. 1

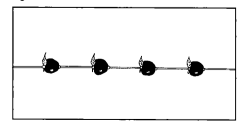

PAPER STOCKINGS
(Shown on page 49)

For each stocking, you will need four 9" x 11" pieces of brown craft paper, thread to match craft paper, tracing paper, pinking shears, craft glue, raffia, and one 3½" x 4" piece of wrapping paper.

1. Trace stocking pattern, page 103, onto tracing paper; cut out.
2. Place all craft paper pieces together; pin edges so paper will not shift when sewing. Center pattern on craft paper and use a pencil to draw around pattern. Leaving top edge open, sew ¼" inside pencil line. Cutting through all thicknesses of paper, use pinking shears to cut out stocking on pencil line.
3. For bow, begin at one short edge of wrapping paper and fanfold paper; tie center with raffia. Referring to photo, glue bow to stocking.

SIMMERING POTPOURRI
(Shown on page 53)

You will need ½ cup dried apple slices (cut into small pieces), ½ cup whole cranberries, four cinnamon sticks and one whole nutmeg (broken into small pieces), and two tablespoons **each** whole cloves and whole allspice.

1. Allow apples and cranberries to air dry for several days.
2. Mix all ingredients together.
3. To simmer potpourri, place ½ cup mixture and 2 cups water in a small saucepan. Place pan over low heat and simmer several hours. Add more water as needed.

GINGERBREAD PEOPLE (Shown on pages 48 and 51)

Note: This is a decorative project and should not be eaten.

You will need Gingerbread dough (recipe follows), paring knife, tracing paper, ¾"w heart-shaped cookie cutter, drinking straw, fork, small paintbrush, red and black acrylic paint, and 9" of florist wire, hot glue gun, and glue sticks for each hanger (optional).

GINGERBREAD

   1 cup butter or margarine, softened
   ¾ cup firmly packed light brown sugar
   ½ cup granulated sugar
   ⅓ cup molasses
   ¾ cup dark corn syrup
   3 eggs
   8½ cups all-purpose flour
   1 tablespoon baking soda
   1 teaspoon salt
   1 teaspoon **each** ground allspice, ground cinnamon, ground cloves, and ground ginger

Cream butter and sugars. Add molasses, corn syrup, and eggs. Beat until smooth. Sift together flour, soda, salt, and spices. Stir into creamed mixture (dough will be stiff).

Divide dough in half and form into two balls. Wrap each half in plastic wrap and chill at least 2 hours.

Follow Gingerbread People instructions to complete project.

GINGERBREAD PEOPLE

1. Trace desired pattern(s), on this page or page 58, onto tracing paper and cut out.
2. Preheat oven to 325 degrees for large gingerbread people or 350 degrees for small gingerbread people. On a lightly floured surface, use a floured rolling pin to roll out one-half of dough ⅜" thick for large gingerbread people or ⅛" thick for small gingerbread people. Place pattern(s) on dough and use paring knife to cut out desired number of gingerbread people.

3. Carefully transfer gingerbread people to lightly greased baking sheet. Referring to photo, use fork, cookie cutter, and drinking straw to lightly imprint dough.
4. Bake large gingerbread people 30 to 35 minutes or until lightly browned. Bake small gingerbread people 8 to 10 minutes or until lightly browned. Place on wire rack to cool.
5. Referring to photo, paint gingerbread people.
6. If hanger is desired, form a 2" loop at one end of florist wire. Glue loop to center back of gingerbread figure. Twist wire around branch of tree to secure.

SMALL BOY

LARGE BOY

Patterns continued on page 58

GINGERBREAD PEOPLE (continued)

LARGE GIRL

SMALL GIRL

PAPER GINGERBOYS (Shown on page 50)

For each paper gingerboy, you will need four 14" x 18" pieces of brown craft paper, two 14" x 18" pieces of craft batting, thread to match craft paper, pinking shears, craft glue, flat paintbrush, felt-tip pen, tracing paper, transparent tape, and one 3½" x 6" piece of wrapping paper and raffia for optional bow (see Step 3 of Paper Stockings instructions, page 56).

1. Use body and legs patterns, page 59, and follow **Transferring Patterns**, page 156.

Matching arrows to form one pattern, tape patterns together.
2. Place all craft paper pieces together; pin edges so paper will not shift when cutting. Center pattern on craft paper and draw around pattern. Cutting through all thicknesses of paper, cut out.
3. Place batting pieces together and center pattern on top. Use pen to draw around pattern. Cutting through both thicknesses of batting, cut ½" inside pen line.
4. Dilute 2 parts craft glue with 1 part water.

Using paintbrush to apply glue, glue edges of two paper pieces together. Repeat for remaining paper pieces. Glue batting pieces together. Center and glue batting pieces between paper pieces. Allow to dry.
5. Using a ⅜" seam allowance, sew pieces together. Use pinking shears to trim paper close to stitching.
6. If desired, glue bow at neck of gingerboy.

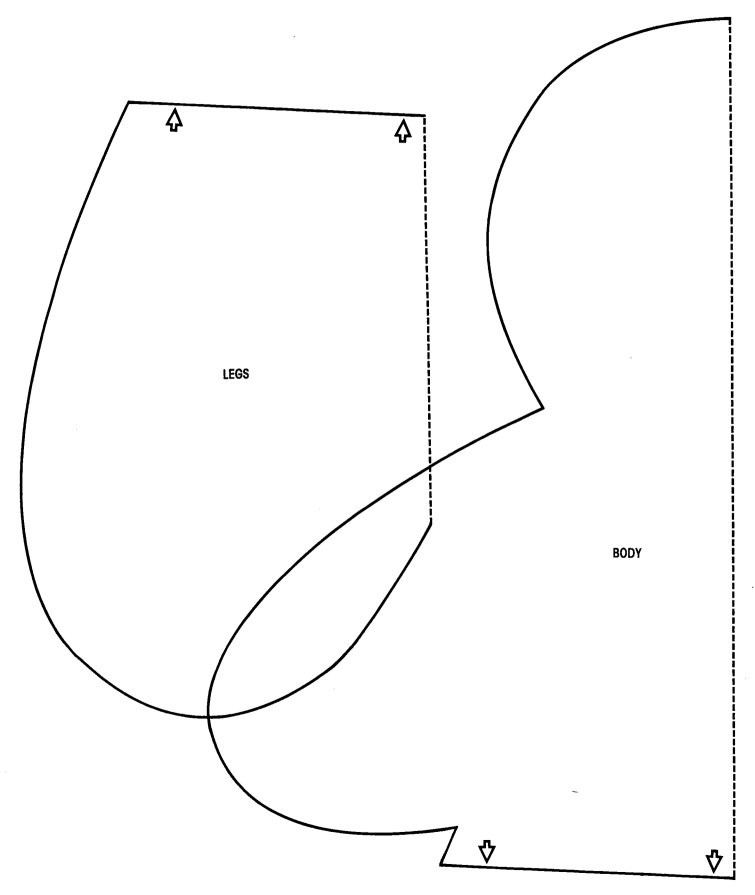

LEGS

BODY

T he holiday spirit invites us to make Christmas a grand occasion marked by splendid ornamentation. In this collection, lots of shiny trimmings are contrasted with simple elements of nature to achieve a balanced elegance befitting any home decor.

Hues of rose and gold are accented by copper beads and metallic mesh ribbon to bring opulence to the tree. Borrowing from nature, we group glass ball ornaments together to resemble clusters of grapes. Gold-tipped pinecones and twig sprays complement the ornaments, while tiny white lights twinkle like stars. Strips of shimmering floral lamé fabric wind through the branches and swirl around the base of the tree in a golden cloud. To coordinate with the tree, arrangements of poinsettias fashioned from gold lamé are enhanced by bead garlands, ribbons, twigs, and pinecones. The rich beauty of the decorations is illuminated by the warm glow of golden tapers.

Instructions for the projects shown here and on the next four pages begin on page 66. If your tastes run to the lavish but your pocketbook doesn't, this collection is for you. Enjoy a splendid Christmas!

Shades of rose and gold lend opulent color to the **Splendid Holiday Tree** *(page 66)*. Strips of rich floral lamé, strands of metallic mesh ribbon, and a garland of copper beads loop through the branches with shimmering color. Cascades of **Glass Ball Clusters** *(page 66)* in varying hues of burgundy and rose add richness to the tree. Gold-tipped pinecones and miniature white lights provide sparkle. Beneath the tree, lengths of gold and floral lamé create the illusion of an elegant tree skirt *(shown on page 60)*.

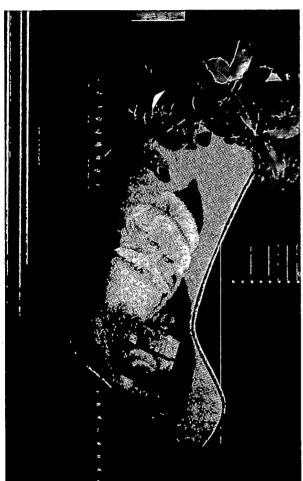

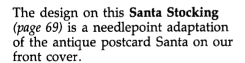

The design on this **Santa Stocking** *(page 69)* is a needlepoint adaptation of the antique postcard Santa on our front cover.

Flanked by golden tapers and boughs of evergreen, a graceful cascade of **Poinsettias** *(page 68)* spills over the mantel. To create the bouquet, arrange the flowers in a floral foam base along with curved twigs cut from a twig wreath. For extra richness, loop a copper bead garland through the poinsettias and wind metallic mesh ribbon through both the cascade and the greenery.

Stunning in its simplicity, a **Standing Poinsettia** *(page 68)* crafted of lamé is a dramatic accent for a table or shelf.

Our needlepoint **Santa Door Hanger** *(page 69)* hangs from a tasseled gold cord.

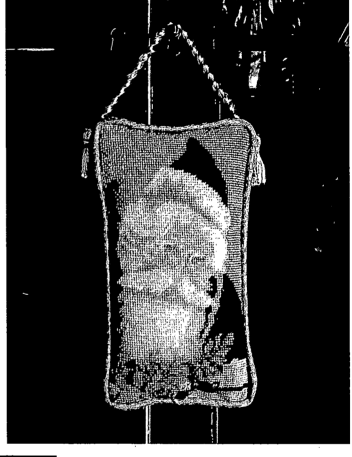

An eye-pleasing blend of elegance and simplicity, this **Twig Tree** *(page 67)* is decorated with pink and gold berries, green eucalyptus, and curls of golden ribbon.

A sprinkling of gold glitter brings sparkle to **Winter Potpourri** *(page 66)*. Filled with bay leaves, pinecones, painted cedar chips, and other offerings from nature, the mixture is both aromatic and attractive. A gleaming **Poinsettia** *(page 68)* and golden tapers complement the potpourri-filled vase.

Greet holiday visitors with a striking double **Poinsettia Wreath** *(page 69)*. Painted gold lamé poinsettias and metallic mesh ribbon shimmer against the dark twig wreaths. Sprigs of evergreen and gilded berries complete the decoration.

Keeping a record of your Christmas card and gift lists will be a pleasure with this elegant book. To create it, we glued **Marbled Paper** *(page 66)* to a purchased address book.

Adorned with frosty poinsettias, this lovely **Etched Wine Set** *(page 67)* has the look of expensive glassware. Filled with your favorite wine, the set is perfect for a Christmas toast. **Marbled Paper** *(page 66)* and narrow gold ribbon make elegant wrappings for small gifts.

This glowing basket holds an array of **Poinsettias** *(page 68)*, twig sprays, and evergreen in a floral foam base. To enhance it, we nestled gold-tipped pinecones *(see Splendid Holiday Tree, page 66)* among the flowers and looped metallic mesh ribbon and copper bead garland through the arrangement.

SPLENDID HOLIDAY TREE

(Shown on page 60)

Striking a delicate balance between gleaming glass, shimmering fabric, and muted natural elements, this Splendid Holiday tree sets the tone for elegant Christmas decorating. The seven foot tall Noble fir provides a lush deep green background for decorations that emphasize shades of rose, burgundy, and gold. The items decorating this tree are readily available or easy to handcraft.

In this section, instructions are included for assembling glass ball clusters from three sizes of balls. Semicircular twig pieces cut from a 9" dia. wreath accent each cluster. Nothing could be simpler to make than the fabric strips used as a garland. Sumptuous floral lamé fabric is cut into 6" wide strips, and the edges are treated with fray preventative. Pinecones are given a golden glow by brushing the tips of the scales with metallic gold paint. Purchased items such as strings of miniature white lights, copper bead garland, and 1¼" wide metallic mesh ribbon round out the list of decorations.

To decorate the tree, the white lights are strung among the branches to provide sparkle from within the tree. Starting at the top of the tree and repeating throughout, each cluster of glass balls is arranged to fall in a cascade of color. The twig vines placed among the clusters give a natural touch.

Also starting at the treetop, lamé fabric strips are placed in the tree. Unlike traditional Christmas garland which goes around the tree, the fabric moves along more vertical lines; it is twisted and tucked gracefully to show off the contrasting sides of the fabric.

Once the fabric strips are in place, the copper beads are draped and looped over the branches in traditional garland fashion. The gold-tipped pinecones are then nestled among the branches and the metallic ribbon is cut into lengths and hung in ringlets over the ends of the branches. For a dramatic tree skirt, several yards of gold lamé fabric are entwined with more floral lamé around the base of the tree.

The result is a combination of elegant decorations that will add richness and vibrant color to all your Splendid Holiday celebrations.

GLASS BALL CLUSTERS

(Shown on page 62)

For each ball cluster, you will need one 3" dia. glass ball, three 2½" dia. glass balls, and three 2" dia. glass balls (we used five coordinating colors of balls); craft glue; and one 18" length of 18-gauge florist wire.

1. Remove hanger from each ball and set aside. Glue metal caps in place.
2. Referring to **Fig. 1**, bend wire around a pencil to form seven loops.

Fig. 1

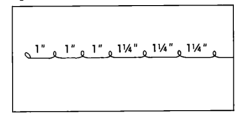

3. Beginning at looped end of wire, attach one 2" dia. ball to wire by placing a hanger through loop and replacing hanger in cap. Placing smallest to largest balls along wire, repeat to attach remaining balls to wire.
4. Referring to photo, place ball cluster on tree. Bend end of wire around tree branch to secure; arrange balls as desired.

WINTER POTPOURRI

(Shown on page 64)

You will need large pieces of cedar chips, small pieces of preserved cedar and pine bark, small dried white flowers, rock salt, bay leaves, small pinecones, gold spray paint, assortment of nuts in shells (we used almonds, hickory nuts, and pecans), copper beads, white acrylic paint, gold glitter, adhesive spray, jar with tight-fitting lid, almond oil or desired essential oil, and a clear glass container to display potpourri.

1. Spray nuts and pinecones with gold paint; allow to dry. Lightly spray pine bark with gold paint; allow to dry.
2. Spray bay leaves with adhesive spray and sprinkle with glitter.
3. In a small bowl, dilute white paint with an equal amount of water. Add cedar chips to diluted paint; stir until chips are well coated. Remove chips from paint and allow to dry.
4. Place cedar chips, bay leaves, pine bark, pinecones, rock salt, nuts, cedar, and flowers in jar. Add desired amount of oil (we used 7 drops in a quart jar of potpourri). Secure lid on jar and place in a cool, dark, dry place for two weeks. Every few days, shake jar to mix contents.
5. Place potpourri in glass container. Add beads and sprinkle potpourri with glitter.

MARBLED PAPER

(Shown on pages 64 and 65)

You will need one gallon liquid starch, one 12" x 18" disposable aluminum foil roasting pan, 8½" x 11" pieces of white paper, desired colors of acrylic paint (we used burgundy, dark green, pink, and cream), paper towels, waxed paper, and a small paintbrush.

1. Pour starch into pan to a depth of 1".
2. To apply paint to starch surface, hold bottle of paint near surface and gently squeeze out a small dot of paint (paint will float and begin to spread). Repeat to apply several dots of each color of paint. Remove any dots of paint that do not spread with a corner of a paper towel or the tip of a finger.
3. To form paint design, pull the wooden end of the paintbrush through the starch across the length and the width of the pan (**Fig. 1**).

Fig. 1

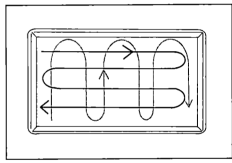

4. Gently place a piece of paper on starch surface (paper will float); immediately pick up paper by two corners and lay paper painted side up on paper towels.
5. Using dry paper towels, blot excess starch and paint from marbled paper. Lay paper on waxed paper; allow to dry.
6. (**Note:** To remove buildup of paint or to change colors, place a layer of paper towels on starch surface. Lift paper towels from starch and discard.) For each sheet of paper, repeat Steps 2 – 5 using desired colors of paint and adding more starch to pan as needed.
7. Use a warm, dry iron to press marbled paper.

ETCHED WINE SET (Shown on page 65)

You will need wine glasses and a decanter, white self-adhesive plastic covering (Con-tact® paper), graphite transfer paper, tracing paper, masking tape, craft knife, paper towels, 1"w foam brush, glass etching cream (available at craft stores), and rubber gloves.

1. Trace wine glass and decanter poinsettia patterns onto tracing paper.
2. For each wine glass, cut one piece of plastic 4½" x 3½". For decanter, cut one piece of plastic 5½" x 4½".
3. Using transfer paper, center and transfer pattern to plastic side of each plastic piece.
4. Remove backing from one plastic piece. Referring to photo for position, place plastic on glassware; press bubbles and wrinkles flat. Cover edges of plastic with masking tape. Repeat for remaining plastic pieces.
5. Use craft knife to cut out each design. Use paper towel to gently clean design areas on glass.

6. Wearing rubber gloves and following manufacturer's instructions, use foam brush to apply etching cream to design areas. After 1 minute, remove cream under running water.
7. Remove tape and plastic pieces from glassware. Wash and dry glassware (a dishwasher may be used).

WINE GLASS POINSETTIA

DECANTER POINSETTIA

TWIG TREE (Shown on page 63)

For an approx. 18"h tree, you will need one 16" Styrofoam® cone, two 24" dia. twig wreaths, brown spray paint, wire cutters or desired tool to cut twigs, brown acrylic paint, paintbrush, hot glue gun, glue sticks, ⅛"w metallic gold ribbon, clusters of dried pink berries, pieces of green eucalyptus, and clusters of gold-painted berries.

1. Spray paint entire cone; allow to dry.
2. For glue guidelines, use a pencil to lightly score around cone at 4" intervals; score around cone 2" from bottom (**Fig. 1**).

Fig. 1

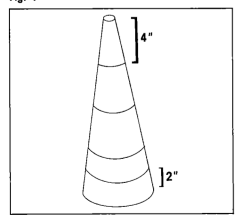

3. (**Note:** Cut twigs that are no more than ¼" in diameter at thickest point.) Use wire cutters to cut 2" long straight twigs, 4" long straight twigs, and 6" long curved twigs from wreaths. Use acrylic paint to paint cut areas of twigs; allow to dry. Cut and paint more twigs as needed.

4. (**Note:** Large amounts of hot glue may melt cone. When gluing twigs to cone, apply a ½" long line of glue to larger end of each twig; glue twig to cone at guideline.) Using scored line 2" from bottom of cone as a guide, glue 2" twig lengths around cone.
5. (**Note:** Refer to photo for Steps 5 – 9.) Using scored line 4" from bottom of cone as a guide, glue 4" lengths around cone (**Fig. 2a**). Using same scored line as a guide, glue 6" lengths on top of 4" lengths (**Fig. 2b**).

Fig. 2a   **Fig. 2b**

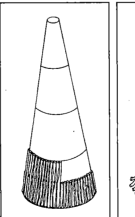 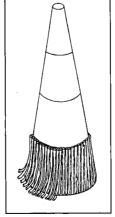

6. Repeat Step 5 to glue 4" and 6" lengths around cone along remaining scored lines.
7. With ends of twigs even with top of cone, glue 4" lengths around cone.
8. Applying glue approximately 2½" from larger end of each twig, glue 6" lengths around top of cone (**Fig. 3**).

Fig. 3

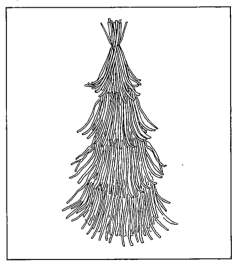

9. To decorate tree, glue eucalyptus and berries to tree. Use ribbon to form a multi-loop bow with streamers. Glue bow to top of tree. Cut several 24" lengths of ribbon; glue one end of each length to top of tree. Twist ends of lengths; glue in place.

POINSETTIAS (Shown on pages 62 and 65)

For each poinsettia, you will need ½ yd of 44"w gold lamé fabric, spray adhesive, 18-gauge and 20-gauge florist wire, green crepe florist tape, small piece of dried yellow yarrow, wire cutters, tracing paper, burgundy and green acrylic paint, flat paintbrush, and paper towels.

1. For leaf wires, use wire cutters to cut thirteen 9" lengths of 20-gauge wire.
2. From lamé, cut ten 3" x 5" pieces, ten 3½" x 6" pieces, and six 4" x 7" pieces.
3. For leaf pieces, spray one side of two 3"x 5" lamé pieces with adhesive. Referring to **Fig. 1**, center one 9" wire length on adhesive side of one lamé piece. With adhesive sides facing, place lamé pieces together; smooth to adhere. Repeat for remaining wire and lamé pieces.

Fig. 1

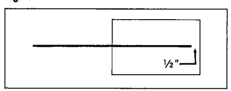

4. Trace small, medium, and large leaf patterns onto tracing paper and cut out.
5. Matching wires and edges of lamé, place 3" x 5" leaf pieces together and pin long edges so that pieces will not shift when cutting. Center small leaf pattern on top of pieces (**Fig. 2**); pin in place. Cutting through all layers of fabric, cut out leaves; remove pattern. Repeat to cut out five medium leaves from 3½" x 6" leaf pieces and three large leaves from 4" x 7" leaf pieces.

Fig. 2

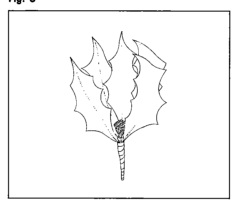

6. To paint leaves, dip bristles of paintbrush into burgundy paint and remove excess paint on paper towels. Lightly paint both sides of one small leaf. Repeat to paint remaining small and medium leaves. Using green paint, repeat to paint large leaves.
7. To assemble poinsettia, use florist tape to tape yarrow to one end of 18" length of 18-gauge wire (stem). Overlapping long edges, place small leaves around stem with bottom of leaf fabric below yarrow; tape leaf wires to stem (**Fig. 3**). Place medium leaves around stem below small leaves; tape leaf wires to stem. Continue wrapping stem with tape, and at the same time, tape large leaves to stem at desired intervals.

Fig. 3

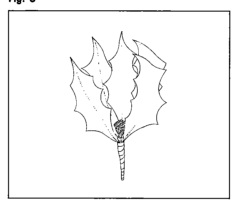

8. Referring to photo, bend wires to arrange leaves into poinsettia shape.

STANDING POINSETTIA

(Shown on page 63)

You will need one Poinsettia (on this page), two 18" lengths of 18-gauge florist wire, and green crepe florist tape.

1. To reinforce poinsettia stem, place wire lengths along stem and wrap with tape. Referring to **Fig. 1**, bend end of stem to form a 4" dia. circle; tape in place.

Fig. 1

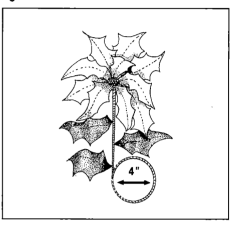

2. Referring to photo, use circle as a base and arrange stem so poinsettia will stand.

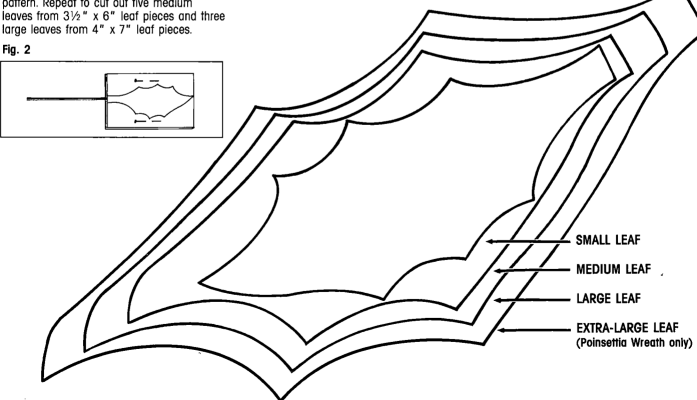

SMALL LEAF

MEDIUM LEAF

LARGE LEAF

EXTRA-LARGE LEAF
(Poinsettia Wreath only)

POINSETTIA WREATH

(Shown on page 64)

For poinsettias, you will need 1 yd of 44"w gold lamé fabric, spray adhesive, 18-gauge and 20-gauge florist wire, brown crepe florist tape, two small pieces of dried yellow yarrow, wire cutters, burgundy and green acrylic paint, flat paintbrush, tracing paper, and paper towels.

For wreath, you will also need one 18" dia. twig wreath, artificial greenery, sprays of artificial gold berries, burgundy spray paint, hot glue gun, glue sticks, and 2½ yds of 1¼"w peach metallic mesh ribbon.

1. For leaf wires, use wire cutters to cut twenty-six 9" lengths of 20-gauge wire.
2. From lamé, cut ten 3" x 5" pieces, twenty 3½" x 6" pieces, sixteen 4" x 7" pieces, and six 4½" x 8" pieces.
3. For leaf pieces, follow Step 3 of Poinsettias instructions, page 68.
4. Trace small, medium, large, and extra-large leaf patterns, page 68, onto tracing paper and cut out.
5. (**Note:** Do not cut out more than five leaves at a time.) Follow Step 5 of Poinsettias instructions, page 68, to cut out five small leaves, ten medium leaves, eight large leaves, and three extra-large leaves.
6. Use burgundy paint and follow Step 6 of Poinsettias instructions, page 68, to paint small leaves, medium leaves, and five large leaves. Use green paint to paint remaining leaves.
7. To assemble small poinsettia, use five small leaves, five medium leaves, and three large green leaves and follow Steps 7 and 8 of Poinsettias instructions, page 68. Using remaining leaves, repeat to assemble large poinsettia.
8. Wrap several lengths of 20-gauge wire with tape; cut into 6" lengths. Remove ties or wires that hold wreath together. Referring to photo, pull twigs apart to form two wreaths (one wreath should be slightly larger in diameter and thickness than other wreath). Use 6" wire lengths to secure twigs in wreath shapes.
9. (**Note:** Refer to photo for Steps 9 – 13.) Place small wreath on large wreath; wire wreaths together.
10. Form ribbon into a large multi-loop bow with streamers; wire bow to bottom of wreaths.
11. Arrange small poinsettia at top of wreaths; wrap stem around wreaths to secure. Repeat to arrange large poinsettia on top of bow.
12. Glue greenery to wreaths.
13. Use spray paint to lightly spritz berries; allow to dry. Wire or glue berries to wreaths.

SANTA STOCKING (Shown on page 62)

You will need one 16" x 22" piece of 14 mesh needlepoint canvas, Paternayan Persian yarn (see color key, page 71), #22 Tapestry needle, masking tape, one 14" x 20" piece of fabric (for backing), one 1½" x 45" bias strip of fabric and 1¼ yds of ⅛" dia. cord (for cording), one 2" x 5" piece of fabric (for hanger), two 14" x 20" pieces of fabric (for lining), thread to match fabric, fabric marking pencil, blocking board, water in spray bottle, and T-pins.

1. Cover edges of canvas with masking tape.
2. Center and work design on canvas following chart on pages 70 and 71. Use two strands of yarn and Tent Stitch (**Fig. 1** and **Fig. 2** on this page).
3. To block stitched piece, dampen with water. Place stitched piece on blocking board and align canvas threads with horizontal and vertical lines on board. Use T-pins, spaced ½" apart, to pin stitched piece to board. Allow to dry. Remove pins.
4. Trim canvas ½" from stitching.
5. Place stitched piece and backing fabric right sides together. Using stitched piece as a pattern, use fabric marking pencil to draw around stitched piece; cut out backing. Place lining pieces right sides together and repeat to cut out lining pieces.
6. For cording, lay cord along center on wrong side of bias strip. Matching long edges, fold strip over cord. Use zipper foot and machine baste along length of strip close to cord.
7. Matching raw edges, baste cording to side and bottom edges on right side of stitched piece; clip seam allowance as needed along curves. Cut off remaining cording.
8. (**Note:** Use a ½" seam allowance throughout.) For stocking, place stitched piece and backing piece right sides together. Leaving top edge open, use zipper foot and sew as close as possible to stitched design. Clip curves and turn right side out; press. Fold top edge of stocking ½" to wrong side (unworked canvas should not show); press.
9. For lining, place lining pieces right sides together. Leaving top edge open, use regular presser foot and sew pieces together.
10. With wrong sides together, insert lining into stocking. Fold top edge of lining ½" to wrong side and pin to stocking.
11. For hanger, fold long edges of 2" x 5" piece ½" to wrong side and press. With wrong sides together, fold hanger piece in half lengthwise and press. Sew long edges together. Fold hanger in half to form a loop. Place ends of hanger between lining and stocking at left seam line with approximately 2" of hanger extending above stocking; pin in place.
12. Slipstitch lining to stocking and, at the same time, securely sew hanger in place.

SANTA DOOR HANGER (Shown on page 63)

You will need one 8" x 10" piece of 18 mesh needlepoint canvas, Paternayan Persian yarn (see color key, page 71), #24 Tapestry needle, masking tape, one 6" x 8" piece of fabric (for backing), one 1½" x 21" bias strip of fabric and 21" of ⅛" dia. cord (for cording), 7½" of ⅛"w satin drapery cord, two 1" long tassels, polyester fiberfill, thread to match fabric and satin cord, blocking board, water in spray bottle, and T-pins.

1. Cover edges of canvas with masking tape.
2. Working **inside heavy black lines only,** center and work design following chart on pages 70 and 71. Use 1 strand of yarn and Tent Stitch (**Fig. 1** and **Fig. 2**).
3. To block stitched piece, follow Step 3 of Santa Stocking instructions on this page.
4. Trim canvas ½" from stitching. Cut backing same size as stitched piece.
5. For cording, follow Step 6 of Santa Stocking instructions on this page.
6. Matching raw edges and starting 1" from end of cording, baste cording to right side of stitched piece; clip seam allowance at corners. Open ends of cording and cut cording to fit exactly. Fold fabric around cord. Overlap cording and turn ends toward raw edge of stitched piece; stitch in place.
7. For door hanger, place stitched piece and backing piece right sides together. Leaving an opening for turning, use zipper foot and sew as close as possible to stitched design. Cut corners diagonally and turn right side out; press. Stuff door hanger with fiberfill and sew final closure by hand.
8. Referring to photo, tack ends of satin cord to back of door hanger. Tack tassels to top corners.

TENT STITCH

Work a Tent Stitch to correspond to each square on the chart. When working a single row of Tent Stitches horizontally, vertically, or diagonally, use the Continental method (**Fig. 1**). When working an area having several rows of stitches, use the Basketweave method (**Fig. 2**).

Fig. 1

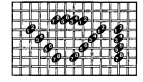

Fig. 2

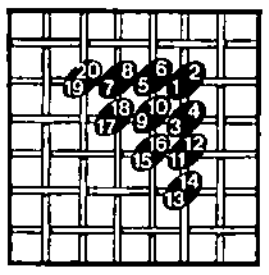

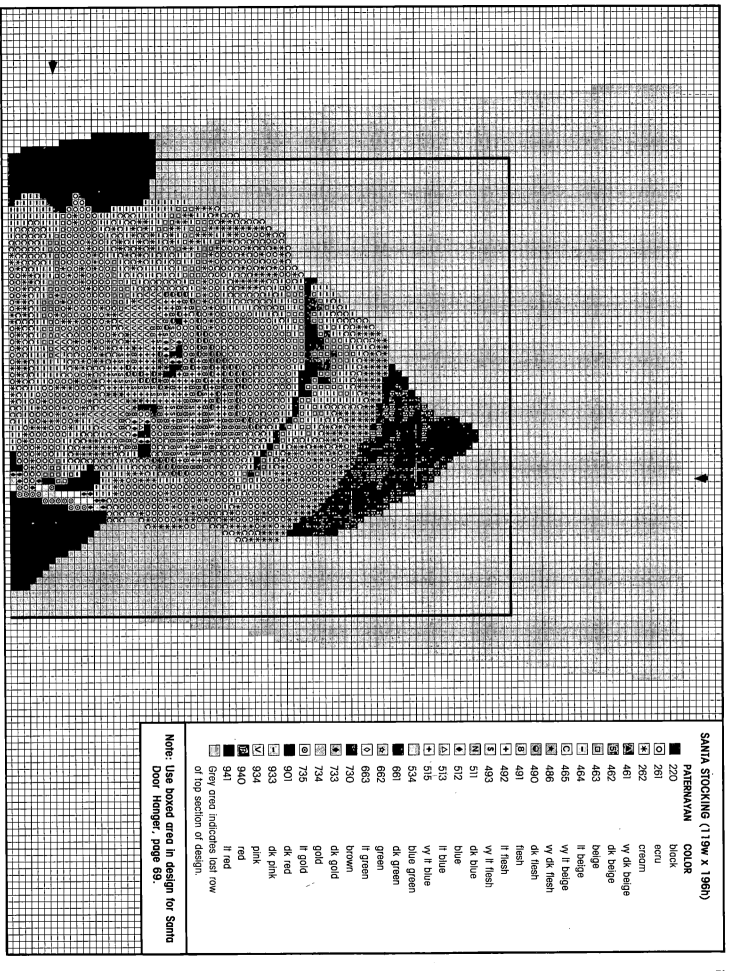

SANTA STOCKING (119w x 196h)

PATERNAYAN	COLOR
■ 220	black
◙ 261	ecru
✱ 262	cream
◪ 461	vy dk beige
462	dk beige
▣ 463	beige
464	lt beige
◨ 465	vy lt beige
◧ 486	vy dk flesh
▣ 490	dk flesh
◙ 491	flesh
◙ 492	lt flesh
➕ 493	vy lt flesh
◈ 511	dk blue
◆ 512	blue
◭ 513	lt blue
➕ 515	vy lt blue
▣ 534	blue green
■ 661	dk green
◇ 662	green
◈ 663	lt green
■ 730	brown
▧ 733	dk gold
■ 734	gold
◉ 735	lt gold
■ 901	dk red
933	dk pink
◨ 934	pink
■ 940	red
▣ 941	lt red

Grey area indicates last row
of top section of design.

**Note: Use boxed area in design for Santa
Door Hanger, page 69.**

THE BIRDS OF CHRISTMAS

Т

he song of a bird
in the dark of December is a
magical thing that's sweet to
remember. Taken for granted
during the sunny days of
spring and summer, the
cheerful melody of a bird is a
rare pleasure in winter.
Because legend says that the
birds sang all through the
night when Christ was born,
these little creatures have
earned a place of honor in our
Christmas celebrations.

This collection is dedicated
to the simple beauty and
warmth that birds add to our
lives. We chose four colorful
birds — the chickadee,
cardinal, goldfinch, and
bluebird — to showcase in a
variety of cross stitch projects.
To enhance the natural beauty
of the birds, we kept our tree
decorations simple, adding
only gold bead garland, holly,
berries, and a big red bow. A
lifelike Father Christmas bears
gifts for his winged friends,
and an evergreen wreath
frames an enchanting cross-
stitched verse. Woodsy
potpourris and scented fire
starters provide an aromatic
touch of the outdoors.

Instructions for the projects
shown here and on the next
six pages begin on page 80.
Have a magical Christmas!

"I heard a bird sing in the dark of December — a magical thing, and sweet to remember."
Framed in our evergreen **Bird Song Wreath** *(page 80)*, this verse by Oliver Herford celebrates the rare pleasure of hearing a bird's sweet melody in the wintertime.

A warm fire on a chilly winter evening can be even cozier with **Scented Fire Starters** *(page 82)*. Coated with tinted paraffin, the ordinary pinecones will burn easily in your fireplace. A few drops of cinnamon oil added to the paraffin create a light, pleasing aroma when the starters are used.

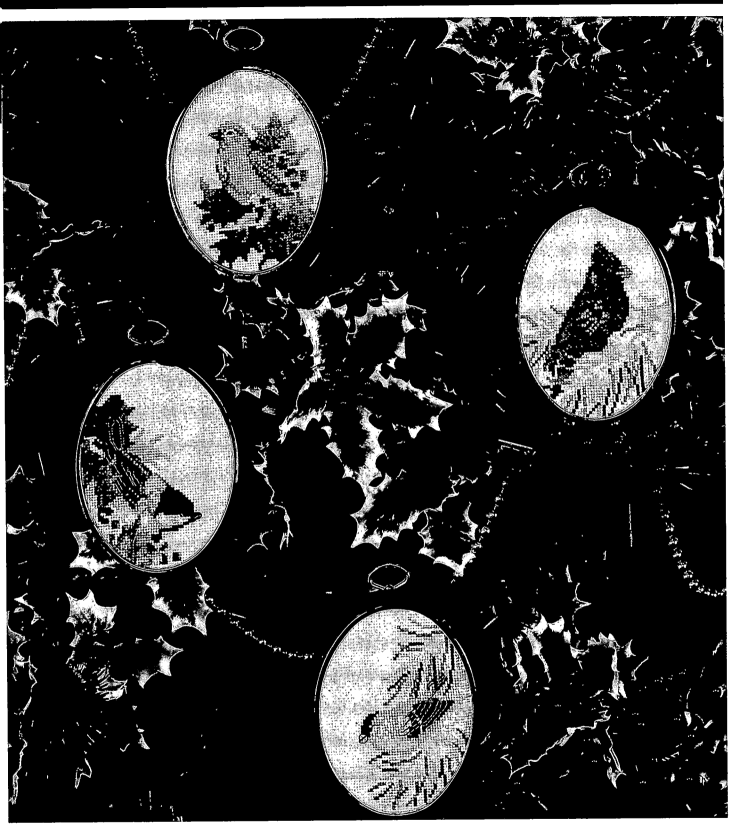

As sweet as a bird's song, the **Birds of Christmas Tree** *(page 80)* features four favorite birds in cross-stitched **Tree Ornaments** *(page 82)*. The natural beauty of the bluebird *(clockwise from top left)*, cardinal, goldfinch, and chickadee is enhanced by a few simple decorations. A garland of gold beads, sprigs of variegated silk holly, and sprays of shiny red berries are all you need to complete this handsome tree. Shown on page 72, a red multi-loop bow with streamers makes a graceful tree topper, while the base of the tree is hidden inside a large painted basket.

Flocking together for a cross stitch portrait, the **Birds of Christmas** *(page 82)* are shown off in fine style. We dressed up the frame with a festive bow for the holidays, but you'll want to display this beautiful design all winter long!

Its shape resembling a Christmas tree, this **Scented Jumbo Pinecone** *(page 82)* makes a fragrant, festive accent.

These charming **Nested Potpourris** *(page 80)* will fill the house with your favorite fragrances. We used a variety of woodsy elements to create three distinctive mixtures and decorated the nests with colorful birds, ribbon, cedar, holly, and berries.

With a cheerful pair of cardinals perched on its handle, our pretty **Card Basket** *(page 82)* is a lovely way to display your holiday greeting cards. Variegated holly, red ribbon, and small pinecones add the finishing touches.

Any of the cross stitch birds in our **Tree Ornaments** collection *(page 82)* can be showcased in a favorite frame. We inserted the cardinal design in a small candlescreen.

The bright red and green ruffles on our **Bird Pillows** *(page 80)* give them a touch of holiday color. With their classic cross stitch designs, these beautiful accent pillows can be used all year long.

You can almost imagine this lifelike **Father Christmas** *(page 81)* walking through the woods on his yearly journey. Along with gifts for good children, he also bears a basket of treats for his little feathered friends.

BIRDS OF CHRISTMAS TREE

(Shown on page 72)

Charming cross stitched birds have flocked together on this Birds of Christmas tree. Stitched on 18 count fabric, these feathered friends sit on snow-covered boughs or among branches of bright holly. Each bird is shown off in fine style when framed in a simple gold oval frame and trimmed with a bow made from ¼" wide satin ribbon. Charts and instructions for these classic designs are found in the pages of this section.

The remainder of the tree decorations are kept sweet and simple. Finished off with long streamers, a multi-loop bow made from 2¾" wide craft ribbon makes an easy and elegant treetop decoration. Purchased gold bead garland provides an additional gold accent to the framed pieces. Stems of silk variegated holly are placed between the branches of the tree to provide a further dash of Christmas spirit, while airy touches of red come from placing purchased sprays of shiny red berries among the clusters of holly.

For an unusual container for the tree, the tree stand was placed in a large, red basket. Even after the holidays are over, such an unusual basket would be sure to find a use in any decor. And like the basket, the Birds of Christmas will bring their beauty to your home throughout the year.

BIRD SONG WREATH

(Shown on page 74)

You will need an approx. 20" dia. artificial evergreen wreath with twigs, one 16" square of Ivory Aida (14 ct), embroidery floss (see color key), embroidery hoop (optional), one 15" dia. piece of cardboard, ⅞"w red satin ribbon, three large artificial cardinals, clusters of artificial red berries, silk variegated holly, pinecones, hot glue gun, and glue sticks.

1. Center and stitch design on fabric. Use 2 strands of floss for Cross Stitch and 1 for Backstitch.
2. Referring to photo, glue birds, ribbon, holly, pinecones, and berries to wreath.
3. With design centered, cut stitched piece same size as cardboard circle. Glue edges of stitched piece to cardboard. Center and glue right side of stitched piece to back of wreath.

BIRD PILLOWS

(Shown on page 78)

For each pillow, you will need one 10" square of Ivory Aida (18 ct), embroidery floss (see color key, page 84 or 85), embroidery hoop (optional), one 2" x 80" piece of fabric for ruffle (pieced if necessary), one 10" square of fabric for backing, polyester fiberfill, and thread to match fabric.

1. For placement of Goldfinch or Bluebird, page 85, place bottom and right side of design 1¾" from edges of fabric. For placement of Chickadee, page 84, place bottom and left side of design 1¾" from edges of fabric.
2. For pillow top, stitch design on fabric using 2 strands of floss for Cross Stitch and 1 for Backstitch.
3. For ruffle, fold short edges of ruffle fabric ½" to the wrong side; press. With wrong sides together, fold fabric in half lengthwise; press. Baste close to raw edge. Make another basting seam ¼" from the first. Pull basting threads, drawing up gathers to fit pillow top.
4. Matching raw edges and overlapping ends of ruffle, baste ruffle to right side of pillow top.
5. **(Note:** Use a ½" seam allowance.) With right sides together and leaving an opening for turning, sew pillow top and backing together. Turn right side out, carefully pushing corners outward. Stuff with fiberfill; sew final closure by hand.

NESTED POTPOURRIS

(Shown on page 76)

For potpourris, you will need small pieces of pine bark, sunflower seeds, clusters of red canella berries or artificial red berries, small pinecones, ½"w shapes cut from orange peel, an assortment of nuts in shells (we used hickory nuts and almonds), small pieces of preserved cedar, desired scented oil, and three jars with tight-fitting lids.
You will also need three artificial bird nests (we used 5¼", 4½", and 3½" dia. nests), one large artificial cardinal, two small artificial red birds, ¼"w red satin ribbon, silk holly, small pieces of preserved cedar, clusters of red canella berries or artificial red berries, hot glue gun, and glue sticks.

1. Fill one jar with bark, sunflower seeds, and clusters of berries. Fill another jar with pinecones and orange peel shapes. Fill remaining jar with nuts, cedar, individual berries, and orange peel shapes. Add desired amount of oil to each jar. Secure lids on jars and place in a cool, dark, dry place for two weeks. Every few days, shake the jars to mix contents.
2. **(Note:** Refer to photo for Steps 2 – 4.) Fill one nest with bark mixture potpourri. Glue holly and cardinal in nest.
3. Glue holly, clusters of berries, and red birds to second nest. Fill nest with pinecone mixture potpourri.
4. Glue holly and cedar to third nest. Tie ribbon in a bow and glue to greenery. Fill nest with nut mixture potpourri.

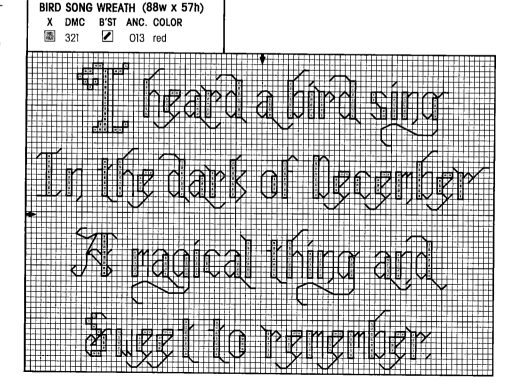

BIRD SONG WREATH (88w x 57h)

X	DMC	B'ST	ANC.	COLOR
▓	321	✎	013	red

You will need one 24"h Styrofoam® cone, 1 yd of 44"w muslin, ⅛ yd of 44"w terry cloth, thread to match muslin, instant papier mâché, tracing paper, fabric marking pencil, polyester fiberfill, 24½" length of 18-gauge wire, two 2¼" x 10" pieces of craft batting, craft glue, 8 oz. bottle of fabric stiffener, masking tape, gesso, desired paintbrushes, acrylic paint (see Steps 17 and 18 for colors), dark brown water base wood stain, a soft cloth, one 12" square of black felt, one 15" length of cotton cord, and items to decorate Santa (we used a twig basket, birdseed, Spanish moss, twigs, artificial birds, pinecones, ½"w shapes cut from orange peel, birdhouse, sheet moss, artificial greenery, hot glue gun, and glue sticks).

1. For arms, insert wire through cone 4" from top, leaving equal lengths of wire at each side of cone (**Fig. 1a**). Bend each end of wire 2¼" from cone to form shoulders; tightly wrap a piece of batting around each shoulder and tape in place (**Fig. 1b**).

Fig. 1a   **Fig. 1b**

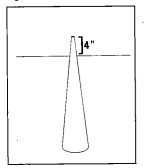

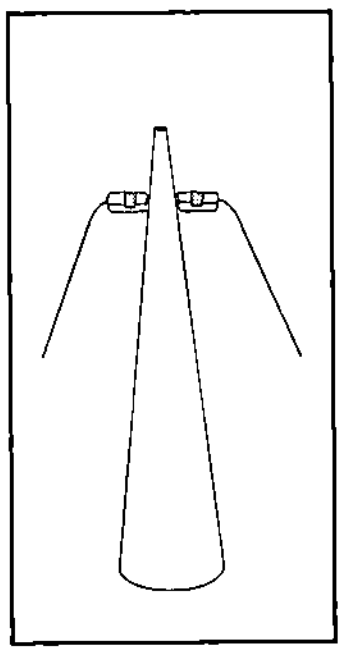

2. For head, follow manufacturer's instructions to make approximately 1 cup of papier mâché. Reserving a small amount for nose and cheeks, mold papier mâché in an approximately 2¼" wide egg shape around the top 3" of cone (**Fig. 2**). With bottom of nose at center of head, use small pieces of papier mâché to form nose and cheeks. Allow to dry.

Fig. 2

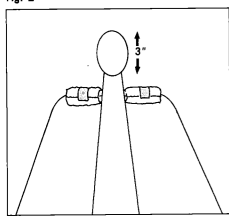

3. Cut the following pieces from muslin: one 14" x 43" piece for coat, two 5½" x 6¼" pieces for sleeves, one 4½" x 11½" piece for hood, four 4" squares for mittens, and two 7" x 10" pieces for sack.
4. (**Note:** Use a ¼" seam allowance throughout unless otherwise stated.) For coat, follow Steps 7 and 8 of Jolly St. Nick instructions, page 16 (do not fold lower edge of coat to wrong side).
5. Referring to **Fig. 3a**, cut neck opening in coat through both layers of fabric. Referring to **Fig. 3b**, cut front opening in coat through one layer of fabric.

Fig. 3a

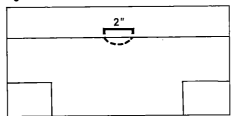

Fig. 3b

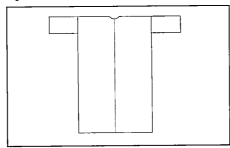

6. For hood, match short edges and fold fabric in half. Sew along one long edge. Cut corner diagonally and turn right side out.
7. Using mitten and sack patterns and fabric pieces, follow **Transferring Patterns** and **Sewing Shapes**, page 156. Set sack aside. Stuff each mitten with a small amount of fiberfill. Place one mitten over each end of wire; tape in place.
8. Follow manufacturer's instructions to apply stiffener to coat.
9. (**Note:** Refer to photo for Steps 9 – 13.) Place coat on body, pulling arms through sleeves. Overlap front edges of coat ¼". Secure fabric at neck opening by inserting several straight pins into cone. Fold bottom edge of coat to wrong side even with bottom of cone.
10. Repeat Step 8 to apply stiffener to hood. Fold raw edges of hood ½" to wrong side. Place hood on head with seam at back of head and front of hood extending ½" from head.
11. For coat and hood trim, refer to photo for placement and measure length of areas to be trimmed. Cut terry cloth 1" wide by the determined lengths. Repeat Step 8 to apply stiffener to lengths of trim. With right sides

up, place lengths of trim on Santa and smooth in place.
12. Use paintbrush to apply stiffener to mittens.
13. Position arms as desired and arrange folds on coat. Arrange hood, covering pins at sides and back of neck. Allow fabric to dry completely.
14. Repeat Step 8 to apply stiffener to sack. Fold raw edge of sack ¼" to wrong side. Arrange sack on back of Santa with top edge approximately 2½" below right shoulder (leave sack open to hold desired decorative items). Allow fabric to dry completely.
15. For hair, eyebrows, mustache, and beard, refer to photo and glue small pieces of fiberfill around face and on front of coat; allow to dry.
16. Paint entire Santa and length of cord with gesso. For mouth, make a small indentation below mustache. Allow to dry. Apply a second coat of gesso to hair, eyebrows, mustache, and beard; allow to dry.
17. (**Note:** For even coverage, apply two coats of paint to each area, allowing paint to dry between coats.) Apply paint in the following order:
    Coat and hood – red
    Mittens – brown
    Sack and cord – lt brown
    Trim – dk ivory
    Face – flesh
    Cheeks – lt pink
    Hair, eyebrows, mustache, and beard – lt ivory
    Mouth – pink
18. Referring to **Fig. 4**, paint eyes blue and black with white highlights. Allow to dry.

Fig. 4

19. To antique Santa, thin stain with water. Working on small areas at a time, use paintbrush to apply stain to Santa; remove excess stain with soft cloth, leaving stain in recessed areas. Allow to dry.
20. Place Santa on felt; draw around bottom of coat with fabric marking pencil. Cut out felt slightly inside pencil line. Glue felt to bottom of cone.
21. Glue one end of cord to sack; arrange cord on Santa as desired. Trim remaining end as needed; glue to Santa.
22. Referring to photo, decorate Santa as desired. (**Note:** It may be necessary to hot glue items to Santa.)

CARD BASKET
(Shown on page 76)

You will need desired basket with handle, green spray paint, glossy wood tone spray (available at craft stores), silk variegated holly, ¼"w red satin ribbon, small pinecones, clusters of red canella berries or desired artificial berries, two artificial cardinals, hot glue gun, and glue sticks.

1. Paint basket green; allow to dry. Use wood tone spray to darken basket to desired shade; allow to dry.
2. (**Note:** Refer to photo for Steps 2 – 5.) Cut individual leaves from holly. Referring to **Fig. 1**, glue leaves to basket handle and basket rim.

Fig. 1

3. Cut two 18" lengths of ribbon. Referring to **Fig. 2**, form each ribbon into a double bow; glue to secure. Glue one bow to greenery on handle. Glue remaining bow to greenery on rim.

Fig. 2

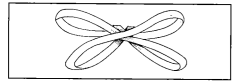

4. Glue cardinals to bows. Glue one end of remaining ribbon to bow on handle. Referring to **Fig. 3**, continue gluing ribbon to basket, ending at bow on rim; trim excess.

Fig. 3

5. Glue pinecones and berries to greenery.

82

SCENTED FIRE STARTERS
(Shown on page 74)

You will need pinecones, paraffin, double boiler or electric frying pan and a can (for melting paraffin), tongs, red crayons with paper removed (to color wax), cinnamon oil (1 teaspoon per 1½ lbs of paraffin), and newspaper.

1. **Caution: Do not melt paraffin over an open flame or directly on burner.** Cover work area with newspaper. Melt paraffin in double boiler over hot water or in a can placed in an electric frying pan filled with water. Add pieces of crayon to melted paraffin until desired color is obtained. Add cinnamon oil.
2. Holding pinecones with tongs, dip cones in paraffin. Allowing paraffin to dry between coats, continue dipping cones until well coated. Allow paraffin to harden completely.
3. To use fire starters, place several pinecones under logs and light cones.

SCENTED JUMBO PINECONE
(Shown on page 77)

You will need a large pinecone (we used a 9"h pinecone), circle of felt to fit bottom of pinecone, craft glue, large double boiler or electric frying pan and a large can (for melting paraffin), and supplies listed in Scented Fire Starters on this page.

1. Follow Steps 1 and 2 of Scented Fire Starters instructions on this page, dipping one-half of pinecone at a time into paraffin.
2. Glue felt to bottom of pinecone to protect surfaces from paraffin.

TREE ORNAMENTS
(Shown on page 75)

For each bird, you will need one 7" square of Ivory Aida (18 ct), embroidery floss (see color key, page 84 or 85), embroidery hoop (optional), 18" of ¼"w red satin ribbon, and one 3¼" x 4¼" gold oval frame with hanger.

1. Center and stitch desired design on fabric. Use 2 strands of floss for Cross Stitch and 1 for Backstitch.
2. Insert stitched piece in frame. Tie ribbon in a bow around hanger; trim ends.

BIRDS OF CHRISTMAS
(Shown on page 77)

You will need one 12" x 15" piece of Ivory Aida (18 ct), embroidery floss (see color key on this page), embroidery hoop (optional), and desired frame.

1. Center and stitch design over two fabric threads. Use 6 strands of floss for Cross Stitch and 2 for Backstitch.
2. Frame stitched piece as desired (we used a custom frame).

X	DMC	¼X	B'ST	ANC.	COLOR
▒	blanc	▒	◪	02	white
■	310	◪	◪	0403	black
B	318			0399	grey
S	350			046	lt red
◎	352			010	vy lt red
+	367			0216	green
C	368			0214	lt green
▨	402			0347	vy lt brown
4	434			0944	dk tan
R	436			0363	tan
▨	535		◪	0400	dk grey
✦	642			0392	beige grey
△	727			0293	yellow
E	729	◪		0890	dk yellow
8	738			0361	lt tan
▢	739			0366	vy lt tan
N	760			09	pink
◙	761			08	lt pink
2	762		◪	0397	lt grey
▣	775	◪		0158	vy lt blue
▨	801			0359	dk brown
■	816			044	dk red
■	817			047	red
◪	890			0212	dk green
■	895			0218	vy dk olive
■	930	◪		0922	vy dk blue
3	931			0921	dk blue
A	932			0920	blue
■	938		◪	0381	vy dk brown
▨	975			0355	brown
▨	976			0349	lt brown
6	986	◪		0246	dk olive
H	987			0244	olive
5	989		◪	0242	lt olive
◙	3325			0159	lt blue
✦	3328			011	dk pink
▢	3348			0265	vy lt olive

BIRDS OF CHRISTMAS (70w x 98h)

BIRDS OF CHRISTMAS (70w x 98h)

Aida 11	6⅜"	x	9"
Aida 14	5"	x	7"
Aida 18	4"	x	5½"
Hardanger 22	3¼"	x	4½"

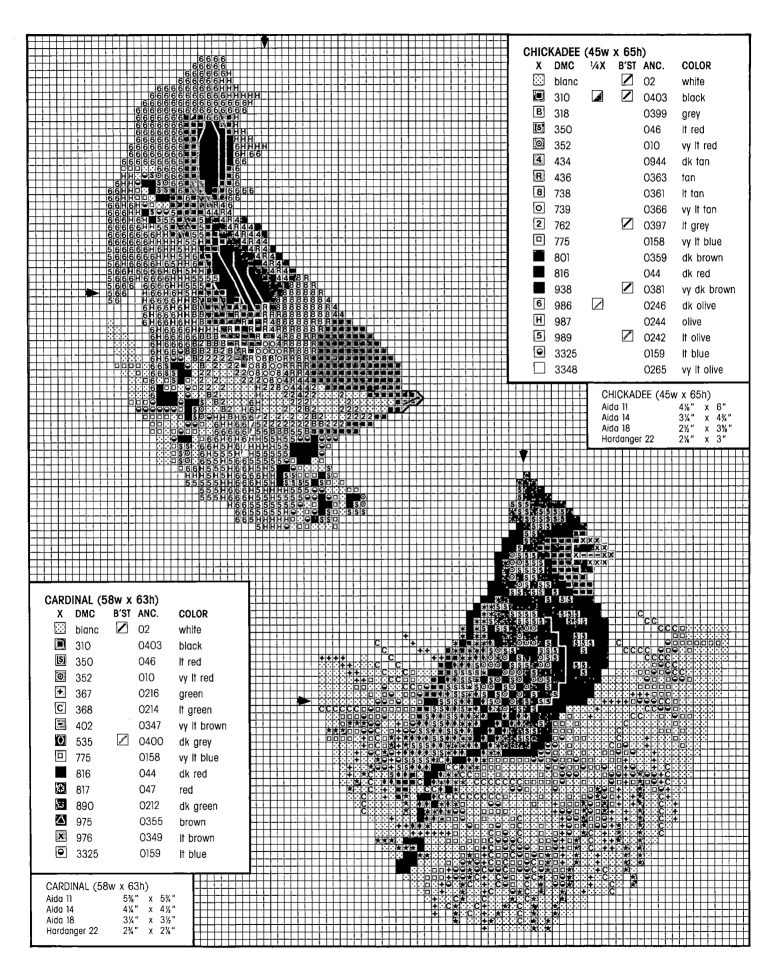

CHICKADEE (45w x 65h)

X	DMC	¼X	B'ST	ANC.	COLOR
⠿	blanc		╱	02	white
◼	310	◢	╱	0403	black
B	318			0399	grey
S	350			046	lt red
◎	352			010	vy lt red
4	434			0944	dk tan
R	436			0363	tan
8	738			0361	lt tan
o	739			0366	vy lt tan
2	762		╱	0397	lt grey
▫	775			0158	vy lt blue
◼	801			0359	dk brown
◼	816			044	dk red
◼	938		╱	0381	vy dk brown
6	986	╱		0246	dk olive
H	987			0244	olive
5	989		╱	0242	lt olive
◉	3325			0159	lt blue
☐	3348			0265	vy lt olive

CHICKADEE (45w x 65h)
Aida 11	4⅛"	x	6"
Aida 14	3¼"	x	4¾"
Aida 18	2½"	x	3⅝"
Hardanger 22	2⅛"	x	3"

CARDINAL (58w x 63h)

X	DMC	B'ST	ANC.	COLOR
⠿	blanc	╱	02	white
◼	310		0403	black
S	350		046	lt red
◎	352		010	vy lt red
+	367		0216	green
C	368		0214	lt green
▦	402		0347	vy lt brown
◐	535	╱	0400	dk grey
▫	775		0158	vy lt blue
◼	816		044	dk red
▩	817		047	red
▨	890		0212	dk green
◿	975		0355	brown
✕	976		0349	lt brown
◒	3325		0159	lt blue

CARDINAL (58w x 63h)
Aida 11	5⅜"	x	5¾"
Aida 14	4¼"	x	4½"
Aida 18	3¼"	x	3½"
Hardanger 22	2¾"	x	2⅞"

84

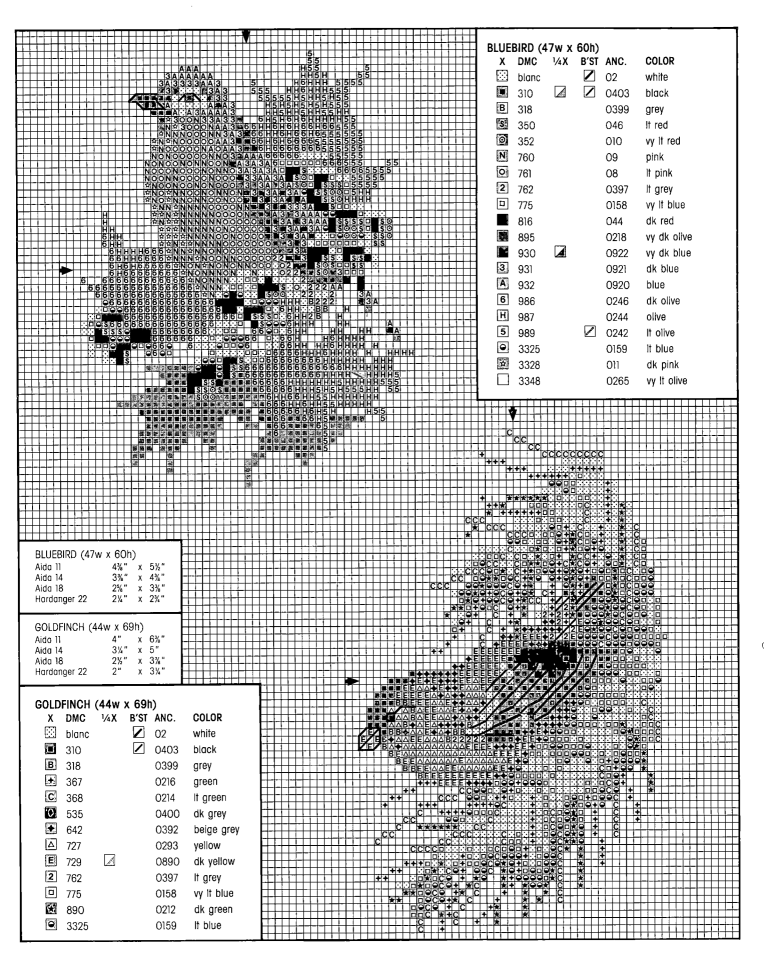

BLUEBIRD (47w x 60h)

X	DMC	1/4X	B'ST	ANC.	COLOR
⠃	blanc		⟋	02	white
■	310	◪	⟋	0403	black
B	318			0399	grey
S	350			046	lt red
◎	352			010	vy lt red
N	760			09	pink
◌	761			08	lt pink
2	762			0397	lt grey
⬜	775			0158	vy lt blue
■	816			044	dk red
▦	895			0218	vy dk olive
◤	930	◪		0922	vy dk blue
3	931			0921	dk blue
A	932			0920	blue
6	986			0246	dk olive
H	987			0244	olive
5	989		⟋	0242	lt olive
◙	3325			0159	lt blue
✿	3328			011	dk pink
☐	3348			0265	vy lt olive

BLUEBIRD (47w x 60h)

Aida 11	4⅜"	x	5½"
Aida 14	3⅜"	x	4⅜"
Aida 18	2⅝"	x	3⅜"
Hardanger 22	2¼"	x	2¾"

GOLDFINCH (44w x 69h)

Aida 11	4"	x	6⅜"
Aida 14	3¼"	x	5"
Aida 18	2½"	x	3⅞"
Hardanger 22	2"	x	3¼"

GOLDFINCH (44w x 69h)

X	DMC	1/4X	B'ST	ANC.	COLOR
⠃	blanc		⟋	02	white
▣	310		⟋	0403	black
B	318			0399	grey
✦	367			0216	green
C	368			0214	lt green
◉	535			0400	dk grey
◆	642			0392	beige grey
△	727			0293	yellow
E	729	◪		0890	dk yellow
2	762			0397	lt grey
⬜	775			0158	vy lt blue
✪	890			0212	dk green
◙	3325			0159	lt blue

THE
SHARING
OF
CHRISTMAS

◆

A season of secrets and surprises, Christmas brings out a childlike excitement in us all. With a flurry of activities, we prepare for the special day, focusing our energy on choosing the right presents for those we love. Handcrafted gifts hold a unique joy, giving twofold to everyone concerned. For the giver there is both satisfaction in creating something special and pleasure in seeing our gift appreciated. And for those who accept our handmade offering, there is a double reward as well — for with our gift, they also receive a portion of our heart.

◆

JOLLY PAPER JEWELRY

This handcrafted jewelry will spread Christmas cheer wherever it's worn! Great for last-minute gifts, the jewelry is fashioned from painted paper and bits of ribbon, cotton, and beads. The Santa and mitten earrings are simple cutouts; the wreath pin and earrings are made with the circles created by a paper hole punch. Teenagers will enjoy crafting these colorful accessories for their friends — and for themselves!

For Santa Earrings, you will need two 3" squares of 140 lb. cold press watercolor paper; red, black, flesh, and pink acrylic paint; three cotton balls; two ear wires; craft glue; large, sharp needle; tracing paper; small round paintbrush; flat paintbrush; and glossy clear acrylic spray.

1. Using flat paintbrush and red paint, paint front and back of one paper square; allow to dry. Apply second coat of paint; allow to dry. Using flesh paint, repeat to paint remaining paper square.
2. Trace Santa hat and face patterns, page 89, onto tracing paper and cut out. Use patterns to cut two hat pieces from red paper square and two face pieces from flesh paper square.
3. Referring to Diagram, glue hats to faces. Use round paintbrush to paint eyes black and cheeks pink; allow to dry.
4. Shape two cotton balls into approximately 1" x 1½" pieces. Apply a line of glue to lower edge of each face. Insert glued edge of one face into center of one cotton ball along one short edge; repeat for remaining face. Allow to dry.
5. For hat trim, refer to photo and glue a small amount of cotton along lower edge of each hat.
6. Use needle to make a hole in top center of each earring. Apply three coats of acrylic spray to earrings, allowing to dry between coats.
7. Place ear wires through holes in earrings.

For Mitten Earrings, you will need one 3" square of 140 lb. cold press watercolor paper; white, red, blue, green, and black acrylic paint; small round paintbrush; flat paintbrush; tracing paper; large, sharp needle; glossy clear acrylic spray; and two ear wires.

1. Using flat paintbrush and white paint, paint front and back of paper square; allow to dry. Apply second coat of paint; allow to dry.
2. Trace mitten pattern, page 89, onto tracing paper and cut out. Use pattern to cut out two mitten pieces from paper square.
3. Referring to photo, use round paintbrush to paint details on each mitten. Outline each mitten with black paint; allow to dry.
4. To complete earrings, follow Steps 6 and 7 of Santa Earrings instructions.

For Wreath Pin and Earrings, you will need one 8" square of 140 lb. cold press watercolor paper, small red beads, flat paintbrush, paper hole punch, craft glue, green acrylic paint, 1/16"w red satin ribbon, two earring posts and backs, one 1" long pin back, tracing paper, and glossy clear acrylic spray.

1. Use green paint and follow Step 1 of Mitten Earrings instructions.

2. Trace pin and earring patterns, page 89, onto tracing paper and cut out. Use patterns to cut out one pin piece and two earring pieces from green paper square.
3. Use hole punch to punch circles from paper square. Referring to photo, glue circles to pin and earring pieces.
4. Make three small bows from ribbon. Referring to photo, glue bows and beads to pin and earrings.
5. Apply three coats of acrylic spray to pin and earrings, allowing to dry between coats.
6. Glue pin back to top center on back of pin. Glue earring posts to back of earrings.

Diagram

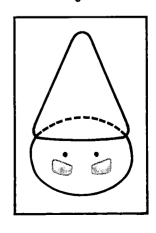

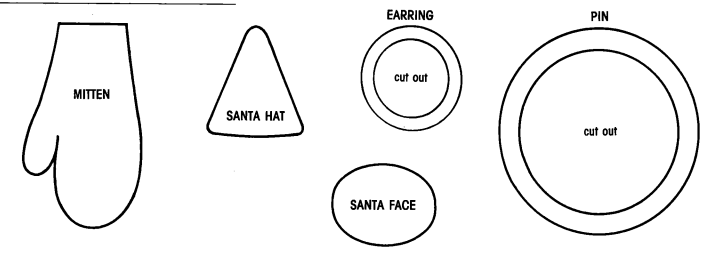

MITTEN

SANTA HAT

EARRING

cut out

SANTA FACE

PIN

cut out

CHRISTMAS COASTERS

With their festive shapes, these coasters will be favorites during the holidays. Sewn of cheery red and green plaids, the Christmas tree and star shapes have holiday charm with country style. Give individual coasters to your coffee-break pals, or tie a matching set together with jute for an extra-special gift.

For each coaster, you will need two 7" squares of fabric for tree or two 9" squares of fabric for star, thread to match fabric, tracing paper, craft batting, fabric marking pencil, crochet hook (to turn fabric), and 8" of jute and thread to match jute (for bow on tree coaster).

1. Trace desired pattern, page 90, onto tracing paper and cut out.

2. With right sides of fabric together, place squares on batting. Follow **Sewing Shapes,** page 156, to make one tree or star coaster, trimming batting close to seam. Sew final closure by hand; press.
3. Topstitch ¼" from edge of coaster.
4. For bow on tree, tie 8" length of jute in a bow and tack to top center of tree.

Patterns on page 90

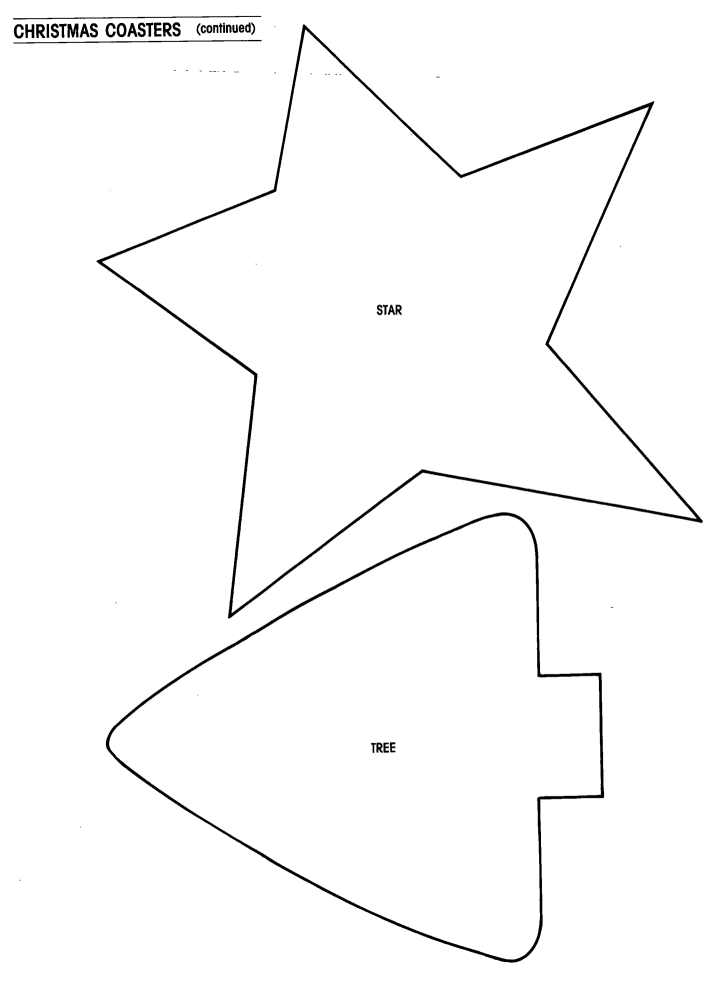

STAR

TREE

ELEGANT STATIONERY

Presented in a matching ribbon-tied folder, this hand-embossed stationery is an elegant gift. To make it, we simply placed ordinary writing paper over a stencil cutout and rubbed in the indentations with a plastic burnisher. The patterns are included for making our quilt block stencils, but any small stencil will do. To make your gift even more attractive, tuck in a pretty pen. Your friends won't believe you embossed these papers yourself!

You will need sheets of colored stationery (we used 6¼" x 9" sheets; one sheet will make one notecard or four gift enclosures); envelopes to match stationery; one sheet of Mylar® or clear, flexible plastic; black permanent felt-tip pen with fine point; craft knife or electric stencil cutter; cardboard; plastic burnisher with pointed tip (available at art supply stores); removable tape; one 9" x 12" sheet of heavyweight colored drawing paper (for folder); thread to match drawing paper; and 16" of ⅛"w satin ribbon.

1. Use permanent pen to trace quilt pattern onto Mylar®. To cut stencil, place Mylar® on cardboard and use craft knife or stencil cutter to cut out design.
2. For each notecard, fold one sheet of stationery in half from top to bottom. Place stencil in desired position on front of notecard; tape in place. Place notecard stencil side down on a smooth, hard surface. Unfold notecard. Use side of burnisher tip to gently rub over design to produce outline. To emphasize design, use point of burnisher to trace over outline of design. Remove stencil. If desired, move stencil on notecard and repeat to emboss design on another area of notecard.
3. For gift enclosure, fold one sheet of stationery in half from top to bottom and

again from left to right; cut along fold lines. Matching short edges, fold each piece in half. Repeat Step 2 to emboss front of each gift enclosure.
4. For folder, fold one long edge of drawing paper 1½" to one side (inside). Fold one short edge 5¾" to inside; repeat for remaining short edge.
5. To emboss design on front of folder, refer to photo and repeat Step 2. On inside of folder, use pencil to mark center on each short edge. Cut ribbon in half. Tape one end of each ribbon length at a pencil mark. Stitch ¼" from all edges of paper, catching taped ends of ribbon in stitching (**Fig. 1**) Remove tape.

Fig. 1

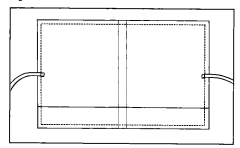

6. Place stationery in folder and tie ribbons together in a bow.

  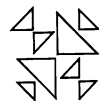 

ARGYLES FOR MEN

Outfit the men on your gift list with these handsome appliquéd argyle sweatshirts. Variations of the classic pullover and cardigan sweaters, they offer stylish warmth around the house, out in the woods, or out on the town. Whatever his lifestyle, he'll enjoy these comfy sweatshirts.

For Cardigan Sweatshirt, you will need one men's sweatshirt one size larger than is normally worn; one package of coordinating wide bias tape; one package of soutache braid; two 12" x 16" pieces of coordinating colors of knit fabric; lightweight fusible interfacing; fusible webbing; reusable pressing sheet; fabric marking pencil; five buttons; tracing paper; ruler; fabric glue; and thread to match sweatshirt, fabrics, braid, and buttons.

1. Find center of shirt by folding shirt in half lengthwise; press. Use fabric marking pencil to draw line down center front of shirt on fold line.
2. Referring to **Fig. 1**, measure 10" from neckband at center front of shirt and mark with fabric marking pencil. Referring to dashed lines in **Fig. 1**, draw lines to connect mark to lower edge of neckband at shoulders.

Fig. 1

3. Beginning at bottom of shirt, cut along drawn lines and around lower edge of neckband (neckband will be cut off).
4. Fold one short edge of bias tape ½" to wrong side and press. With right sides together and beginning with folded short edge of tape at one lower edge of shirt, match long edges and pin tape to shirt. Fold tape to wrong side even with bottom of shirt; trim excess to ½". Sew tape to shirt along fold line in tape; remove pins. Fold tape to wrong side of shirt and pin in place; press. Stitching on right side of shirt, sew through all thicknesses ⅛" from edge of shirt; remove pins. Press shirt.
5. Cut two pieces of interfacing and webbing slightly smaller than knit fabric pieces. Following manufacturer's instructions,

fuse interfacing pieces to wrong sides of fabric pieces. Using pressing sheet and following manufacturer's instructions, fuse webbing to wrong sides of fabric pieces.
6. (**Note:** It may be necessary to adjust diamond pattern. Four diamonds should touch end to end from shoulder seam to top of waistband.) Use diamond pattern, page 93, and follow **Transferring Patterns,** page 156.
7. Matching arrow on pattern to grain of fabric, cut out four diamonds from one piece of knit fabric. Repeat for remaining piece of knit fabric.
8. Referring to photo and alternating colors, fuse diamonds in place. Using a medium width zigzag stitch with a short stitch length and thread to match fabric, appliqué diamonds to shirt.
9. Use fabric marking pencil and ruler to draw lines intersecting through center of diamonds as shown in **Fig. 2.**

Fig. 2

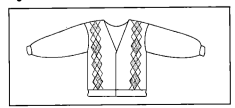

10. Use fabric glue to glue soutache braid along marked lines. Allow to dry. Using thread to match braid, stitch in place.
11. Referring to photo, work five buttonholes on left side of shirt. Sew buttons on right side of shirt.

For Pullover Sweatshirt, you will need one sweatshirt, one package of soutache braid, two 12" x 16" pieces of coordinating colors of knit fabric, lightweight fusible interfacing, fusible webbing, reusable pressing sheet, fabric marking pencil, fabric glue, tracing paper, ruler, and thread to match knit fabric pieces and braid.

1. Cut two pieces of interfacing and webbing slightly smaller than knit fabric pieces. Following manufacturer's instructions, fuse interfacing pieces to wrong sides of fabric pieces. Using pressing sheet and following manufacturer's instructions, fuse webbing to wrong sides of fabric pieces.
2. (**Note:** It may be necessary to adjust diamond pattern. Five diamonds should touch side to side from one side of shirt to other side.) Use diamond pattern, page 93, and follow **Transferring Patterns,** page 156.
3. Matching arrow on pattern to grain of fabric, cut out three diamonds from one piece of knit fabric and two diamonds from remaining piece of knit fabric.

4. Referring to photo and alternating colors, fuse diamonds in place. Using a medium width zigzag stitch with a short stitch length and thread to match fabric, appliqué diamonds to shirt.

5. Use fabric marking pencil and ruler to draw lines intersecting through center of diamonds as shown in **Fig. 1**.

6. Use fabric glue to glue soutache braid along marked lines. Allow to dry. Using thread to match braid, stitch in place.

Place on grain

Fig. 1

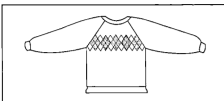

APPLE KITCHEN ACCENTS

A set of stenciled kitchen accessories will make an enchanting gift for someone who's the apple of your eye! Charming red apples painted on a recipe box, index cards, and dish towels transform these ordinary kitchen helpers into cheerful accent pieces. A joy to make as well as to give, this cute collection is a delightful way to help a friend put her kitchen in apple-pie order!

You will need one metal index file box; fine sandpaper; matte white spray paint; red and black acrylic paint; stencil brushes; toothbrush; one 2½" square and one 2" x 6" piece of Mylar® or clear, flexible plastic; black permanent felt-tip pen with fine point; craft knife or electric stencil cutter; cardboard; paper towels; small piece of screen wire; matte clear acrylic spray; index cards; two cotton dish towels; and a pressing cloth.

1. Lightly sand outside surface of box. Use white paint to spray paint box; allow to dry.
2. Use permanent pen to trace apple pattern onto 2½" square of Mylar®. To cut stencil, place Mylar® on cardboard; use craft knife or stencil cutter to cut out apple. Repeat for checked pattern and remaining piece of Mylar®.
3. Referring to photo, position apple stencil on top of box. Hold stencil firmly in place while stenciling. Dip stencil brush into red paint and remove excess paint on a paper towel. Apply paint in a stamping motion;

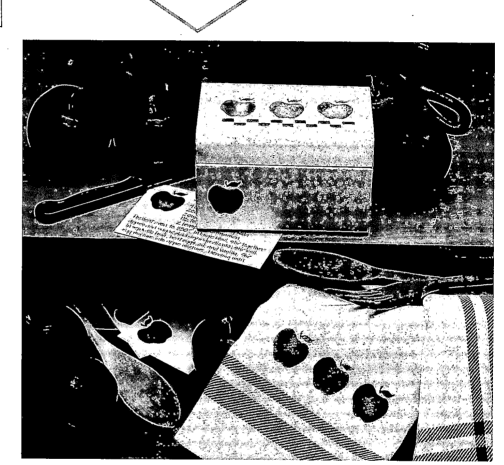

allow to dry. Move stencil and repeat as desired.
4. Repeat Step 3, using black paint to stencil checked design on box.
5. (**Note:** Practice spattering technique on paper before applying paint to box.) To spatter top and all sides of box, dip tip of toothbrush in black paint and brush downwards against edge of screen wire; allow to dry.
6. Spray box with acrylic spray; allow to dry.
7. To stencil each index card, repeat Step 3.

8. To stencil each towel, repeat Step 3. To heat-set paint, use pressing cloth and press over design area with a hot iron.

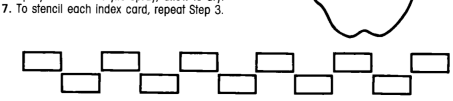

STITCHER'S ORGANIZER

With this handy organizer, stitchers can carry their needlework wherever they go. Easy to make from reversible quilted fabric, the organizer has pockets to store needles, embroidery floss, and more. Two large clear plastic pockets keep charts and patterns neat and visible. There's even a ribbon loop to hold scissors so they'll always be close at hand. Perfect for working at home or for traveling, this organizer will make an indispensible gift for your favorite stitcher!

You will need ¾ yd of reversible quilted fabric, two packages of extra wide double fold bias tape, thread to match fabric and bias tape, ½ yd of heavyweight clear plastic (available at fabric stores), ¾ yd of ⅜"w grosgrain ribbon, one small snap, tracing paper, and two sets of ¾" dia. self-gripping fasteners.

1. Use flap pattern, page 95, and follow **Transferring Patterns**, page 156.
2. From quilted fabric, cut one 13½" x 30½" piece (back) and one 8½" x 10½" piece (center section). Using flap pattern, cut two flaps from quilted fabric.
3. From plastic, cut one 6¼" x 10½" piece (center section) and two 8½" x 13½" pieces (sides).
4. Bind the following pieces with bias tape: one long edge of 6¼" x 10½" plastic piece, one long edge of each 8½" x 13½" plastic piece, one long edge of 8½" x 10½" fabric piece, and the curved edge of each flap piece.
5. (**Note:** Determine which side of fabric will be the outside of organizer. All fabric pieces will then have an outside and inside.) For center section, place the center section fabric piece with outside fabric facing up. Matching raw edges, place center section plastic piece on top of center section fabric piece; baste long raw edges together (bottom). Referring to **Fig. 1**, sew plastic piece to fabric piece through center of plastic piece.

Fig. 1

6. Place back piece with inside fabric facing up. Matching raw edges, center the center section on one long edge of back piece. Baste side and bottom edges of center section to back piece.
7. Matching raw edges, place each side piece on back piece (**Fig. 2.**); baste edges in place.

Fig. 2

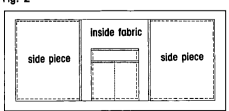

8. Bind all edges of back piece with bias tape, being careful to catch center section and side pieces between bias tape.
9. For scissors holder, cut a 4½" length from ribbon. Fold under ends ¼"; fold under again ¼" and stitch in place. Sew snaps to folded ends of ribbon. Matching ends and snaps, fold ribbon in half. Refer to **Fig. 3** and pin ribbon to center section.

Fig. 3

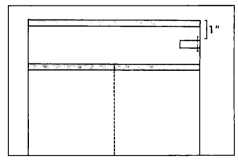

10. Matching raw edges, place one flap on center section with inside fabric facing up. Sew ⅛" from raw edge (**Fig. 4a**). Fold flap over seam and sew ¼" from fold (**Fig. 4b**). Repeat for remaining flap.

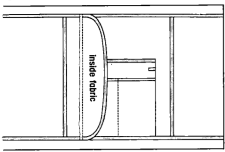

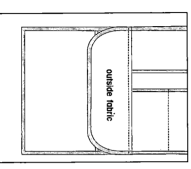

11. On inside fabric, whipstitch loop side (soft side) of one fastener to center of one flap close to bias tape. Whipstitch hook side (firm side) of one fastener to center of side piece to match fastener on flap. Repeat for remaining flap and side piece.

12. Fold organizer with left side over right side. Cut remaining length of ribbon in half. Fold under one end of each length ¼"; fold under again ¼" and pin in place. Refer to **Fig. 5** and sew folded ends of each length of ribbon to outside of back piece; remove pins and reinforce stitching.

Fig. 5

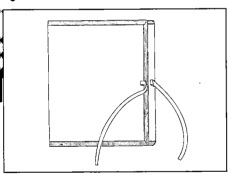

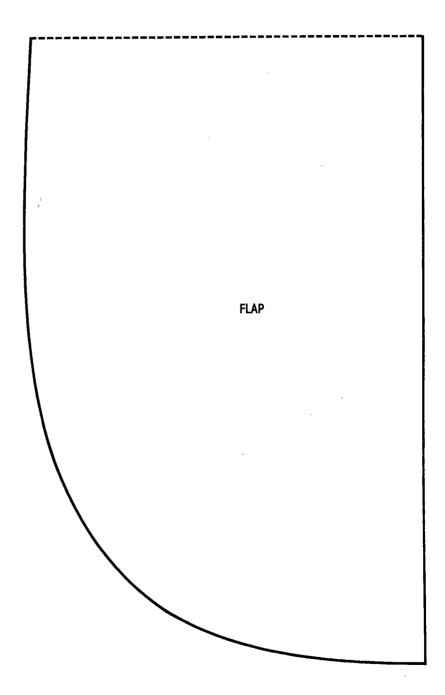

FLAP

HOLIDAY HAIR BOWS

Little girls (and big ones, too!) will be sitting pretty with these handmade hair accessories. Full of Christmas cheer, they're perfect accents for holiday attire. The red and green many-loop bow has festive feminine appeal for dressy occasions. The bright Ho-Ho-Ho ribbon and the plastic bow filled with miniatures offer a touch of whimsy. You'll find a style to fit every girl's fancy!

For Many-Loop Bow, you will need 2 yds each of ¹⁄₁₆"w red, ⅛"w red, ¹⁄₁₆"w green, and ⅛"w green satin ribbon; thread to match ribbon; 26-gauge wire; 2½" long flat barrette; and four 6mm jingle bells.

1. Beginning at open end of barrette and leaving ½" of ribbon extending past end of barrette (**Fig. 1**), layer ribbons on barrette. Wrap wire tightly around ribbons several times, but do not cut wire.

Fig. 1

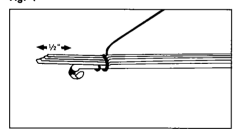

2. Make a 1½" loop with layered ribbons; secure loop with wire (**Fig. 2**).

Fig. 2

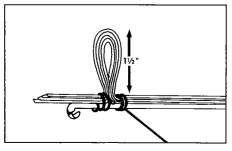

3. Continue forming loops the length of barrette, leaving approximately 8" long streamers at end of barrette (**Fig. 3**).

Fig. 3

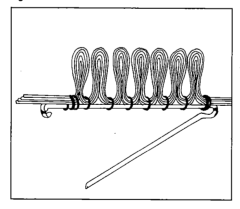

4. Separate ribbons in each loop. Tack one jingle bell to end of each streamer.

For HO-HO-HO Bow, you will need 1¼ yds of 2¼"w red grosgrain ribbon, 3" of 26-gauge wire, 2½" of ¼"w red grosgrain ribbon, 3" long spring-type barrette, hot glue gun, glue sticks, three "H" and three "O" ¾"h wooden letters, and white spray paint.

1. Spray paint letters; allow to dry.
2. Beginning 4½" from one end of 2¼"w ribbon, follow **Fig. 1** to form a 4" long loop; gather ribbon between fingers. Place gathers

next to, but not on top of, each other throughout entire assembly. Form a second loop, same size as first, on the bottom; then gather and hold (**Fig. 2**).

Fig. 1

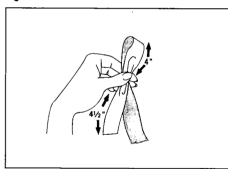

Fig. 2

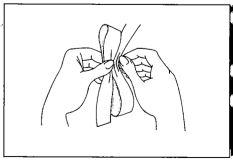

3. Repeat Step 2 to form a third and fourth loop. Leaving a 4½" length of ribbon, trim end (**Fig. 3**).

Fig. 3

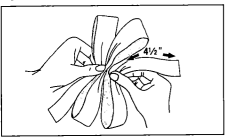

4. Wrap wire tightly around center of bow. Glue ¼"w ribbon over wire, overlapping ends at back of bow.
5. Referring to photo, separate loops and streamers. Glue letters to bow.

6. With opening of barrette on the left, glue bow to barrette (**Fig. 4**).

Fig. 4

For See-Through Bow, you will need ⅛ yd of clear lightweight plastic (available at fabric stores), one 3" long spring-type barrette, 3½" of ⅜"w ribbon, 5" of 26-gauge wire, miniature items and various sizes and colors of sequins to place in bow, hot glue gun, and glue sticks.

1. Cut a piece of plastic 7" x 18". Overlap long edges ¼" and glue together to form a tube.
2. Place miniature items and sequins in tube.
3. Overlap short edges of tube 1" to form a loop. Keeping overlapped area in center of loop, gather center to form a bow; wrap wire tightly around gathered area. Glue ribbon over wire, overlapping ends at back of bow.
4. Glue bow to barrette.

COMFY CUSHION

Great for lounging in front of the TV or chatting on the phone, this denim floor pillow is sure to please a special teen on your gift list. For the varied shades of blue, cut squares from several pairs of faded jeans and stitch them together with the seams on the outside. Before sewing the pillow top and backing together, run the patchwork through several cycles in the washer and dryer to give the clipped edges a soft, worn look. The attached jeans pocket is handy for holding magazines, candy, or other goodies.

You will need sixteen 7¼" squares of denim for pillow top (we used several pairs of faded denim jeans to create color variation), 26" square of fabric for backing, polyester fiberfill, thread to match fabric, and one pocket from denim jeans.

1. (**Note:** Use a ½" seam allowance throughout. Reinforce stitching at beginning and ending of all seams.) For first row, match **wrong** sides and sew two denim squares together along one edge. Repeat to join third and fourth squares to first two squares.
2. Repeat Step 1 to make a total of four rows of four squares each.
3. Matching seams and one long edge, place two rows **wrong** sides together. Sew rows together, breaking stitching at seams and being careful not to catch seams in stitching (**Fig. 1**).

Fig. 1

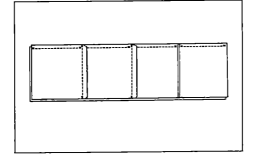

4. Repeat Step 3 to join remaining rows to form pillow top.
5. Clip all seam allowances to within ⅛" of seams at ½" intervals.
6. To fringe pillow top, machine wash and dry top several times.
7. Referring to photo, sew bottom and sides of pocket to pillow.
8. With right sides facing, place pillow top and backing fabric together. Leaving an opening for turning, sew pieces together; cut corners diagonally and turn right side out. Stuff with fiberfill. Sew final closure by hand.

JUST FOR BABY

This carry-along play quilt is just the thing for a baby on the go! The 40" by 40" quilt folds into a 20" square with a handy carrying strap. Lengths of ribbon secure toys to their storage pockets. Baby will love the bright colors and teddy bear appliqués, and Mom will appreciate the convenience of a traveling play area. The quilt makes any spot on the floor a comfortable place for playing or napping!

You will need one 16" x 24" piece and two 8" squares of brown sport suede fabric, one 12" x 15" piece and one 25½" square of red print fabric, scrap of black fabric, 1 yd of 44"w yellow fabric, one 40" square of blue quilted fabric, four 7" squares of blue fabric, four 7" squares of green fabric, two 9" lengths of ⅜"w blue grosgrain ribbon, two 9" lengths of ⅜"w green grosgrain ribbon, one 12" length of ¼"w red grosgrain ribbon, polyester bonded batting, thread to match fabric, 5½ yds of red double fold quilt binding (pieced if necessary), seam ripper, washable fabric marking pen, reusable pressing sheet, lightweight fusible interfacing, fusible webbing, one 1⅜6"w red plastic button, polyester fiberfill, black embroidery floss, tracing paper, and three purchased infant toys (we used plastic keys on a ring, a rattle, and an infant mirror).

1. From interfacing and webbing, cut pieces slightly smaller than 12" x 15" red fabric piece, 16" x 24" brown fabric piece, and black fabric scrap. Following manufacturer's instructions, fuse interfacing pieces to wrong sides of fabric pieces. Using pressing sheet and following manufacturer's instructions, fuse webbing to wrong sides of fabric pieces.
2. Using tracing paper and bear pattern, page 99, trace one pattern each for bear, overalls, and nose; cut out. Using interfaced and webbed fabrics, cut out five bears from brown fabric, five overalls from red fabric, and five noses from black fabric. Referring to pattern, use fabric marking pen to transfer eyes to bears.
3. To assemble each bear, place pressing sheet on ironing board. Referring to pattern, layer bear, overalls, and nose pieces on pressing sheet; fuse pieces together. Peel off pressing sheet while fabric is still hot.

4. From yellow fabric, cut two 8¼" x 40 pieces for top and bottom borders and two 8¼" x 25½" pieces for side borders.
5. Center one bear on right side of one border with bottom of feet ¾" from one long edge (lower edge); fuse in place. Repeat for remaining borders.
6. Referring to **Fig. 1**, use ruler to position remaining bear on right side of one corner of quilted fabric square (backing); fuse in place.

Fig. 1

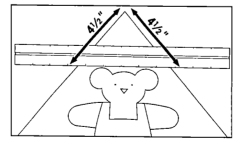

7. Using a medium width zigzag stitch with a short stitch length and thread to match fabric, appliqué bears to fabric pieces. For eyes, use black thread and follow **Fig. 2** to make approximately 5 stitches (shown in grey); pivot and make approximately 5 more stitches (shown in black) over previous stitches. Pull all loose threads to wrong side of fabric; knot and trim ends.

Fig. 2

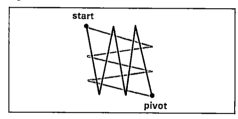

8. (Note: Use a ½" seam allowance throughout.) To assemble quilt front, match right sides and sew lower edge of one side border to one edge of 25½" red fabric square. Repeat to attach remaining side border to opposite side of fabric square. Press seam allowances toward center.
9. Repeat Step 8 to attach top and bottom borders to center fabric square and attached borders.
10. For pockets, place two 7" blue fabric squares right sides together. Leaving an opening for turning, sew pieces together. Cut corners diagonally and turn right side out; press. Sew final closure by hand. Repeat for remaining blue and green squares.
11. Referring to **Fig. 3**, page 99, center one blue pocket on right side of quilt front. Place 1" of one blue ribbon end between pocket and quilt front as shown in **Fig. 3**. Following dashed lines in **Fig. 3**, sew pocket and ribbon end to quilt front. Alternating pocket colors, repeat to sew remaining pockets and ribbons to quilt front.

Fig. 3

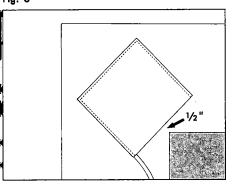

½"

12. Cut batting the same size as backing. Place backing right side down on a flat surface. Matching edges, layer batting and quilt top on backing. Baste layers together, making sure all pieces lay smooth.

13. Use fabric marking pen to draw a line 2" from edge of center fabric square (**Fig. 4**). Referring to dashed lines in **Fig. 4**, machine stitch layers together.

Fig. 4

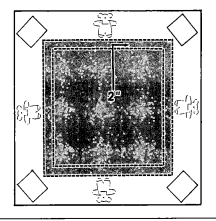

14. To bind edges of quilt, place edges of quilt between folded edges of quilt binding and baste in place. Overlap ends of binding ¾" and trim excess; turn top end ¼" to wrong side. Stitching through all thicknesses of fabric, stitch binding in place. Remove all basting threads.

15. For carrying strap, cut one 23" length from remaining bias binding. Unfold binding and fold short edges ½" to wrong side; press. Refold binding and topstitch along all edges. Make one 1⅜" long buttonhole ½" from one short edge.

16. On corner with bear appliquéd to backing, center strap on quilt front with short end 1" from pocket; securely sew end in place (**Fig. 5**).

Fig. 5

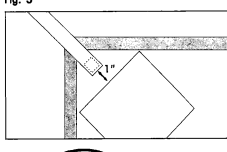

1"

17. On back of quilt, firmly sew button over area where strap was stitched.

18. On remaining corners, make 1⅜" long buttonholes through all layers of fabric with one end of each buttonhole 1" from corners of quilt. Use seam ripper to cut open all buttonholes.

19. For stuffed bear toy, use brown fabric squares and bear pattern and follow **Sewing Shapes**, page 156. Stuff toy with fiberfill; sew final closure by hand. Referring to pattern, use 3 strands of embroidery floss and Satin Stitch to work eyes and nose. Tie red ribbon in a bow around neck; trim ends. Securely tack bow in place.

20. Securely sew one ribbon length to each toy (we whipstitched ribbon to back of bear toy; we threaded ribbon through each purchased toy and machine stitched ribbon together).

21. Place toys in pockets. To fold quilt, match right sides of quilt top and fold in half from top to bottom and again from left to right (bear appliquéd to corner should be on outside). Thread carrying strap through buttonholes in quilt; button strap to quilt.

ANGEL PICTURE FRAME

A dainty handcrafted frame makes a wonderful Christmas gift for a grandmother. And when it's presented with a photograph of her favorite grandchild, this frame is one she'll want to display all year long. To give the memento its soft charm, we covered a mat and frame with lace fabric and added angel cutouts, stars, and a pretty bow. The pastel finish is created with a special painting technique.

You will need one 8" x 10" wood frame, one 8" x 10" mat with 5" x 7" opening, acrylic paint (see Steps 11 and 12 for colors), one 13" x 15" piece of lace fabric, 1 yd of ¼"w twill tape, poster board, ½" gummed stars, 5" of ½"w pre-gathered lace trim, scrap of yarn, gesso, craft glue, tracing paper, graphite transfer paper, paper towels, flat paintbrushes, small bowl, and matte clear acrylic spray.

1. Trace patterns onto tracing paper. Use transfer paper to transfer patterns to poster board; cut out pieces.
2. Glue mat to inside of frame; allow to dry.
3. (**Note:** When frame is used in instructions, it refers to both mat and frame.) Apply an even coat of glue to front and sides of frame. Glue lace fabric to frame and smooth out wrinkles; allow to dry. Fold remaining lace to back of frame and glue in place; allow to dry.
4. Referring to **Fig. 1**, cut lace fabric covering frame opening; trim to within 1" of frame. Fold lace fabric to back of frame and glue in place.

Fig. 1

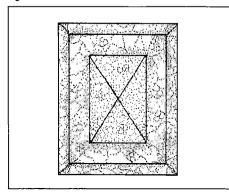

5. (**Note:** Refer to photo for Steps 5 – 9.) Apply a thin coat of glue to backs of all pieces except arms; glue pieces to frame.
6. Pour glue into bowl. Tie twill tape into an approximately 5"w bow with 10" streamers. Dip bow in glue. Remove bow from glue and pull tape through fingers to remove excess glue. Arrange bow on frame; allow to dry.
7. Apply a thin coat of glue to backs of arm pieces; glue to frame. Glue stars to frame.
8. For trim on dresses, cut two 1⅜" lengths of lace trim; glue to lower edges of dresses. For cuffs on dresses, cut two ⅛" x ⅜" pieces from lace trim; glue to wrists.
9. For haloes, cut two 1½" lengths of yarn; dip in bowl of glue. Remove yarn from glue and pull yarn through fingers to remove excess glue. Form each length into an oval and glue to frame; allow to dry.
10. Apply one coat of gesso to entire project; allow to dry.
11. (**Note:** For even coverage, apply two coats of paint to each area, allowing to dry between coats. Some colors may require more than two coats.) Referring to photo, apply paint in the following order:
    Frame — lt blue
    Hair — lt brown
    Faces and hands — flesh
    Dresses — pink
    Wings — lt yellow
    Stars and haloes — gold
    Bow — rose

12. Use ivory paint to dry brush entire frame. To dry brush, use a dry paintbrush and dip tips of bristles in paint. Brush tips across paper towels. Lightly stroke brush across surface of frame, highlighting prominent areas. Allow to dry.
13. Spray entire frame with two coats of acrylic spray, allowing to dry between coats.

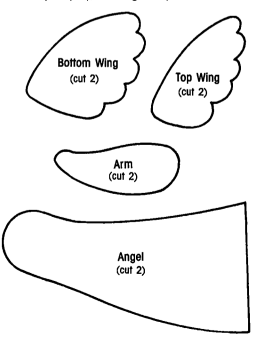

Bottom Wing
(cut 2)

Top Wing
(cut 2)

Arm
(cut 2)

Angel
(cut 2)

FOR YOUR NUMBER 1 GOLFER

If golf is a favorite pastime of the Number 1 man in your life, these golf club covers will make him feel like a pro! Worked in simple stockinette stitch, the knitted pieces are perfect for identifying and protecting his lucky clubs. To make the gift a family affair, Mom can knit the covers, and the kids can use enamel paints to personalize a set of golf balls with their own designs and messages. This special gift will suit Dad to a tee!

ABBREVIATIONS

CC   Contrasting Color
K   knit
MC   Main Color
mm   millimeters
P   purl
st(s) stitch(es)

( ) – contains explanatory remarks

MATERIALS

MC – Worsted weight yarn, approximately:
   5 ounces (140 grams, 315 yards)
CC – Worsted weight yarn, approximately:
   2 ounces (60 grams, 125 yards)
Straight knitting needles, sizes 6 (4.25 mm)
   and 7 (4.50 mm) **or** sizes needed for
   gauge
Yarn needle

GAUGE: With larger size needles,
      in Stockinette Stitch,
      5 sts and 7 rows = 1"
      **DO NOT HESITATE TO CHANGE
      NEEDLE SIZE TO OBTAIN CORRECT
      GAUGE.**

CLUB COVER (Make 4)

RIBBING
With smaller size needles and MC, cast on 36 sts **loosely**.

Work in K2, P2 ribbing for 5" increasing 5 sts evenly spaced across last row: 41 sts.

BODY
Change to larger size needles.
Beginning with a knit row, work in Stockinette Stitch (knit one row, purl one row) until cover measures approximately 10¾" from cast on edge.
Cut yarn, leaving an 18" end.

FINISHING
Thread yarn needle with yarn end and separately slip each stitch from the knitting needle onto the yarn, gathering the stitches tightly.
Secure end.
Using CC, follow chart to center and work Duplicate Stitch (page 30) with bottom of number 1" above ribbing.
Weave seam.
Using MC and CC, make Pom-Pom (**Fig. 1** and **Fig. 2**).
Sew pom-pom to top of Cover.

POM-POM
Cut a 3½" square of cardboard. Wind yarn around cardboard until it is approximately ½" thick in the middle. Slip the yarn off the cardboard and tie an 18" length of MC around the middle (**Fig. 1**). Leave yarn ends long enough to attach the pom-pom. Cut the loops on both ends and trim the pom-pom into a smooth ball (**Fig. 2**).

Fig. 1

Fig. 2

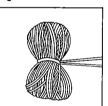

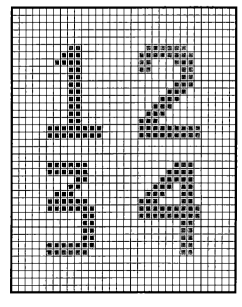

PET STOCKINGS

With their very own Christmas stockings, your pets will really feel like part of the family this holiday season. Decorated with dog and cat shapes in bright red and green, these adorable pet stockings are easy to make using simple sewing and appliqué techniques. You'll have fun choosing pet toys and snacks to stuff inside, and the children will enjoy having their faithful companions share in the holiday festivities!

For each stocking, you will need two 12" fabric squares for stocking; two 12" fabric squares for lining; the following fabric pieces for pet appliqué: one 7" x 8" piece for body, one 3" x 2" piece for bow, and a scrap of black fabric for nose; two 3mm black beads; ½ yd of ⅜"w satin ribbon; thread to match fabric and ribbon; lightweight fusible interfacing; fusible webbing; reusable pressing sheet; tracing paper; fabric marking pencil; and desired gift tag.

1. Using tracing paper and desired pattern, page 103 or 104, trace one pattern each for body, bow, nose, and stocking; cut out.
2. Place stocking fabric pieces right sides together and center stocking pattern on top. Use fabric marking pencil to draw around pattern; cut out. Repeat for lining fabric pieces.
3. Cut interfacing and fusible webbing slightly smaller than the body, bow, and

nose fabric pieces. Following manufacturer's instructions, fuse interfacing to wrong sides of fabric pieces. Using pressing sheet, follow manufacturer's instructions to fuse webbing to wrong sides of fabric pieces.
4. Center body pattern on fabric piece and draw around pattern with fabric marking pencil; cut out. Repeat for bow and nose patterns.
5. Referring to pattern for placement, fuse body piece to right side of one stocking piece (front); repeat to fuse bow and nose pieces to body.
6. Using a medium width zigzag stitch with a short stitch length and thread to match fabric, appliqué fabric pieces to stocking piece. For eyes, refer to pattern and tack beads to body.

7. (**Note:** Use a ¼" seam allowance throughout.) With right sides facing and leaving top edge open, sew stocking pieces together. Trim seam allowance and clip curves. Repeat for lining pieces. Turn stocking only right side out and press.
8. With wrong sides together, insert lining into stocking. Fold top edges of stocking and lining ½" to wrong side; press. Slipstitch lining to stocking.
9. For hanger, cut a 4" length of ribbon; fold in half to form a loop. Place ends of hanger at heel side of stocking with approximately 1¼" of loop extending above stocking; tack in place.
10. For gift tag, thread remaining piece of ribbon through a hole in tag and tie in a bow; trim ends. Tack bow to hanger.

Patterns continued on page 104

MINIATURE CHRISTMAS SAMPLER

Create remembrances of yesteryear with this miniature cross stitch Christmas sampler. Stitched in rich holiday colors, the 2¼" by 3" design is filled with tiny yuletide motifs. Presented with a small wooden easel for display, this petite creation will make a welcome gift for a friend or relative. With its old-fashioned charm, it's sure to become a treasured keepsake.

You will need one 6" x 7" piece of Ivory Aida (18 ct), embroidery floss (see color key), embroidery hoop (optional), and desired frame.

1. Center and work design on fabric. Use 2 strands of floss for Cross Stitch, 1 for Backstitch, and 1 for French Knots.
2. Frame stitched piece as desired (we used a purchased frame with a 2½" x 3½" opening).

SAMPLER (40w x 54h)

X	DMC	¼X	B'ST	ANC.	COLOR
⊟	224			0893	pink
▨	433	◿	◿	0371	brown
◆	501			0878	dk green
△	502			0876	green
◙	729		◿	0890	gold
▩	816		◿	044	red
▲	930			0922	blue
◉	816	red French Knot			

SAMPLER (40w x 54h)

Aida 11	3¾"	x 5"
Aida 14	2⅞"	x 3⅞"
Aida 18	2¼"	x 3"
Hardanger 22	1⅞"	x 2½"

WINTER WOODLAND TABLE SCARF

Bring lacy elegance to holiday gatherings with our easy-to-make filet crochet table runner. This lovely heirloom piece will enhance cherished dinnerware or complement a favorite centerpiece. The winter woodland design makes the scarf a lovely seasonal accessory. You'll want to give this gift early so it can be enjoyed throughout the holidays.

GENERAL INSTRUCTIONS

Finished size: approximately 18" x 36"

ABBREVIATIONS
ch(s)   chain(s)
dc   double crochet(s)
rep   repeat
sp(s)   space(s)
st   stitch

★ — work instructions following ★ as many **more** times as indicated in addition to the first time.
( ) or [ ] — work enclosed instructions **as many** times as specified by the number immediately following **or** contains explanatory remarks.

GAUGE

18 dc and 8 rows = 2"

Correct gauge is essential for proper size. Hook size given in instructions is merely a guide and should never be used without first making a sample swatch approximately 4" square in the stitch, yarn, and hook specified. Then measure the swatch, counting your stitches and rows carefully. If you have more stitches per inch than specified, try again with a larger size hook; if fewer, try again with a smaller size. Keep trying until you find the size that will give you the specified gauge. DO NOT HESITATE TO CHANGE HOOK SIZE TO OBTAIN CORRECT GAUGE.

MATERIALS

Bedspread Weight Cotton, approximately:
1130 yards
Steel crochet hook, size 5 (2.00 mm) **or** size needed for gauge

WORKING WITH CHARTS

Each blank square on the chart represents one Space (ch 2, dc) and each grey square represents one Block (3 dc). For right side rows, the chart should be read from right to left; for wrong side rows, the chart should be read from left to right.

INSTRUCTIONS

Ch 164 **loosely**.

Row 1 (Right side): Dc in eighth ch from hook, ★ ch 2, skip 2 chs, dc in next ch; rep from ★ across: 53 ch-2 sps.

Row 2: (Ch 5, turn, dc in next dc **(beginning Space over Space made)**), ★ (work 2 dc in next Space, dc in next dc **(Block over Space made)**); rep from ★ across to last Space, (ch 2, dc in next dc **(Space over Space made)**).

Row 3: Work beginning Space, (dc in next 3 dc **(Block over Block made)**), (ch 2, skip 2 dc, dc in next dc **(Space over Block made)**), follow chart across.

Row 4-144: Follow chart; do not finish off.

EDGING

Turn; (slip st, ch 3, 2 dc) in same sp, (slip st, ch 3, 2 dc) in each ch-2 sp around table runner; join with a slip st to first slip st; finish off.

MERRY NIGHTWEAR

'Twas the night before Christmas, when all through the house ... children and grown-ups alike wore nightclothes adorned with festive cross stitch designs. Perfect for Christmas Eve, these nightclothes are quick and easy to create using purchased gowns, nightshirts, and pajamas. We stitched the reindeer design over the waffle grid on thermal pajamas. The other designs were stitched on a variety of nightwear using waste canvas, a removable evenweave canvas that allows you to cross stitch on ordinary fabric. With these merry nightclothes, the whole family can wait for Santa in style!

For Twas The Night, Santa and Sleigh, or Santa sleepwear, you will need desired garment, embroidery floss (see color key, page 109), #24 Tapestry needle, 8.5 mesh waste canvas (refer to Step 1 for amount needed), lightweight non-fusible interfacing, masking tape, embroidery hoop (optional), tweezers, and a spray bottle filled with water.

1. Cut waste canvas 2" larger than design size on all sides. Cut interfacing same size as canvas. Cover edges of canvas with masking tape.
2. Refer to photo for placement of design; mark center of design on garment with a straight pin.
3. Match center of canvas to pin. Use blue threads in canvas to pin canvas straight on garment. Pin interfacing to wrong side of garment under canvas. Baste securely around edges of canvas through all three thicknesses. Then baste from corner to corner and from side to side.
4. **(Note:** Using a hoop is recommended when working on large garments.) Work design on canvas, stitching from large holes to large holes. Use 6 strands of floss for Cross Stitch, 2 for Backstitch, and 3 for French Knots.
5. Trim canvas to within ¾" of design and

remove basting threads. Use spray bottle to dampen canvas until it becomes limp. Pull out canvas threads one at a time using tweezers.
6. Trim interfacing close to design.

For Reindeer sleepwear, you will need desired thermal garment, embroidery floss (see color key, page 109), #24 Tapestry needle, lightweight non-fusible interfacing, and an embroidery hoop (optional).

1. Cut interfacing 2" larger than design size on all sides.
2. Refer to photo to determine placement of design; mark center of design on garment with a straight pin.
3. On wrong side of garment, match center of interfacing to pin; pin interfacing to garment. Baste around edges of interfacing through both thicknesses. Then baste from corner to corner and from side to side.
4. **(Note:** Using a hoop is recommended when working on large garments.) Work design on garment over fabric ribs, using indented squares for Cross Stitch corners. Use 6 strands of floss for Cross Stitch, 2 for Backstitch, and 3 for French Knots.
5. Trim interfacing close to design and remove basting threads.

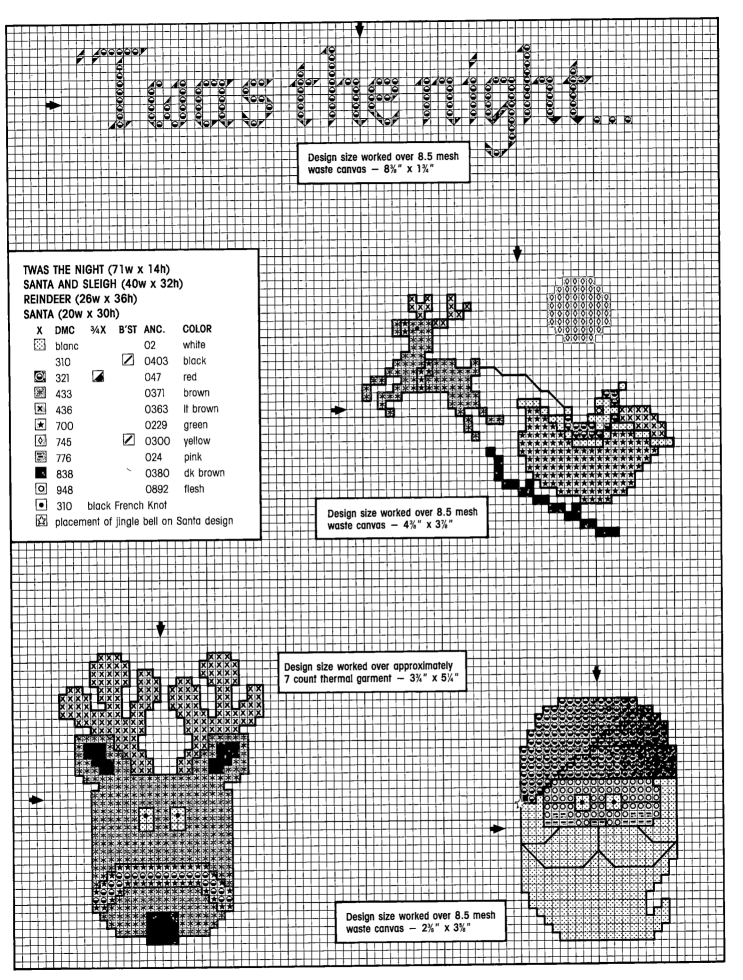

Design size worked over 8.5 mesh
waste canvas — 8⅜" x 1¾"

TWAS THE NIGHT (71w x 14h)
SANTA AND SLEIGH (40w x 32h)
REINDEER (26w x 36h)
SANTA (20w x 30h)

X	DMC	¾X	B'ST	ANC.	COLOR
⊞	blanc			02	white
	310		∕	0403	black
◉	321	◢		047	red
✳	433			0371	brown
✕	436			0363	lt brown
★	700			0229	green
◊	745		∕	0300	yellow
▦	776			024	pink
■	838		`	0380	dk brown
⊙	948			0892	flesh
⦿	310		black French Knot		
☆	placement of jingle bell on Santa design				

Design size worked over 8.5 mesh
waste canvas — 4⅜" x 3⅞"

Design size worked over approximately
7 count thermal garment — 3¾" x 5¼"

Design size worked over 8.5 mesh
waste canvas — 2⅜" x 3⅞"

109

THE
TASTES
OF
CHRISTMAS

♦

Surrounded by family and friends, we find that the wonderful foods of Christmas are made better with the sharing. Aromas of holiday baking stir memories of bygone Christmas gatherings and hold the promise of yet another happy celebration. Gift packages of favorite cookies and candies tell special friends how much we care. Christmas dinner, with both old dishes and new, becomes an opportunity to delight the ones we love. With hearts full of hospitality, we specialize in tempting hors d'oeuvres and rich desserts to turn even the simplest visit into a festive occasion. And in each of our heartfelt gestures, there resides the essential ingredient — love!

♦

KEEPING CHRISTMAS

As family and friends gather for Christmas dinner, sounds of happy conversation and laughter fill the air. When we open our hearts and homes for this joyous occasion, we experience the "keeping" of Christmas that Charles Dickens wrote about in his classic story, A Christmas Carol. Though our lives are very different from those in the nineteenth century London that Dickens knew, English and American families alike continue to build their own cherished traditions — many centered on the family Christmas dinner. Roasted to golden perfection, turkey has always been popular with Americans, while a succulent beef rib roast has been a favorite of the English. Both of these traditional entrées are featured here, along with a selection of salads, soup, vegetables, pie, and other dishes. Whether you use just a few of the recipes or plan a complete menu with them, these distinctive foods are sure to please those gathered 'round your table.

(Top) Thin slices of Standing Rib Roast with Madeira Mushroom Gravy make an elegant serving. Individual Yorkshire Puddings are a unique accompaniment for this traditional English entrée.

(Bottom) Roast Turkey Glazed with Honey is a moist, delicious main course. A distinctive touch is added when Cornbread Dressing is nestled in grape leaves and served with Sour Cream Giblet Gravy.

STANDING RIB ROAST WITH MADEIRA MUSHROOM GRAVY

ROAST
    1 standing rib of beef
        (about 10 pounds or 4 ribs)
    2 teaspoons salt
    1 teaspoon freshly ground pepper
    1 teaspoon ground thyme

GRAVY
    ⅔ cup water
    2 tablespoons butter or margarine
    2 tablespoons lemon juice
    ½ pound fresh mushrooms, sliced
    ¼ cup butter or margarine
    ½ cup finely chopped onion
    1½ cups beef broth
    2 tablespoons tomato paste
    ½ cup Madeira wine
    2 tablespoons all-purpose flour
        Salt and freshly ground pepper

Sprinkle roast with 2 teaspoons salt, 1 teaspoon pepper, and thyme; rub into roast. Place roast on rack in roasting pan. Insert meat thermometer into thickest portion of meat without touching bone. Allow to stand at room temperature 30 minutes.

Preheat oven to 500 degrees. Roast meat 10 minutes. Reduce temperature to 350 degrees. Continue roasting until meat thermometer registers 130 degrees (about 17 minutes per pound). Transfer roast to serving platter.

Combine water, 2 tablespoons butter, and lemon juice in saucepan. Bring to a boil over medium-high heat. Reduce heat to low and add mushrooms. Cover and cook 5 minutes. Pour off fat from roasting pan, reserving for Yorkshire Pudding, if desired. Add ¼ cup butter to roasting pan and place over medium-high heat, stirring to melt. Add onion and sauté until transparent. Drain mushroom liquid into pan. Add beef broth, tomato paste, and Madeira; blend well. Stir in mushrooms and flour. Stir until gravy is slightly thickened and mushrooms are heated through. Salt and pepper to taste. Serve with roast.
Yield: 8 to 10 servings

YORKSHIRE PUDDING

        Hot drippings from roast or melted margarine
    1½ cups all-purpose flour
    1 teaspoon salt
    ¾ cup milk at room temperature
    3 eggs at room temperature, lightly beaten
    ¾ cup water at room temperature

Preheat oven to 400 degrees. Pour ¼-inch of drippings or margarine into each cup of a 12-cup muffin pan. Place muffin pan in oven to heat drippings while preparing batter. In a medium mixing bowl, combine flour and salt. Make a well in the center and stir in milk. Beat in eggs. Add the water, beating until bubbly. Remove muffin pan from oven and immediately fill each cup slightly less than half full with batter. Bake 20 minutes. Reduce heat to 350 degrees; bake 15 minutes more. Serve immediately.
Yield: 12 servings

ROAST TURKEY GLAZED WITH HONEY

    1 turkey (12 to 14 pounds)
        Salt and freshly ground pepper
    ¼ cup butter or margarine, melted
    ½ cup honey

Preheat oven to 350 degrees. Remove giblet packet from turkey and reserve for another use. Rinse turkey and pat dry with paper towels. Liberally salt and pepper turkey inside and out. Tie ends of legs to tail with kitchen twine; lift wing tips up and over back so they are tucked under bird. Place on rack in roasting pan with breast side up. Insert meat thermometer into thickest part of thigh without touching bone. Pour 1 cup water into the pan. Brush turkey with butter. Loosely cover with aluminum foil and roast 2½ hours. Remove foil from turkey. Reduce heat to 325 degrees. Roast uncovered until done (about 1 hour), basting often with honey. To test for doneness, meat thermometer should register 180 degrees, or the juices should run clear when the thickest part of the thigh is pierced with a fork. Remove from oven and allow turkey to stand 20 minutes before carving.
Yield: 10 to 12 servings

CORNBREAD DRESSING IN GRAPE LEAVES

    ½ cup butter or margarine
    ½ cup chopped celery
    1 small onion, coarsely chopped
    2 tablespoons minced parsley
    5 cups cornbread crumbs
    2 cups white bread crumbs
    1½ cups chicken broth
    1 teaspoon ground sage
    ½ teaspoon poultry seasoning
    1 teaspoon salt
    ½ teaspoon freshly ground pepper
    1 egg, lightly beaten
    14 grape leaves in brine, rinsed and separated

Preheat oven to 350 degrees. Melt butter in skillet. Add celery, onion, and parsley and sauté until onion is transparent. Remove from heat; pour into large mixing bowl. Stir in all bread crumbs and chicken broth. Add sage, poultry seasoning, salt, and pepper, adjusting seasoning as desired. Stir in egg. Place about ½ cup stuffing in the center of each grape leaf; gently press sides of each leaf around mound of stuffing. Place stuffed leaves in a baking dish with sides touching. Cover and bake 25 to 30 minutes or until stuffing is heated through.
Yield: 14 servings　Continued on page 115

113

KEEPING CHRISTMAS

ACORN SQUASH SOUP

4 cups water
2 medium acorn squash, scrubbed, halved, and seeds removed
1 large onion, sliced
1 yellow bell pepper, sliced
3 tablespoons butter or margarine
3 apples, cored and diced
1 teaspoon curry powder
1 tablespoon Worcestershire sauce
3 cups chicken broth
Salt and freshly ground pepper
2 cups half and half

In large saucepan, bring water to a boil. Add squash, cover, and boil 15 to 20 minutes or until tender. Remove squash and allow to cool; reserve liquid. When cool enough to handle, scoop out squash with a spoon and discard skin.

In a large saucepan, sauté onion and bell pepper in butter until onion is transparent. Add squash, reserved liquid, apples, curry, Worcestershire, and chicken broth. Salt and pepper to taste. Bring to a boil. Reduce heat to simmer. Partially cover and cook 15 minutes, stirring occasionally.

Place squash mixture in a blender or food processor and purée. Return to saucepan. Stir in half and half, adjust seasonings, and cook over medium heat just until heated through; do not allow to boil.
Yield: 8 to 10 servings

CARAMELIZED NEW POTATOES

20 small new potatoes, scrubbed
½ cup butter or margarine
½ cup brown sugar

Cook unpeeled potatoes in well-salted boiling water 15 to 20 minutes, or until tender. Remove from heat, drain, and allow to cool slightly; peel.

Melt the butter in a large, heavy skillet over medium heat. Stir in the brown sugar and cook, stirring constantly, until the mixture bubbles and thickens slightly (about 5 minutes). Add the potatoes and cook 2 to 3 minutes, stirring constantly until the potatoes are thoroughly coated with the caramel. Place in a heated serving dish and serve immediately.
Yield: 8 to 10 servings

SPINACH SALAD WITH WARM DRESSING

DRESSING
½ cup red wine vinegar
¼ cup water
2 teaspoons lemon juice
1 teaspoon Dijon-style mustard
1 teaspoon Worcestershire sauce
1 tablespoon granulated sugar
¾ teaspoon garlic salt
¼ teaspoon freshly ground pepper
½ cup olive oil

SALAD
½ cup slivered almonds, toasted
½ pound fresh mushrooms, sliced
3 green onions, chopped
4 slices bacon, cooked and crumbled
1 bunch fresh spinach, rinsed and torn into pieces
1 bunch red leaf lettuce, rinsed and torn into pieces

Combine dressing ingredients in a jar with a tight-fitting lid. Close jar and shake vigorously.

Toss salad ingredients together in serving bowl. Before serving, pour the dressing into a non-aluminum saucepan and stir over medium heat until heated through. Serve warm dressing with salad.
Yield: 8 to 10 servings

CORN-STUFFED TOMATOES

5 medium tomatoes
2 tablespoons butter or margarine
2 tablespoons all-purpose flour
1 teaspoon salt
¼ teaspoon freshly ground pepper
1 cup milk
5 slices bacon, cooked and crumbled
½ cup finely chopped green onion
3 cups frozen corn, cooked in salted water
Salt and freshly ground pepper

Cut tomatoes in half. Scoop out as much flesh as possible, invert on paper towels, and drain.

Preheat oven to 350 degrees. Melt butter in saucepan over medium-low heat. Stir in flour, 1 teaspoon salt, and ¼ teaspoon pepper. Continue cooking until mixture is smooth and bubbly. Slowly pour in milk, stirring constantly. Increase heat to medium and continue cooking and stirring until mixture thickens (about 1 minute). Remove from heat and stir in bacon, green onion, and corn. Salt and pepper to taste. Fill each tomato half with corn mixture and place on baking sheet. Cover with aluminum foil and bake 25 to 30 minutes or just until heated through.
Yield: 10 servings

Continued from page 113

SOUR CREAM GIBLET GRAVY

Neck and giblets from turkey
1 medium onion, chopped
3 tablespoons butter or margarine
4 cups water
1 teaspoon paprika
2 tablespoons chopped parsley
½ cup all-purpose flour
½ cup water
½ cup sour cream
Salt and freshly ground pepper

Clean and wash neck and giblets; set aside. In large saucepan, sauté onion in butter until transparent. Add neck and giblets and 4 cups water. Simmer over medium heat until meat is tender (1 to 1½ hours). Add paprika and parsley and simmer 10 minutes more. Remove neck and giblets from pan, reserving liquid and onion. Remove meat from neck; discard bone. Chop meat and giblets and return to saucepan with reserved liquid and onion. In small bowl, combine flour with ½ cup water. Beat in sour cream until smooth. Stir ½ cup liquid from saucepan into sour cream mixture and stir sour cream mixture into giblets. Salt and pepper to taste. Cook over medium-low heat 15 to 20 minutes or until thickened and heated through.
Yield: about 4½ cups gravy

(Top) Garnished with sage leaves and apple slices, Acorn Squash Soup makes an attractive first course for an elegant dinner. A subtle blend of apples and curry complements the squash and adds delicate flavor to this rich soup.

(Bottom left) Spinach Salad with Warm Dressing features fresh mushrooms, toasted almonds, and crisp bacon. Warming the dressing intensifies its spicy vinegar flavor.

(Bottom right) Corn-Stuffed Tomatoes bring exciting new flavors to the table. Caramelized New Potatoes offer a taste of Old World ingenuity.

KEEPING CHRISTMAS

CANDIED GINGER BISCUITS

- 2 cups all-purpose flour
- 1 teaspoon salt
- 1 tablespoon baking powder
- ⅓ cup vegetable shortening
- ½ cup finely minced crystallized ginger
- 2 tablespoons brown sugar
- 1 teaspoon ground ginger
- ½ teaspoon ground cinnamon
- 1 cup milk
- 2 tablespoons butter, melted

Preheat oven to 450 degrees. In mixing bowl, combine flour, salt, and baking powder. Cut in shortening with a pastry blender or two knives until mixture resembles coarse meal. Stir in crystallized ginger, brown sugar, ground ginger, and cinnamon. Add milk and stir just until blended. Turn out on a lightly floured board and gently knead just until dough holds together. Pat out dough until it is about ½-inch thick. Cut with 2½-inch round cutter and place on ungreased baking sheet. Bake 15 to 20 minutes or until golden brown. Remove from oven and brush with melted butter.
Yield: about 20 biscuits

CRANBERRY-APPLE RELISH

- 2 cups granulated sugar
- 2 cups water
- 4 cups fresh or frozen cranberries
- 1 apple, cored and finely chopped
- 1 teaspoon grated orange peel
- ½ cup raisins

In a large saucepan, bring sugar and water to a boil over medium-high heat. Boil 5 minutes. Add cranberries and apple; boil 10 to 15 minutes or until cranberries pop and mixture begins to thicken. Remove from heat and stir in orange peel and raisins; cool.
Yield: about 4½ cups of relish

PUMPKIN-APPLE PIE

- ¼ cup butter or margarine
- 3 medium apples, peeled, cored, and coarsely chopped
- 1 teaspoon ground cinnamon
- ¼ teaspoon ground allspice
- ¼ teaspoon ground nutmeg
- 1 tablespoon all-purpose flour
- ¼ cup apple juice
- 2 tablespoons granulated sugar
- 1 unbaked 9-inch pie shell
- 1 cup pumpkin
- 1 egg
- ⅓ cup granulated sugar
- ½ teaspoon ground cinnamon
- ¼ teaspoon ground nutmeg
- ¼ teaspoon ground cloves
- ½ cup half and half

Preheat oven to 425 degrees. Melt butter in a skillet over medium heat. Stir in apples, 1 teaspoon cinnamon, allspice, and ¼ teaspoon nutmeg; cook 5 minutes. Stir in flour, apple juice, and 2 tablespoons sugar. Cook 1 minute and remove from heat. Pour into pie shell.
In a medium mixing bowl, combine pumpkin, egg, ⅓ cup sugar, ½ teaspoon cinnamon, ¼ teaspoon nutmeg, and cloves. Beat until well blended. Stir in half and half. Carefully pour pumpkin mixture over apple mixture. Bake 15 minutes. Reduce heat to 350 degrees and bake 30 minutes more or until center is set.
Yield: 8 servings

GREEN BEANS WITH DILL SAUCE

- 1 tablespoon chopped dried chives
- 1½ teaspoons lemon pepper
- 1 teaspoon dill weed
- 6 slices bacon, cooked and crumbled
- 1 cup sour cream, room temperature
  Salt
- 2 packages (10 ounces each) frozen French-style green beans

Combine first 5 ingredients in small saucepan. Salt to taste and set aside (do not refrigerate). Cook green beans according to package directions. At the same time, gently warm sour cream mixture over low heat, stirring constantly. Drain green beans well and place about ½ cup on each serving plate. Indent center of beans with the back of spoon. Place a heaping tablespoon of sour cream mixture in center of beans.
Yield: 8 servings

PEACH ASPIC WITH CREAM CHEESE DRESSING

ASPIC
- 2 packages (3 ounces each) peach-flavored gelatin
- 1½ cups boiling water
- 1 cup orange juice
- ½ teaspoon grated lemon peel
- 3 tablespoons lemon juice
- 1 can (1 pound 13 ounces) peaches in syrup, drained, puréed, and divided
- 2 tablespoons granulated sugar

DRESSING
- 1 package (8 ounces) cream cheese, softened
- 3 tablespoons mayonnaise
- 1 tablespoon granulated sugar

In mixing bowl, combine peach gelatin and boiling water; stir until gelatin is dissolved. Stir in orange juice, lemon peel, lemon juice, 1½ cups puréed peaches, and 2 tablespoons sugar. Pour into lightly oiled 1½-quart ring mold and chill 4 to 6 hours or until set.
In small mixing bowl, combine cream cheese, mayonnaise, 1 tablespoon sugar, and ½ cup puréed peaches. Beat until smooth. Remove aspic from mold to serving platter; serve with dressing.
Yield: 8 to 10 servings

SPINACH-SQUASH CASSEROLE

- 6 medium yellow squash, scrubbed and stems trimmed
- 2 packages (10 ounces each) frozen chopped spinach, thawed
- 1 package (8 ounces) cream cheese, softened
- 2 eggs, lightly beaten
- 6 tablespoons butter or margarine, melted
- 1 tablespoon granulated sugar
- ½ teaspoon salt
- ½ teaspoon garlic salt
- 1 teaspoon freshly ground pepper
- 1 cup Ritz Bits™ cheese cracker crumbs
- 6 slices bacon, cooked and crumbled
  Paprika

Preheat oven to 350 degrees. Cook squash in salted boiling water until tender (about 10 minutes); drain. Place squash in large mixing bowl and mash. Add next eight ingredients to squash and stir well. Pour into lightly greased 2-quart baking dish and top with cracker crumbs, bacon, and paprika. Cover and bake 45 minutes. Remove cover and bake 15 minutes more or until center is set.
Yield: 8 to 10 servings

Brighten your holiday meal with these flavorful accents: *(Top left)* Green Beans with Dill Sauce and Candied Ginger Biscuits offer easy preparation. *(Top right)* Pumpkin-Apple Pie is a layered dessert combining two delicious favorites. *(Bottom left)* A ring mold brings holiday elegance to Peach Aspic with Cream Cheese Dressing. *(Bottom right)* Cranberry-Apple Relish (left) is a tangy alternative to traditional cranberry sauce. Bacon and cheese cracker crumbs top our Spinach-Squash Casserole.

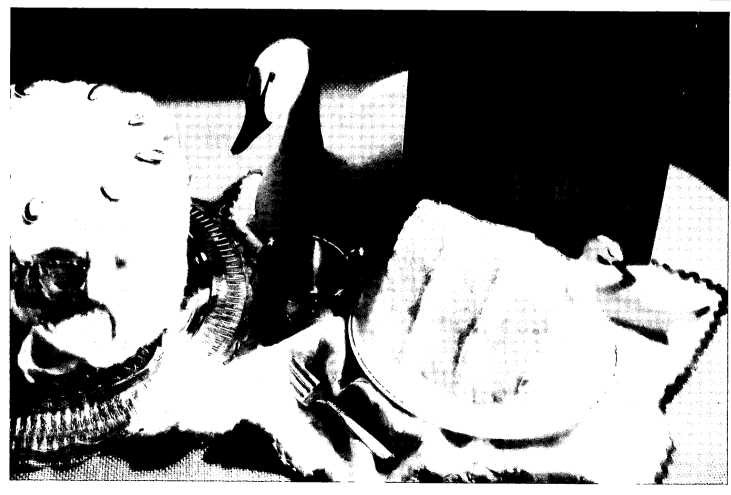

HOLIDAY SWEETS

Although many things change with the passage of time, one thing remains the same — the fascination that Christmas holds for children. There's nothing more thrilling to a child than to wake up on Christmas Day and discover the toys, books, and goodies that Santa has left under the tree. Though today's toys are different from those we and our parents before us received, the appeal of Christmas cookies and candies has never changed. We hope our selection of sweets will rekindle memories of your childhood and enrich your holiday celebration.

SWAN CAKE

Beating the dry ingredients with an electric mixer may be an unusual step, but it blends and aerates the ingredients, giving the cake its sponge-like texture.

CAKE
- 2¼ cups cake flour
- 1¾ cups granulated sugar
- 2 teaspoons baking powder
- ½ teaspoon salt
- ½ cup vegetable oil
- 7 egg yolks
- ¾ cup orange juice
- 2 teaspoons grated orange peel
- 2½ teaspoons orange extract
- 1 teaspoon vanilla extract
- 10 egg whites
- 1 teaspoon cream of tartar

FROSTING
- 1 package (8 ounces) cream cheese, softened
- 2 tablespoons milk
- 1 cup butter, softened
- 8 cups confectioners sugar, sifted
- 2 tablespoons orange juice
- 1 tablespoon orange extract

Preheat oven to 325 degrees. For cake, combine flour, sugar, baking powder, and salt in a large mixing bowl. Using an electric mixer, blend at low speed 1 minute. Make a well in the center of dry ingredients and add oil, egg yolks, orange juice, orange peel, and extracts. Beat until smooth. In another large mixing bowl, combine egg whites and cream of tartar. Beat until soft peaks form. Carefully fold egg whites into first mixture. Pour batter into three greased 9-inch round cake pans lined with waxed paper. Bake 25 to 30 minutes or until a toothpick inserted in the center of a cake comes out clean. Cool in pans 10 minutes; then remove cakes from pans and cool on wire racks.

For frosting, combine all frosting ingredients in a large bowl and beat until smooth. Frost between layers and on top and sides of cake.

Yield: 10 to 12 servings

COCONUT CREAM

This fluffy, old-fashioned dessert is a snap to make during the busy holiday season. We decorated the mold with fresh greenery and shiny candy dragées.

- 3 envelopes unflavored gelatin
- ⅓ cup water
- 5 cups whipping cream, divided
- 1 cup granulated sugar
- 1½ teaspoons coconut extract
- 2 cups coconut

  Purchased chocolate syrup to serve, optional

Dissolve gelatin in water. In a heavy saucepan, bring 2 cups cream to a boil over medium heat. Add gelatin mixture and sugar, cooking and stirring constantly until sugar dissolves; cool.

Beat remaining 3 cups of cream with coconut extract until soft peaks form. Fold whipped cream and coconut into gelatin mixture. Pour into a lightly greased 8-cup mold. Chill 6 to 8 hours or until firm. If desired, serve with a small amount of chocolate syrup.

Yield: 8 to 10 servings

ROCKY ROAD MOUSSE

Studded with marshmallows and almonds, this mousse is a wonderful adult version of the classic childhood treat. It makes plenty for a hungry crowd!

- 3 cups semisweet chocolate chips
- ½ cup prepared coffee
- 1 teaspoon vanilla extract
- 4 eggs, separated
- 1 cup whipping cream
- ¼ cup granulated sugar
- ⅛ teaspoon salt
- 1½ cups miniature marshmallows
- 1 cup sliced almonds, toasted

In a heavy saucepan, combine chocolate chips, coffee, and vanilla over low heat. Stir constantly until chocolate is melted and smooth. Remove from heat; cool mixture to room temperature. Transfer chocolate mixture to a large mixing bowl and add egg yolks one at a time to chocolate mixture, beating well after each addition.

In another large mixing bowl, whip cream with sugar until stiff. In a separate bowl, whip egg whites with salt until stiff. Fold egg whites into whipped cream. Stir 1 cup of the cream mixture into chocolate mixture. Gently fold remaining cream mixture into chocolate mixture just until combined. Fold in marshmallows and almonds. Pour mousse into serving bowl. Cover and refrigerate until set.

Yield: 10 to 12 servings

(Top left) Our light and fluffy Coconut Cream mold is an elegant dessert that can be prepared ahead of time.

(Top right) A rich chocolate treat filled with marshmallows and nuts, Rocky Road Mousse is a new twist on a childhood favorite.

(Bottom) This orange-flavored Swan Cake is full of old-fashioned goodness. Silvery almond-shaped dragées give it holiday sparkle.

VIENNA TORTE

CAKE
    2 cups granulated sugar
    2 cups all-purpose flour
    1 teaspoon baking soda
    1 cup butter or margarine
    ½ cup cocoa
    1 cup water
    ½ cup buttermilk
    2 eggs, lightly beaten
    2 teaspoons vanilla extract

FROSTING
    2 cups whipping cream
    3 tablespoons green crème de menthe
          liqueur
    2 tablespoons white crème de cocoa
          liqueur
    1½ cups confectioners sugar

Preheat oven to 400 degrees. For cake, combine sugar, flour, and baking soda in a large mixing bowl; set aside. In a saucepan, combine butter, cocoa, and water; bring to a boil. Add the chocolate mixture to the flour mixture and stir until well blended. Beat in buttermilk, eggs, and vanilla. Pour into a greased and floured 15 x 10 x 1-inch jellyroll pan. Bake 20 to 25 minutes or until cake springs back when touched in center. Allow cake to cool in pan.

Combine frosting ingredients, beating until stiff peaks form.

Invert cake onto the back of another jellyroll pan. Cut cake crosswise into four equal sections. Place one section of cake on serving platter. Frost between layers and on top of cake; do not frost sides. Chill torte until serving time.
Yield: 10 to 12 servings

(Top) A traditional French Christmas dessert, this chocolate Yule Log makes a stunning centerpiece, too.

(Bottom left) European-style Vienna Torte is a light chocolate cake with a crème de menthe filling.

(Bottom right) A chocolate cookie crumb crust is a delicious base for Peppermint Pie; the candy ladybugs are a sweet garnish. The filling has a texture similar to frozen custard.

YULE LOG

In France this delicate cake is known as a Bûche de Noël. Plan to make the cake a part of your own family Christmas traditions.

CAKE
    1 cup cake flour
    1¼ teaspoons baking soda
    ¼ teaspoon salt
    6 tablespoons cocoa
    ⅓ cup boiling water
    1½ teaspoons vanilla extract
    ¼ cup butter, softened
    ¼ cup vegetable shortening
    1 cup granulated sugar, divided
    2 eggs, separated
    ½ cup buttermilk

CREAM FILLING
    1 cup whipping cream
    ½ cup granulated sugar
    1½ teaspoons vanilla extract

GLAZE
    2 cups semisweet chocolate chips
    ½ cup butter, softened
    ½ cup whipping cream
          Confectioners sugar

Preheat oven to 325 degrees. For cake, combine flour, baking soda, and salt in a medium mixing bowl. In a small bowl, combine cocoa, water, and vanilla, whisking until smooth.

In a large bowl, cream butter and shortening. Gradually beat in ¾ cup plus 2 tablespoons sugar. Beat in the egg yolks one at a time, beating well after each addition. Beat until mixture is light and fluffy, about 2 to 3 minutes. Beginning with the flour mixture, alternately beat in the flour mixture and buttermilk, beating well after each addition. Beat in the cocoa mixture until smooth.

In a medium bowl, beat egg whites until soft peaks form. Gradually beat in the remaining 2 tablespoons sugar until mixture is stiff. Fold one-fourth of the egg white mixture into the chocolate mixture. Carefully fold in the remaining egg white mixture. Pour the batter into a greased and floured 15 x 10 x 1-inch foil-lined jellyroll pan. Smooth top of batter with a spatula. Bake 12 to 15 minutes until the cake is slightly puffed and just begins to pull away from sides of pan. (Cake will be underdone.) Place pan on wire rack to cool.

For filling, beat cream, sugar, and vanilla in a large mixing bowl until stiff peaks form.

Using a knife, loosen the cake from the edges of the pan. Place a second jellyroll pan on top of the first pan and invert cake onto the back of the second pan. Peel off foil. Invert cake again so cake is right side up. Spread the cream filling over the cake, leaving a 1-inch border around the edges of the cake. Beginning with one long edge, roll the cake up. Wrap cake tightly with aluminum foil and freeze overnight.

For glaze, melt chocolate chips in top of a double boiler over warm water. Remove from heat and cool slightly. Beat in butter and cream. Allow mixture to sit at room temperature until slightly thickened. Remove cake from freezer and unwrap. Place cake, seam side down, on a wire rack placed over waxed paper. Pour glaze over cake, using a spatula to spread glaze evenly over top and sides of cake. Carefully transfer cake to serving platter. Referring to photo, gently pull a fork over the top and sides of the cake to resemble bark. Refrigerate until serving time. Before serving, sprinkle cake with confectioners sugar.
Yield: 10 to 12 servings

PEPPERMINT PIE

The charming ladybug decorations on top of our pie come from a European confectionery, but similar decorations may be found wherever cake decorating supplies are sold.

CRUST
    2 cups chocolate cookie crumbs
    ½ cup granulated sugar
    ⅓ cup butter, melted

FILLING
    10 ounces white chocolate
    ½ cup milk
    24 large marshmallows
    1 teaspoon peppermint extract
    1 cup whipping cream, whipped

Combine crust ingredients and press into bottom of an ungreased 9-inch springform pan.

Combine white chocolate, milk, and marshmallows in top of a double boiler over simmering water. Stir constantly until melted and smooth. Remove from heat. Cool to room temperature. Fold extract and whipped cream into white chocolate mixture. Pour mixture into crust. Cover and freeze overnight.
Yield: 8 to 10 servings

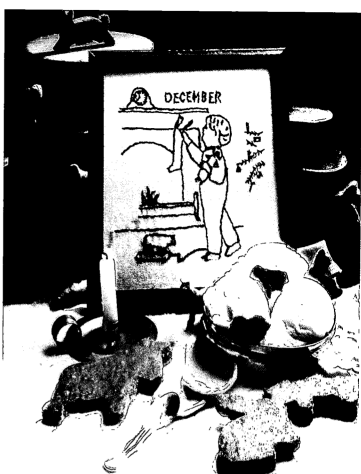

HOLIDAY SWEETS

CARAMEL CREAM

This old-fashioned egg custard has a layer of caramel at the bottom which liquifies during baking.

1½ cups granulated sugar, divided
2 tablespoons water
2 eggs
3 egg yolks
1 tablespoon vanilla extract
2 cups milk

Preheat oven to 350 degrees. Combine 1 cup sugar with water in a heavy pan over medium heat. Swirl pan occasionally until sugar begins to melt and turns golden (do not stir mixture and do not increase temperature). Pour caramel into eight warmed custard cups. Tilt the cups to coat bottoms and sides; set aside.

Beat eggs, yolks, remaining ½ cup sugar, and vanilla until well blended. Slowly beat milk into egg mixture. Pour mixture into caramel-lined cups. Set cups in a 13 x 9 x 2-inch baking pan and add boiling water to baking pan to come halfway up the sides of the cups. Bake 45 minutes or until custard is set in center. Serve warm or chilled.
Yield: 8 servings

(Top left) A sweet caramel surprise is hidden beneath traditional egg custard in our Caramel Cream dessert.

(Top right) Kids will love a menagerie of Gingerbread Cutouts, especially when these moist, spicy treats are served with ice cream.

(Bottom) Reminiscent of old-fashioned jam cake, the Christmas Keeping Cake *(left)* gets more flavorful with each passing day. Date Pinwheels are easy-to-make refrigerator cookies that have all the good, spicy flavor of Grandma's traditional version.

GINGERBREAD CUTOUTS

½ cup vegetable shortening
2 tablespoons granulated sugar
1 egg
1 cup dark molasses
1 cup boiling water
2¼ cups all-purpose flour
1 teaspoon baking soda
½ teaspoon salt
1½ teaspoons ground ginger
1 teaspoon ground cinnamon
½ teaspoon ground cloves

Ice cream to serve

Preheat oven to 325 degrees. In a large mixing bowl, cream shortening, sugar, and egg. Blend in molasses and water. Combine flour, baking soda, salt, ginger, cinnamon, and cloves and add to molasses mixture. Beat until smooth. Pour into a 15 x 10 x 1-inch waxed paper-lined jellyroll pan. Bake 30 to 35 minutes or until cake springs back when touched in center. Cool cake in pan. Cut out shapes using desired cookie cutters (we used 1-inch long cookie cutters to cut shapes out of scraps). Serve with ice cream, if desired.
Yield: about 3 dozen 3-inch cutouts

DATE PINWHEELS

½ cup butter or margarine, softened
1 cup firmly packed brown sugar
1 egg
1½ teaspoons vanilla extract
2 cups all-purpose flour
½ teaspoon baking soda
½ teaspoon salt
½ teaspoon ground cinnamon
¼ teaspoon ground nutmeg
1 package (8 ounces) chopped dates
½ cup water
¼ cup granulated sugar
¼ teaspoon ground cinnamon

In a large bowl, cream butter, brown sugar, egg, and vanilla. In a separate bowl, combine flour, baking soda, salt, ½ teaspoon cinnamon, and nutmeg. Stir flour mixture into creamed mixture. Cover and refrigerate dough at least 2 hours or until well chilled.

In a saucepan, combine dates, water, sugar, and ¼ teaspoon cinnamon over low heat. Cook, stirring constantly, until thickened; cool. Preheat oven to 350 degrees. Divide dough into three equal parts. Roll each third of dough into a rectangle 8 x 10-inches long and ¼-inch thick. Spread one-third of date mixture over each rectangle. Starting with one long end, roll up dough. Cut into ½-inch thick slices. Place on lightly greased baking sheets. Bake 14 to 16 minutes or until lightly browned. Cool on wire racks.
Yield: about 5 dozen cookies

CHRISTMAS KEEPING CAKE

Be sure to try this delicious alternative to traditional fruit cake. To make the pretty garnish, brush artificial Christmas holly with egg white and sprinkle with sugar.

1 cup butter or margarine, softened
2 cups granulated sugar
3 eggs, separated
1 teaspoon baking soda
½ cup buttermilk
3 cups all-purpose flour, divided
1½ teaspoons ground cinnamon
½ teaspoon ground nutmeg
½ teaspoon ground cloves
1 cup red plum jam
1 cup coarsely chopped pecans
1 cup golden raisins
1 cup quartered dates
1 cup brandy, bourbon, or sherry

Preheat oven to 300 degrees. Cream butter and sugar. Beat in egg yolks until fluffy. Dissolve baking soda in buttermilk. Beat buttermilk into butter mixture. Combine 2½ cups flour with spices. Add to creamed mixture alternately with jam. Beat egg whites until stiff; fold into batter. Combine remaining flour with pecans, raisins, and dates. Fold into batter. Pour into a well-greased and floured 10-inch tube pan. Bake 3 to 3½ hours or until a toothpick inserted in center of cake comes out clean. Place pan on wire rack to cool. When completely cool, cut a piece of cheesecloth large enough to wrap around cake. Soak cheesecloth in liquor. Remove cake from pan and wrap cheesecloth around cake. Wrap cheesecloth-covered cake tightly with aluminum foil. Allow to age 4 to 6 weeks before serving.
Yield: 12 to 14 servings

HOLIDAY SWEETS

RUM-RAISIN CHEESECAKE

Rum-raisin, a popular ice cream flavor, lends itself nicely to the creamy richness of our cheesecake.

CRUST
- 2 cups vanilla wafer cookie crumbs
- 1 tablespoon granulated sugar
- 2 tablespoons butter or margarine, melted

FILLING
- 1¼ cups raisins
- 1 cup dark rum
- 5 packages (8 ounces each) cream cheese, softened
- 1½ cups granulated sugar
- 1 tablespoon vanilla extract
- 6 eggs
- 4 egg yolks
- ⅓ cup whipping cream

In a small bowl, combine raisins with rum. Marinate at least 2 hours.

Combine crust ingredients. Press into the bottom of a lightly greased 10-inch springform pan.

Preheat oven to 350 degrees. For filling, beat cream cheese until smooth. Add sugar and vanilla. Beat in eggs and yolks one at a time, beating well after each addition. Drain raisins, reserving rum. Stir rum and cream into cream cheese mixture. Stir in raisins. Pour filling over crust. Place springform pan in a larger pan and add water to larger pan to come halfway up side of springform pan. Bake 1½ hours or until center is set. Remove

(Top) Southern Pecan Pie *(left)* is an old-fashioned favorite. Crunchy Pecan Nuggets flavored with brown sugar are great for snacking or entertaining.

(Bottom left) Raisins marinated in rum add festive spirit to Rum-Raisin Cheesecake.

(Bottom right) Macadamia nuts, toasted coconut, and fresh bananas give tropical appeal to this Safari Pie.

cheesecake from oven and pan of water and allow to cool completely. Cover and refrigerate overnight.

To serve, use a knife to loosen sides of cheesecake from pan; remove springform.
Yield: 12 to 14 servings

SOUTHERN PECAN PIE

CRUST
- 1¼ cups all-purpose flour
- ¼ teaspoon salt
- 7 tablespoons butter, chilled and cut into pieces
- 3 tablespoons ice water

FILLING
- 4 eggs
- 1 cup pecan halves
- 1¼ cups granulated sugar
- ¼ cup butter or margarine
- ½ cup light corn syrup

Preheat oven to 350 degrees. For crust, sift flour and salt into a mixing bowl. Using a pastry blender or two knives, cut butter into flour until mixture resembles coarse meal. Sprinkle ice water over dough, mixing quickly just until dough forms a ball (dough will be soft). On a lightly floured surface, use a floured rolling pin to roll out dough. Place the dough in an ungreased 9-inch pie pan. Trim and crimp edges of dough.

For filling, combine eggs and nuts in a medium mixing bowl and beat well by hand. In a saucepan, combine sugar, butter, and corn syrup. Bring mixture to a boil. Beating constantly by hand, gradually add sugar mixture to egg mixture. Pour mixture into pie shell. Bake 40 to 45 minutes or until a knife inserted in the center comes out clean.
Yield: 8 servings

PECAN NUGGETS

- 1 cup firmly packed brown sugar
- 2 tablespoons all-purpose flour
- 1 tablespoon cornstarch
- 1 tablespoon dark rum
- 1 egg white
- ⅛ teaspoon cream of tartar
- ⅛ teaspoon salt
- 2 cups pecan halves

Preheat oven to 300 degrees. In a medium mixing bowl, combine brown sugar, flour, cornstarch, and rum. In a separate bowl, beat egg white with cream of tartar and salt until stiff peaks form. Stir one-third of the egg white into the rum mixture; fold in the remaining egg white. Stir in pecans. Drop individual pecan halves coated with some of the mixture 2 inches apart on a lightly greased baking sheet. Bake 12 to 15 minutes or until puffed and golden brown. Remove from pan and cool on wire rack.
Yield: about 6 dozen nuggets

SAFARI PIE

CRUST
- 1¼ cups all-purpose flour
- ¼ teaspoon salt
- 7 tablespoons butter, chilled and cut into pieces
- 3 tablespoons ice water

FILLING
- 2½ cups milk
- ½ cup banana liqueur
- 2 tablespoons vanilla extract
- ½ teaspoon coconut extract
- 4 egg yolks
- ⅔ cup granulated sugar
- ½ cup all-purpose flour
- 2 bananas, cut into ¼-inch thick slices, divided
- 1 cup chopped macadamia nuts, divided
- 1 cup toasted coconut, divided

MERINGUE
- 4 egg whites
- ⅛ teaspoon salt
- ¼ cup granulated sugar
- 1 tablespoon toasted coconut

Preheat oven to 400 degrees. For crust, sift flour and salt into a mixing bowl. Using a pastry blender or two knives, cut butter into flour until mixture resembles coarse meal. Sprinkle ice water over dough, mixing quickly just until dough forms a ball (dough will be soft). On a lightly floured surface, use a floured rolling pin to roll out dough. Place the dough in an ungreased 9-inch pie pan. Trim and crimp edges of pie, and prick bottom of shell with a fork. Bake 15 to 20 minutes or until lightly browned.

For filling, make a custard by combining milk, liqueur, and extracts in a medium saucepan. Bring to a boil. Cover and remove from heat. In a medium bowl, beat egg yolks with sugar until thickened and pale yellow. Add flour and beat until well blended. Gradually whisk milk mixture into egg yolk mixture. Return mixture to saucepan and bring to a boil over medium heat, whisking constantly. Continue cooking and whisking until mixture is thickened and smooth. Remove from heat.

Layer half of the banana slices, ½ cup of the nuts, and ½ cup of the coconut in bottom of pie shell. Pour half of the custard over the bananas. Layer the remaining bananas, nuts, and coconut over the custard and top with the remaining custard. Cover and refrigerate at least 2 hours or until the custard is set.

Preheat oven to 400 degrees. For meringue, beat egg whites with salt until soft peaks form. Gradually beat in sugar until stiff peaks form. Spoon the meringue on top of the pie, sealing edges. Sprinkle top of meringue with coconut. Bake 3 to 5 minutes or until meringue is lightly browned. Serve warm or chilled. Store in refrigerator.
Yield: 8 servings

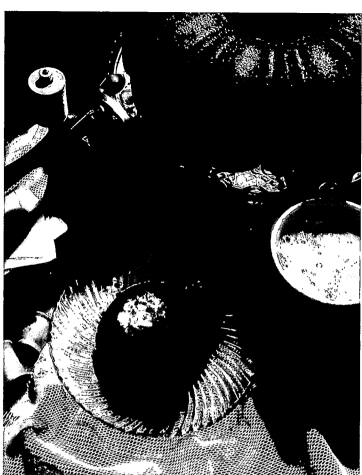

HOLIDAY SWEETS

BAKED FUDGE DESSERT WITH KAHLÚA CREAM

Like a soft, gooey brownie in a cup, this warm dessert will chase away the chill on a cold winter's night.

BAKED FUDGE
- 2 cups granulated sugar
- ½ cup all-purpose flour
- ¾ cup cocoa
- 5 eggs, beaten
- 1 cup plus 2 tablespoons butter or margarine, melted
- 2 teaspoons vanilla extract
- 1½ cups chopped pecans

KAHLÚA CREAM
- ½ cup confectioners sugar
- 3 tablespoons kahlúa liqueur
- 1 cup whipping cream

Preheat oven to 300 degrees. For baked fudge, combine sugar, flour, and cocoa in a medium mixing bowl. Add eggs and beat until smooth. Combine butter and vanilla. Beat into cocoa mixture. Stir in pecans. Pour into eight individual custard cups. Set cups in a 13 x 9 x 2-inch baking pan and add water to come halfway up the sides of the custard cups. Bake 40 to 45 minutes or until tops are crusty.
Combine kahlúa cream ingredients and beat until soft peaks form. Serve cream with warm baked fudge.
Yield: 8 servings

(Top left) Baked Fudge Dessert with Kahlúa Cream *(left)* is a moist brownie-like treat served warm with a topping of sweet, liqueur-flavored whipped cream. Amaretto-Peach Cheesecake gets its delicious flavor combination from dried peaches marinated in amaretto.

(Top right) This yummy chocolate Tunnel Cake has a double surprise inside — a rich cream cheese filling loaded with miniature chocolate chips!

(Bottom) Our Coconut Snowball is rich through and through, from the moist white cake made with cream of coconut and sour cream to the white chocolate frosting sprinkled with shredded coconut. We used more shredded coconut, snow babies, and miniature trees to create this playful snow scene.

TUNNEL CAKE

FILLING
- 11 ounces (one 8-ounce and one 3-ounce package) cream cheese, softened
- 1 egg
- ⅓ cup granulated sugar
- 1 cup miniature semisweet chocolate chips

CAKE
- 1½ cups all-purpose flour
- 1 cup granulated sugar
- ¼ cup cocoa
- ½ teaspoon salt
- 1 teaspoon baking soda
- ⅓ cup vegetable oil
- 1 tablespoon white vinegar
- 2 teaspoons vanilla extract
- 1 cup water

Preheat oven to 350 degrees. For filling, combine cream cheese, egg, and sugar in a small mixing bowl; beat well. Stir in chocolate chips and set aside.
For cake, combine flour, sugar, cocoa, salt, and baking soda in a large mixing bowl. Add remaining ingredients and beat until well blended. Pour half of the chocolate batter into a well-greased 9½-inch bundt pan. Spoon the filling onto the center of the batter. Top with remaining chocolate batter. Bake 50 to 55 minutes or until toothpick inserted in center of cake comes out clean. Remove cake from pan and cool on wire rack.
Yield: 12 to 14 servings

COCONUT SNOWBALL

CAKE
- 1 package (18½ ounces) white cake mix with pudding in the mix
- ¼ cup vegetable oil
- 3 eggs
- 1 cup sour cream
- 1 can (8.5 ounces) cream of coconut

FROSTING
- 6 bars (1¼ ounces each) white chocolate with almonds
- 4 cups confectioners sugar
- 8 tablespoons evaporated milk
- 1½ cups coconut

Preheat oven to 350 degrees. In a medium mixing bowl, combine all cake ingredients, beating until smooth. Pour mixture into a well-greased 2-quart oven-proof bowl. Bake 45 to 50 minutes or until a toothpick inserted in center of cake comes out clean. Cool in bowl 15 minutes. Remove cake from bowl and cool completely on wire rack before frosting.
For frosting, melt white chocolate bars in top of a double boiler over simmering water. Remove from heat and transfer to a mixing bowl. Add confectioners sugar and evaporated milk. Beat until smooth. Place cake on serving platter. Spread frosting over cake. Sprinkle cake with coconut.
Yield: 12 to 14 servings

AMARETTO-PEACH CHEESECAKE

CRUST
- 2 cups vanilla wafer cookie crumbs
- 1 tablespoon granulated sugar
- ¼ cup almond paste
- 2 tablespoons butter, melted

FILLING
- 1 cup diced dried peaches
- 1 cup amaretto liqueur
- 5 packages (8 ounces each) cream cheese, softened
- ¼ cup almond paste
- 1½ cups granulated sugar
- 1 teaspoon almond extract
- 6 eggs
- 4 egg yolks
  Additional amaretto liqueur
- ⅓ cup whipping cream

In a small bowl, combine peaches with 1 cup amaretto. Marinate at least 2 hours.
Combine crust ingredients; press into the bottom of a lightly greased 10-inch springform pan.
Preheat oven to 350 degrees. For filling, beat cream cheese until smooth. Add almond paste, sugar, and almond extract. Beat in eggs and yolks, one at a time, beating well after each addition. Drain marinated peaches, reserving amaretto. Add additional amaretto to reserved amaretto to make 1 cup of liquid. Stir amaretto and cream into cream cheese mixture. Stir in marinated peaches. Pour filling over crust. Place springform pan in a larger pan and add water to larger pan to come halfway up side of springform pan. Bake 1½ hours or until center is set. Remove cheesecake from oven and pan of water and allow to cool completely. Cover and refrigerate overnight.
To serve, use a knife to loosen sides of cheesecake from pan; remove springform.
Yield: 12 to 14 servings

PECAN THIMBLE COOKIES

    2   cups all-purpose flour
 1¼   cups pecans
    1   cup butter, softened
  ¼   cup granulated sugar
  ¼   cup firmly packed brown sugar

Combine the flour and pecans in a blender or food processor. Process until pecans are very fine. In a medium mixing bowl, beat butter and sugars until light and fluffy. Stir in flour mixture. Wrap dough in plastic wrap and refrigerate overnight.

Preheat oven to 300 degrees. On a lightly floured surface, use a floured rolling pin to roll out dough to ¼-inch thickness. Cut out dough using a thimble. Place on foil-lined baking sheet and bake 10 to 12 minutes or until very lightly browned.
Yield: about 50 dozen cookies

Variation: Cookies may be rolled out as directed above and cut out using desired cookie cutters. Bake 20 to 25 minutes.
Yield: about 5 dozen 2½-inch cookies

(Top) Perfect for serving with coffee or tea, Pecan Thimble Cookies *(left)* have a buttery brown sugar crunch. Chocolate Truffles flavored with crème de cassis are extra rich and creamy.

(Bottom left) This attractive Cream Puff Ring gets its delicate orange flavor from the Grand Marnier liqueur in its custard filling and chocolate glaze.

(Bottom right) Light and refreshing, Pink Squirrel Pie is flavored with amaretto and crème de menthe. The chewy crust is made with coconut macaroons and toasted almond pieces.

TRUFFLES

    4   cups semisweet chocolate chips, divided
    1   egg yolk
    3   tablespoons whipping cream
    3   tablespoons crème de cassis liqueur
  ⅓   bar paraffin
    1   ounce white chocolate for decoration
        Red paste food coloring, optional

In top of a double boiler over warm water, melt 2 cups chocolate chips. Stir until smooth. Remove from heat and allow chocolate to cool to room temperature. Beat in egg yolk, cream, and liqueur until smooth. Refrigerate mixture 1 hour or until set. Form heaping teaspoons of mixture into 1-inch balls. Place on cookie sheet and refrigerate 30 minutes.

In top of a double boiler over warm water, melt remaining 2 cups of chocolate chips with paraffin. Remove from heat and cool slightly. Quickly dip candies in chocolate and place on waxed paper to set. Refrigerate until firm.

Melt white chocolate in top of a double boiler over warm water. Remove chocolate from heat. If desired, stir in a small amount of food coloring to tint chocolate a pale pink. Place chocolate in a pastry bag fitted with a small, round tip and pipe initials or bows on tops of candies.
Yield: about 30 truffles

CREAM PUFF RING

PASTRY
    1   cup boiling water
  ½   cup butter or margarine
    1   cup all-purpose flour
  ⅛   teaspoon salt
    4   eggs

PASTRY CREAM
    3   egg yolks
  ½   cup granulated sugar
    2   tablespoons all-purpose flour
  ¾   cup milk
  ¼   cup Grand Marnier liqueur
    1   cup whipping cream, whipped

GLAZE
    2   ounces unsweetened baking chocolate
    1   tablespoon butter or margarine
    2   cups confectioners sugar
  ¼   cup boiling water
    2   tablepoons Grand Marnier liqueur

Preheat oven to 400 degrees. For pastry, combine water with butter in a saucepan over medium heat. Cook until butter is melted. Stir in flour and salt until well blended. Cook, stirring constantly, over medium heat until mixture forms a ball. Remove from heat; cool 10 minutes. Add eggs one at a time, beating after each addition until smooth.

Line a 9-inch round cake pan with aluminum foil. Using about ¼ cup for each, drop eight mounds of dough ½" from edge and ½" apart on pan. Bake 30 minutes. Reduce temperature to 375 degrees, bake 20 minutes more. Cut slits in ring for steam to escape. Bake 20 minutes more. Remove from pan and cool on foil.

For pastry cream, beat egg yolks with sugar until light. Blend in flour and milk. Transfer mixture to a large, heavy saucepan and bring to a boil over medium heat, stirring constantly. Cook until very thick (about 4 minutes). Remove from heat and stir in liqueur; cool completely, stirring occasionally. Fold in whipped cream.

For glaze, melt chocolate with butter in top of a double boiler. Remove from heat and beat in remaining glaze ingredients; set aside.

Carefully slice tops off of pastry. Pull soft dough from inside. Fill with pastry cream. Replace tops and spoon glaze over ring.
Yield: 8 servings

PINK SQUIRREL PIE

CRUST
   14   coconut macaroons, crushed
  ¼   cup finely chopped almonds, toasted
    3   tablespoons butter, melted

FILLING
   24   large marshmallows
  ¾   cup milk
  ½   cup amaretto liqueur
  ½   cup white crème de menthe liqueur
 2½   teaspoons almond extract
    3 to 4 drops red food coloring
    2   cups whipping cream, whipped

Preheat oven to 350 degrees. Combine crust ingredients. Press into the bottom and sides of an ungreased 9-inch pie pan. Bake 10 minutes.

In a heavy saucepan over medium heat, melt marshmallows in milk; cool. Add liqueurs, extract, and food coloring. Fold in whipped cream. Pour into pie shell. Cover and freeze 6 to 8 hours or until firm.
Yield: 8 servings

129

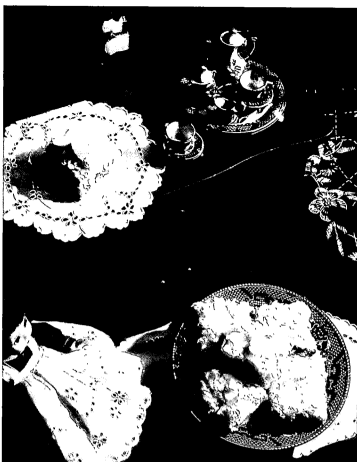

HOLIDAY SWEETS

TEATIME SNOWCAPS

CRUST
- ¾ cup vegetable shortening
- ¾ cup confectioners sugar
- 1½ cups all-purpose flour

TOPPING
- 1¼ cups apricot jam
- 3 egg whites
- ¾ cup granulated sugar
- ¾ cup coconut, divided
- 1 cup sliced almonds, divided

Preheat oven to 350 degrees. For crust, cream shortening and confectioners sugar. Stir in flour and press evenly into the bottom of an ungreased 13 x 9 x 2-inch pan. Bake 12 to 15 minutes or until crust is lightly browned.

For topping, spread jam over hot crust. Beat egg whites until soft peaks form. Gradually beat in sugar a few tablespoons at a time until mixture is stiff and glossy. Fold in ½ cup coconut and ½ cup almonds. Spread mixture over jam. Sprinkle remaining coconut and almonds over top. Bake 20 minutes. Allow to cool and cut into squares. Store in an airtight container.
Yield: about 35 cookies

(Top left) A parade of animal cutouts gives country appeal to tart cranberry-apple Calico Pie.

(Top right) Teatime Snowcaps are sweet bar cookies with a pastry crust and a topping of apricot jam, meringue, coconut, and sliced almonds.

(Bottom) Nostalgic laundry shapes and pastel colored sugar add a touch of whimsy to Jessie's Brickly Cookies. The recipe for these yummy treats was handed down by our food editor's great-grandmother, Jessie England, who called anything crisp "brickly."

CALICO PIE

We used the scraps of dough and miniature cookie cutters to cut out little dogs and cats to decorate the edge and center of the pie. Just bake the cutouts separately 5 to 10 minutes. When the pie is cool, use a little corn syrup to "glue" the cutouts around the edge.

CRUST
- 2¼ cups all-purpose flour
- ½ teaspoon salt
- ¾ cup plus 2 tablespoons butter, chilled and cut into pieces
- ⅓ cup ice water

FILLING
- 1½ cups granulated sugar
- 1 cup golden raisins
- 1½ cups chopped, peeled apple
- 1 cup whole-berry cranberry sauce
- 3 tablespoons lemon juice
- ½ teaspoon salt
- ½ teaspoon ground cinnamon
- ¼ teaspoon ground cloves
- ¼ teaspoon ground ginger

Preheat oven to 400 degrees. For crust, sift flour and salt into a mixing bowl. Using a pastry blender or two knives, cut butter into flour until mixture resembles coarse meal. Sprinkle water over dough, mixing quickly just until dough forms a ball (dough will be soft). Divide dough in half. On a lightly floured surface, use a floured rolling pin to roll out one-half of dough. Place the dough in an ungreased 9-inch pie pan. Roll out the remaining half of dough. If using miniature cookie cutters, center and cut holes in center of top crust; set aside.

For filling, combine ingredients and pour into pie shell. Top pie with remaining dough. Trim and crimp edges of pie. If not using miniature cookie cutters, cut slits in top of pie for steam to escape. Bake 35 to 40 minutes or until crust is golden brown. Serve warm or at room temperature.
Yield: 8 servings

JESSIE'S BRICKLY COOKIES

To make your own colored sugar as we did, shake about ¼ cup of sugar in a jar with 2 or 3 drops of food coloring.

- 1 cup granulated sugar
- 2 eggs
- 1 teaspoon vanilla extract
- 1 cup vegetable shortening
- 4½ cups all-purpose flour
- 1 teaspoon baking soda
- ½ teaspoon baking powder
- ½ teaspoon salt
- ½ cup buttermilk
- Colored sugar

In a large mixing bowl, cream sugar, eggs, vanilla, and shortening. Combine dry ingredients and add to creamed mixture

alternately with buttermilk. Divide dough in half and wrap in plastic wrap. Refrigerate at least 2 hours or until well chilled.

Preheat oven to 375 degrees. On a lightly floured surface, use a floured rolling pin to roll out dough to ⅛-inch thickness. Using patterns given or desired cookie cutters, cut out dough. (To use patterns, trace over patterns with tracing paper. Cut out patterns and use a sharp knife to cut out dough around patterns.) Transfer cookies to an ungreased baking sheet. Sprinkle with colored sugar. Bake 8 to 10 minutes or until lightly browned. Remove from pans and cool on wire racks.
Yield: about 7 dozen 2½-inch cookies

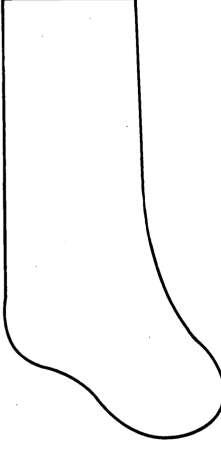

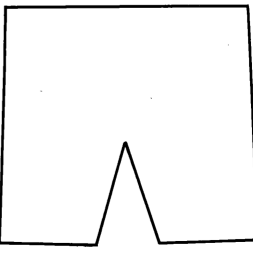

*S*haring *our homes and ourselves with others during the holidays creates a warm glow that remains long after Christmas has passed. As we celebrate the season with friendly gatherings, delicious appetizers and savory snacks enhance the festive mood. Our collection of party foods has something to delight everyone on your guest list. And because we've included several dishes that can be prepared ahead of time, you can spend the evening with your guests — not in the kitchen!*

Your guests will come back for more of these scrumptious treats — and don't be surprised if Santa himself drops in for a bite: *(clockwise from top)* Miniature Corn Muffins with Turkey and Relish are bite-sized sandwiches with the taste of a traditional turkey dinner. Refreshing Kir Royale Punch gets its fruity flavor and pretty color from black currant liqueur. Layers of spinach, cheese, sausage, and pepperoni give our Italian Loaf colorful appeal. Crispy Kielbasa Palmiers have a wonderful spicy-sweet flavor.

ITALIAN LOAF

The spinach and pimientos baked into this spicy loaf make this a colorful Christmas treat.

  1 can (10 ounces) refrigerated prepared pizza crust dough
  4 cups grated mozzarella cheese
  1 pound spicy pork sausage, browned and drained
  ½ cup tomato sauce
  1 teaspoon oregano flakes
  ½ teaspoon basil flakes
  1 package (10 ounces) frozen spinach, thawed and drained
  1 egg, lightly beaten
  1 jar (7 ounces) diced pimientos, drained
  1 package (3 ounces) sliced pepperoni
  12 large pimiento-stuffed green olives, cut in half lengthwise

Preheat oven to 400 degrees. Unroll dough and cut off one-fourth of dough crosswise; set aside. Line a greased 9¼ x 5¼ x 2½-inch loaf pan with the large piece of dough. Moisten the dough with water at corners and press to seal. Place one-half of the cheese on the bottom of the dough and top with sausage. Spoon tomato sauce over sausage and sprinkle with oregano and basil. Combine spinach with egg and spread over tomato sauce. Layer pimientos on top of spinach and top with remaining cheese. Arrange the pepperoni on top of the cheese layer. Top with olive halves. Cover filling with reserved dough and crimp edges of dough to seal. Cut slits in top of dough to allow steam to escape. Bake 50 minutes or until crust is well browned (if crust browns too quickly, cover loosely with aluminum foil). Allow to cool 10 minutes before removing from pan and cutting into slices.
Yield: about 8 servings

KIR ROYALE PUNCH

Crème de cassis (black currant liqueur) gives the champagne in this popular European drink a pretty pink color and a light, fruity flavor.

  1 bottle (750 ml) brut champagne, well chilled
  ¼ cup crème de cassis liqueur

In a serving bowl, combine champagne and liqueur.
Yield: about six 4-ounce servings

MINIATURE CORN MUFFINS WITH TURKEY AND RELISH

  2 eggs
  2 cups buttermilk
  1 teaspoon baking soda
  1½ cups cornmeal
  ½ cup all-purpose flour
  ¼ cup granulated sugar
  1 teaspoon salt
  ¼ pound sliced, cooked turkey breast
      Purchased cranberry relish

Preheat oven to 450 degrees. In a medium mixing bowl, beat eggs with buttermilk. Beat in baking soda, cornmeal, flour, sugar, and salt. Fill lightly greased miniature muffin tins two-thirds full with batter. Bake 10 to 15 minutes or until a muffin springs back when pressed. Remove muffins from pans and cool on wire racks.
Split cooled muffins in half and fill each with a piece of turkey and a small amount of cranberry relish.
Yield: about 45 muffins

KIELBASA PALMIERS

Don't let the sophisticated flavor of this appetizer fool you — it's deceptively simple to make! If you like, make several rolls ahead of time, wrap tightly, and freeze until needed.

  1 pound kielbasa sausage, finely chopped or ground, divided
  1 package (17¼ ounces) frozen puff pastry dough, thawed according to package directions
  1 cup hot and sweet mustard, divided

In a skillet, brown sausage over medium heat. Drain well.
Unfold one sheet of pastry and spread with ½ cup of mustard. Spread half of the sausage over the mustard. Roll each long end tightly and evenly to center of pastry. Repeat with remaining pastry sheet, mustard, and sausage. Wrap tightly in aluminum foil and refrigerate at least 1 hour.
Preheat oven to 450 degrees. Cut palmiers crosswise into ½-inch thick slices. Place on ungreased baking sheets. Bake 15 to 20 minutes or until pastry is puffed and golden. Serve warm or at room temperature.
Yield: about 40 palmiers

MARMALADE CHEESE TARTS

The tangy flavors of marmalade and Cheddar cheese are a winning combination. Definitely give these a try.

    1   cup butter, softened
    2   cups all-purpose flour
    1   cup grated sharp Cheddar cheese
    ¾   cup orange marmalade
    1   egg, lightly beaten

In a medium mixing bowl, combine butter, flour, and cheese. Knead until well combined. Wrap dough in plastic wrap and refrigerate 1 hour.

Preheat oven to 350 degrees. On a lightly floured surface, use a floured rolling pin to roll out dough to ⅛-inch thickness. Cut out dough using a 2-inch round cookie cutter. Place about ½ teaspoon marmalade in center of each circle of dough. Fold dough in half and seal edges by pressing with a fork. Transfer tarts to ungreased baking sheets and brush tops with egg. Bake 10 to 15 minutes or until tarts are set and lightly browned. Remove from pans and cool on wire racks.
Yield: about 5 dozen tarts

(Top) Our Mushroom Paté *(left)* has a creamy, rich texture. The addition of peach schnapps to Spirited Cider *(center)* creates a unique taste sensation. To add pizzazz to your party tray, try our Marinated Olives.

(Bottom left) These tiny Bacon and Lettuce Stuffed Tomatoes were inspired by that all-American sandwich, the BLT.

(Bottom right) Sweet orange marmalade paired with tangy Cheddar cheese makes our Marmalade Cheese Tarts an unusual (and delicious!) treat.

MARINATED OLIVES

These stuffed olives fortified with vinegar and herbs give an everyday treat party flavor. Recipe doubles easily for larger crowds.

    1   jar (8 ounces) green olives stuffed
          with pimientos, drained
    ¼   cup tarragon wine vinegar
    1   tablespoon dried chives
    ¼   cup olive oil
    1   clove garlic, minced
    ¼   teaspoon whole black peppercorns

Place olives in a glass container with a lid. Combine remaining ingredients and pour over olives. Cap jar and shake to coat olives well. Marinate at room temperature 2 days, shaking jar daily. Drain before serving.
Yield: about 1 cup of olives

BACON AND LETTUCE STUFFED TOMATOES

These little appetizers were a big hit with our testing panel. You may make the filling ahead of time, but don't stuff the tomatoes until about an hour or two before serving.

    20 cherry tomatoes
          Salt
    ¼   cup chopped green onion
    10 slices bacon, cooked and crumbled
    ½   cup finely chopped lettuce
    ⅓   cup mayonnaise
          Salt and freshly ground pepper to
            taste

Cut the top off of each tomato. Scoop out pulp and seeds. Salt inside of each tomato. Invert tomatoes and drain 15 minutes.

In a small bowl, combine the remaining ingredients. Fill each tomato with mixture.
Yield: 20 stuffed tomatoes

SPIRITED CIDER

For a non-alcoholic version of this "spirited" drink, simply serve without the peach schnapps. Any leftover cider will refrigerate well.

    3   3-inch long cinnamon sticks
    1   tablespoon whole cloves
    1   tablespoon whole allspice berries
    1   apple, cored and cut into rings
    1   orange, sliced
    1   bottle (48 ounces) unsweetened apple
          cider
          Peach schnapps

Place cinnamon sticks, cloves, and allspice in the center of a square of cheesecloth and tie corners together to make a bag. Combine all ingredients except schnapps in a 2-quart saucepan or slow cooker. Simmer over low heat at least 2 hours to allow flavors to blend. To serve, add 1 jigger (3 tablespoons) peach schnapps to each 8-ounce serving of cider.
Yield: six 8-ounce servings

MUSHROOM PATÉ

For full flavor, serve this simple gourmet paté at room temperature with French bread or crackers.

    1   cup butter
    2   pounds mushrooms, finely chopped
    1   teaspoon salt
    ½   teaspoon lemon pepper
    ½   teaspoon thyme leaves
    3   egg yolks
    1   tablespoon whipping cream or half
          and half

      French bread or crackers to serve

In a skillet, melt butter over medium heat. Add mushrooms. Cook, stirring occasionally, until mushrooms are well-browned and liquid cooks down (about 35 minutes). Stir in salt, pepper, and thyme. Remove from heat.

In a small bowl, combine egg yolks with cream. Add ¼ cup mushroom mixture to yolk mixture, stirring well. Combine yolk mixture with mushroom mixture in skillet. Cook over low heat, stirring constantly, 2 to 3 minutes. Remove from heat and pour into a 3-cup container. Chill until firm. Allow to come to room temperature before serving with crackers or French bread.
Yield: about 3 cups of paté

SPINACH PUFFS

1 sheet frozen puff pastry dough, thawed according to package directions
1 package (12 ounces) frozen spinach soufflé, thawed
1 egg, lightly beaten
Grated Parmesan cheese

Preheat oven to 350 degrees. Unfold puff pastry sheet and cut lengthwise into three equal rectangles. Cut each rectangle into four equal pieces. Place on an ungreased baking sheet and bake 20 to 25 minutes or until golden brown and puffed. Remove tops from puffs and pull out soft dough. Fill each rectangle with about 2 tablespoons of softened soufflé. Replace tops and brush with egg. Sprinkle with Parmesan cheese. Bake 20 minutes. Cut each puff in half diagonally. Serve warm.
Yield: 24 puffs

BRIE EN CROÛTE

Keep your pantry stocked with the ingredients for this quick-to-fix appetizer. You'll be amazed at how delicious something so easy to prepare can be!

1 package (17¼ ounces) frozen puff pastry dough, thawed according to package directions
2 packages (4¼ ounces each) whole, round Brie cheese
¼ cup apricot preserves, divided
¼ cup chopped pecans, toasted and divided
1 egg yolk, lightly beaten

Unfold one sheet of puff pastry and place one Brie in the center. Cover the top with 2 tablespoons preserves and 2 tablespoons pecans. Gather the edges of the dough over the cheese to resemble a bag. Tie top of "bag" with cotton twine. Repeat with remaining sheet of pastry, cheese, preserves, and pecans. Place each bundle on a lightly greased baking sheet and chill 1 hour.
Preheat oven to 400 degrees. Brush the dough with egg yolk. Bake 25 to 30 minutes or until pastry is puffed and golden. (If pastry browns too quickly, reduce temperature to 350 degrees.) Cool slightly and cut into wedges. Serve warm or at room temperature.
Yield: 8 to 10 servings

HOT SEAFOOD DIP

2 cans (14 ounces each) artichoke hearts, drained and coarsely chopped
2¼ cups mayonnaise
2 cups grated Parmesan cheese
2 cans (6 ounces each) lump crab meat, drained
⅓ cup seasoned bread crumbs
1½ teaspoons garlic salt
1 teaspoon lemon pepper

Crackers to serve

Preheat oven to 325 degrees. In a medium mixing bowl, combine all ingredients, blending well. Pour into a greased 3-quart baking dish. Bake 20 to 25 minutes or until heated through. Serve warm or at room temperature with crackers.
Yield: about 6 cups of dip

CINNAMON SNACK MIX

A real departure from the traditional party snack mix, ours has a crispy cinnamon coating.

3 cups apple-cinnamon-flavored cereal
2 cups pecan halves
1 cup whole almonds
1 cup chow mein noodles
2 egg whites
1 cup granulated sugar
2 tablespoons ground cinnamon
½ teaspoon salt

Preheat oven to 300 degrees. Combine first four ingredients and spread on a greased baking sheet. In a small mixing bowl, combine remaining ingredients. Pour over dry ingredients, stirring to coat well. Bake 35 to 40 minutes, stirring frequently to break apart. Pour onto waxed paper to cool.
Yield: about 8½ cups of snack mix

(Top) A sweet alternative to traditional party mixes, our Cinnamon Snack Mix *(left)* features cereal, nuts, and Chinese noodles with a crunchy cinnamon-sugar coating. The Brie en Croûte is made of soft cheese topped with apricot preserves and pecans, all tucked inside a bundle of puff pastry.

(Bottom) Made with canned artichokes and crab meat that can be kept on hand in the pantry, Hot Seafood Dip *(left, on cracker)* is quick to fix for unexpected guests. Our sophisticated Spinach Puffs have gourmet flair, but they're actually simple to prepare using frozen convenience items.

PEANUT BITES

Try our grown-up snack featuring the childhood favorite — peanut butter. Not at all sticky or sweet, these little bites beat the clichéd bowl of peanuts!

  1 loaf (1 pound) thinly sliced whole
      wheat bread
  2 cups creamy peanut butter
  ½ cup vegetable oil
  3 tablespoons brown sugar
  1½ cups honey-flavored wheat germ

Preheat oven to 250 degrees. Trim crusts from bread and discard. Cut each slice of bread in half diagonally. Cut in half again to form triangles. Place triangles on an ungreased baking sheet. Bake 45 to 50 minutes or until light brown and dry.
In a medium saucepan, combine peanut butter, oil, and brown sugar over medium-low heat. Stir occasionally until heated through. Spread wheat germ on a large sheet of waxed paper. Add bread triangles to peanut butter mixture a few at a time, stirring carefully to coat triangles with mixture. Roll triangles in wheat germ. Place on wire racks to dry.
Yield: about 6 dozen bites

(Top left) This attractive Fruit Wreath with Sweet Cheese Dip was inspired by a Della Robbia wreath. Served on your prettiest platter, the wreath is sure to gather compliments.

(Top right) Seasoned with garlic and herbs, Boursin Cheese Spread is a typical French treat. The creamy cheese is best if it's "aged" in the refrigerator overnight.

(Bottom left) A packaged dressing mix seasons our Salmon Mousse with a hint of bacon. Decorated with cherry tomato roses and fresh parsley, the mousse has an elegant look — without a lot of work!

(Bottom right) Peanut Bites *(top)* are a crispy snack that's not too sweet. Garnished with twigs cut from a grapevine wreath and silk grape leaves, this cluster of Cream Cheese Grapes provides a refreshing alternative to heavy party foods.

FRUIT WREATH WITH SWEET CHEESE DIP

A pretty tray of fruit and dip is really quick and easy party fare. The wreath may be prepared ahead of time, but keep the cut fruit fresh by sprinkling with lemon juice.

  2 packages (8 ounces each) cream
      cheese, softened
  1 jar (7 ounces) marshmallow cream
  ¼ cup milk
  1½ teaspoons vanilla extract
  ½ teaspoon ground nutmeg

      Assorted fruits to serve

In a medium mixing bowl, combine cream cheese, marshmallow cream, milk, vanilla, and nutmeg, beating until smooth.
Place dip in a serving bowl. Arrange fruit around bowl.
Yield: about 3½ cups of dip

BOURSIN CHEESE SPREAD

The flavors in this cheese spread improve with age, making it a wonderful "have-on-hand" appetizer for drop-in guests.

  1 cup butter, softened
  2 packages (8 ounces each) cream
      cheese, softened
  2 cloves garlic, minced
  1 teaspoon oregano flakes
  1 teaspoon basil flakes
  ¼ teaspoon dill weed
  ¼ teaspoon marjoram flakes
  ¼ teaspoon thyme leaves
  ¼ teaspoon freshly ground pepper

      Crackers to serve

Combine all ingredients, blending until smooth. Cover and refrigerate overnight to allow flavors to blend. Serve at room temperature with crackers.
Yield: 3 cups of spread

SALMON MOUSSE

We garnished this mousse with cherry tomato roses and leaves of parsley. To make a rose, peel a tomato thinly in a continuous strip. Roll up the strip and secure the base with a toothpick.

  1 envelope unflavored gelatin
  ¼ cup chicken broth
  2 cans (6 ounces each) pink salmon,
      drained
  ⅓ cup mayonnaise
  ¼ cup minced onion
  1 package (1.2 ounces) ranch-style
      dressing mix with bacon
  3 tablespoons sherry
  3 tablespoons minced parsley
  1 tablespoon Dijon-style mustard
  2 cloves garlic, minced
  1 teaspoon Worcestershire sauce
  1 teaspoon lemon juice
      Salt and freshly ground pepper to
      taste

      Crackers to serve

In small saucepan, soften gelatin in chicken broth. Place pan over low heat and stir until gelatin dissolves.
In a large mixing bowl, combine gelatin mixture with remaining ingredients, blending well. Pour mixture into a well-greased 3-cup gelatin mold. Cover with plastic wrap and refrigerate until firm. Serve with crackers.
Yield: about 3 cups of spread

CREAM CHEESE GRAPES

  1 package (8 ounces) cream cheese,
      softened
  2 tablespoons mayonnaise
  1 pound seedless grapes
  1½ cups finely chopped toasted pecans

In a medium mixing bowl, combine cream cheese and mayonnaise, beating until smooth. Add grapes to cream cheese and stir gently just until coated. Spread pecans on a large sheet of waxed paper. Roll the cheese-coated grapes in the pecans until well coated. Place grapes on a baking sheet and chill at least 1 hour. If desired, arrange on a serving platter in the shape of a grape cluster and garnish with grapevine twigs and silk leaves.
Yield: about 6 dozen grapes

FRIED WONTON

1 pound ground pork
8 canned water chestnuts, minced
2 cloves garlic, minced
2 green onions, finely chopped
1 teaspoon ground ginger
¼ teaspoon freshly ground pepper
½ teaspoon garlic salt
1 package (16 ounces) wonton skins
1 egg, lightly beaten
Vegetable oil

Plum Dipping Sauce (recipe follows)

Combine the pork, water chestnuts, garlic, onions, ginger, pepper, and salt, mixing well. Unwrap wonton skins and cover with damp paper towels to keep skins from drying out. Place one wonton skin on work surface with one point facing up. Place 1 heaping teaspoon of filling in center of skin. Bring bottom point up over filling; bring side points over center of filling. Seal seams with egg. Place the wontons on a baking sheet; cover with damp paper towels.
In a Dutch oven, heat 3 inches of oil to 360 degrees over medium-high heat. Fry the wontons three or four at a time, until golden brown (about 2 to 2½ minutes; do not fry too quickly or the pork centers will not be thoroughly cooked). Drain on paper towels. Serve warm or at room temperature with Plum Dipping Sauce.
Yield: about 50 wontons

(Top) Delicate Stuffed Snow Peas *(left)* filled with herbed cheese are an imaginative change from stuffed celery. A delicious appetizer that can be put together early, Shrimp Toast *(center)* is quick-fried just before serving. Tasty Broccoli Dip is especially attractive when served in a hollowed-out loaf of bread.

(Bottom) Crispy pork-filled Fried Wonton *(left)* served with Plum Dipping Sauce makes great party fare. A pita bread crust is a unique base for Party Pizza; spicy tomato sauce, chunks of sausage, and mozzarella cheese top it off.

PLUM DIPPING SAUCE

1 cup red plum jam
1 clove garlic, minced
3 tablespoons white wine
1 tablespoon Dijon-style mustard
1½ teaspoons dry mustard

Combine all ingredients in a small saucepan over low heat. Stir just until jam is melted. Serve with Fried Wonton.
Yield: about 1 cup of sauce

SHRIMP TOAST

½ pound shrimp, peeled, deveined, and minced
6 canned water chestnuts, minced
1 tablespoon minced purple onion
1 egg
1 tablespoon white wine
1 teaspoon ground ginger
½ teaspoon salt
⅛ teaspoon freshly ground pepper
1½ teaspoons cornstarch dissolved in 1 tablespoon water
6 slices day-old bread
Vegetable oil for frying

Combine first nine ingredients, blending well. Trim crusts from bread. Spread shrimp mixture evenly onto bread. Cut each slice of bread in half diagonally. Cut in half again to form triangles.
In a skillet, heat 2" of oil to 360 degrees. Gently place bread, shrimp side down, in hot oil. Fry 1 minute, turn, and fry 15 seconds or until golden brown. Drain on paper towels. Serve immediately.
Yield: 24 toasts

STUFFED SNOW PEAS

Stuffed snow peas are a refreshing appetizer that may be prepared several hours ahead of time. Just wrap airtight and refrigerate until needed.

1 pound fresh snow peas
1 package (8 ounces) cream cheese, softened
1 teaspoon dill weed
½ teaspoon seasoned salt
½ teaspoon lemon pepper
1 teaspoon dried chives
2 tablespoons mayonnaise

Blanch snow peas in lightly salted boiling water 2 to 3 minutes. Drain and rinse in cold water to stop cooking.
Combine remaining ingredients and beat until smooth. Using a sharp knife, split each snow pea open along straight edge. Place cheese mixture in a pastry bag fitted with a small star tip. Pipe a small amount of cheese mixture inside each snow pea.
Yield: about 40 snow peas

PARTY PIZZA

2 pita breads, split into round halves
¼ cup grated Parmesan cheese
1 can (14½ ounces) whole, peeled tomatoes with liquid, chopped
1 can (6 ounces) tomato paste
½ cup chopped mushrooms
1 teaspoon garlic salt
¼ teaspoon minced dried garlic
1½ teaspoons Italian seasoning
1 pound spicy pork sausage, browned and drained
4 cups grated mozzarella cheese

Preheat oven to 400 degrees. Place pita bread halves on a large baking sheet. Sprinkle each half with 1 tablespoon Parmesan cheese. Bake 8 to 10 minutes or until lightly toasted.
In a medium saucepan, combine tomatoes, tomato paste, mushrooms, garlic salt, garlic, and Italian seasoning. Stir over medium heat until heated through.
Generously spread sauce over bread halves. Top with sausage and mozzarella. Return to oven and bake 10 to 12 minutes or until cheese is bubbly and melted. Cut each pizza into 4 wedges to serve.
Yield: 16 servings

BROCCOLI DIP

The special combination of flavors makes this a light and refreshing dip.

1 package (10 ounces) frozen chopped broccoli, thawed and drained
½ cup minced parsley
½ cup chopped green onions
2 celery stalks, chopped
1 tablespoon Worcestershire sauce
1 teaspoon Greek seasoning
1 cup sour cream
1 cup mayonnaise
1 tablespoon lemon juice
1 loaf (1 pound) round Hawaiian bread

Crackers to serve (optional)

In a large mixing bowl, combine first nine ingredients. Blend well and refrigerate overnight.
Before serving, cut the top off the loaf of bread. Hollow out the inside of the bread leaving about a 1-inch shell of bread. Tear bread from inside of loaf into bite-size pieces. Spread bread pieces on an ungreased baking sheet and toast lightly.
Fill hollowed-out round bread with dip. Serve dip with toasted bread or crackers.
Yield: about 3½ cups of dip

SOUTH OF THE BORDER SALSA

Keep this salsa and a package of tortillas in the refrigerator to serve drop-in guests. Just quick-fry our Tortilla Chips and you have a zesty snack in minutes.

 1 can (28 ounces) whole tomatoes with liquid, chopped
 ½ cup minced parsley
 1 medium onion, minced
 2 cloves garlic, minced
 ½ cup olive oil
 ¼ cup chopped jalapeño peppers

 Tortilla Chips to serve (recipe follows)

Combine all ingredients. Refrigerate overnight in a non-metallic container to allow flavors to blend. Serve with Tortilla Chips.
Yield: about 3 cups of salsa

Spice up your holiday get-togethers with a variety of appetizers and snacks: *(clockwise from left)* Hearty Tortilla Chips served with South of the Border Salsa add Mexican flair, while easy-to-make Puff Pastry Sticks combine buttery flavor and crisp texture. Skewers of Marinated Chicken Bites, alternated with chunks of bell pepper, make colorful, delicious hors d'oeuvres. A great make-ahead snack, the Bacon-Cheddar Cheese Ball is sure to be a favorite. The tangy Bacon-Apricot Twists are served with a dipping sauce.

TORTILLA CHIPS

 1 package (12 count) fresh corn tortillas
 Vegetable oil
 1 tablespoon salt
 1 clove garlic, crushed

Cut each tortilla into 6 wedges. Pour oil into a skillet to a depth of 1 inch. Heat oil to 360 degrees over medium-high heat. Fry tortillas about 1 minute or until crisp. Drain on paper towels. Place salt and garlic in a paper bag. Add chips and shake well. Serve warm or at room temperature.
Yield: 6 dozen chips

PUFF PASTRY STICKS

Keep a package of frozen puff pastry dough in the freezer for easy last minute snacks like these.

 1 package (17¼ ounces) frozen puff pastry dough, thawed according to package directions
 ½ cup sesame seeds
 1 cup grated Romano cheese

Preheat oven to 400 degrees. Unfold puff pastry sheet and cut lengthwise into three equal rectangles. Cut each rectangle crosswise into ½-inch wide strips. Sprinkle both sides of strips generously with sesame seeds and cheese, gently pressing seeds and cheese into dough. Place on an ungreased baking sheet and bake 8 to 10 minutes or until puffed and golden.
Yield: about 10 dozen sticks

BACON-APRICOT TWISTS

 12 slices bacon, cut in half
 24 dried apricot halves

DIPPING SAUCE
 ½ cup red plum jam
 ¼ cup soy sauce

Preheat oven to 350 degrees. Wrap one half slice of bacon around an apricot half, securing with toothpick. Repeat with remaining bacon and apricots. Place on ungreased baking sheet and bake 20 to 25 minutes, turning once. Bacon should be brown and crisp.
While twists are baking, combine jam and soy sauce in a small saucepan. Cook over low heat just until jam melts; set aside.
Drain twists on paper towels. Serve warm or at room temperature with dipping sauce.
Yield: 24 twists

BACON-CHEDDAR CHEESE BALL

A miniature cookie cutter is all you need to cut out simple garnishes. We cut out the tiny stars on top of this zesty cheese ball from a red bell pepper.

 2 packages (8 ounces each) cream cheese, softened
 ½ pound sharp Cheddar cheese, grated
 ½ cup chopped green onions
 6 slices bacon, cooked and crumbled
 1 clove garlic, minced
 3 tablespoons diced pimiento
 3 tablespoons minced parsley

 Crackers to serve

Combine all ingredients, blending well. Form into a ball. Cover with plastic wrap. Refrigerate overnight to allow flavors to blend. Serve with crackers.
Yield: about 3 cups of cheese spread

MARINATED CHICKEN BITES

These moist chunks of chicken are perfect to make ahead. Just place the marinated meat and vegetables on the skewers, cover, and refrigerate until ready to broil. Inexpensive bamboo skewers are often available in the party supplies section of most grocery stores.

 1½ pounds boneless, skinless chicken breast, cut into 1" pieces
 ½ cup mango chutney
 ¼ cup olive oil
 ⅓ cup white wine
 1 tablespoon raspberry vinegar
 1 green bell pepper, cut into 1" pieces
 1 red bell pepper, cut into 1" pieces
 ½ cup red plum jam

In a large glass bowl, combine the chicken, chutney, olive oil, wine, and vinegar. Cover and marinate in the refrigerator overnight.
Drain chicken. On each 6-inch skewer, place pieces in the following order: chicken, green bell pepper, chicken, and red bell pepper.
In a small saucepan, melt jam over low heat. Generously brush chicken and peppers with jam. Place on wire rack in baking pan. Brushing often with jam, broil 12 to 15 minutes or until chicken is thoroughly cooked.
Yield: about 24 skewers

*M*aking someone feel special is what gift-giving is all about — and what could be more special than a gift from your kitchen! And when you package your gift in a creative way, it will be remembered for years to come. We've given you a selection of quick and delicious recipes and easy craft projects to please everyone on your list. As you present these tokens of affection, you'll enjoy the warm feeling that comes from giving the best gift of all — a part of yourself.

CHOCOLATE SHORTBREAD

    1   cup butter, softened
    ⅔   cup confectioners sugar
    1   teaspoon vanilla extract
    1½ cups all-purpose flour
    ¼   cup cocoa
    ¼   teaspoon salt
        Confectioners sugar

In a large mixing bowl, cream butter, sugar, and vanilla. In another bowl, combine flour, cocoa, and salt. Stir flour mixture into butter mixture. Wrap dough in plastic wrap and chill 30 minutes.

Preheat oven to 300 degrees. Press dough into a 15 x 10 x 1-inch jellyroll pan. Bake 30 minutes. Remove from oven and cut out warm shortbread in pan using a 2" wide heart-shaped cookie cutter. Remove cookies from pan and cool on wire rack. Sprinkle cookies with confectioners sugar. Store in airtight container.
Yield: about 2 dozen cookies

CHEWY CHOCOLATE BARS

CRUST
    4   cups rolled oats
    ¾   cup dark corn syrup
    1   cup firmly packed brown sugar
    ⅔   cup butter or margarine, melted
    ½   cup chunky peanut butter
    2   teaspoons vanilla extract

TOPPING
    2   cups semisweet chocolate chips
    ⅔   cup chunky peanut butter
    1   cup coarsely chopped peanuts

Preheat oven to 350 degrees. For crust, combine ingredients in a medium mixing bowl, blending well. Pat mixture into a lightly greased 13 x 9 x 2-inch pan. Bake 12 to 15 minutes; cool.

For topping, melt chocolate chips with peanut butter in top of a double boiler over low heat. Stir in peanuts. Spread topping over crust. Cover and refrigerate until chocolate is firm. Store in refrigerator.
Yield: about 4 dozen bars

FRUITCAKE BITES

    ¼   cup golden raisins
    ¼   cup raisins
    ½   cup dark rum
    ¼   cup butter or margarine, softened
    ½   cup firmly packed brown sugar
    2   eggs, beaten
    1½ cups all-purpose flour
    1½ teaspoons baking soda
    1   teaspoon ground cinnamon
    1   teaspoon ground nutmeg
    ½   teaspoon ground allspice
    3   tablespoons milk
    ½   cup chopped green candied cherries
    ½   cup chopped red candied cherries
    ½   cup chopped dates
    2   cups chopped pecans

In a small bowl, combine raisins and rum. Marinate 1 hour.

Preheat oven to 275 degrees. In a large mixing bowl, cream butter and sugar. Beat in eggs. In another bowl, combine flour, baking soda, and spices. Stir into butter mixture. Stir in milk and rum-raisin mixture. Stir in fruit and nuts. Fill paper-lined miniature muffin tins two-thirds full with batter. Bake 10 to 15 minutes or until the top of a muffin springs back when lightly touched.
Yield: about 5 dozen cupcakes

REDWARE-LOOK POTTERY

These containers are for decorative use only. Use for cookies and other dry foods. Wipe clean with a damp cloth.

You will need clay flower pots and plant saucers, gesso, Rusty Nail Folk Art™ acrylic paint for basecoat, yellow and dk blue acrylic paint for designs, 1"w flat and small round paintbrushes, glossy clear acrylic spray, and cellulose sponge and paper towel (for sponged container only).

1. Use flat paintbrush to apply one coat of gesso to containers; allow to dry. Apply two coats of Rusty Nail, allowing to dry between coats.
2. For sponged container only, use small piece of sponge and dip in dk blue paint; blot on paper towel. Referring to photo, apply paint to surface of container. Allow to dry.
3. Referring to photo and using small paintbrushes, paint designs. Allow to dry.
4. Spray containers with two coats of acrylic spray, allowing to dry between coats.

Moist Fruitcake Bites *(clockwise from left)*, flaky Chocolate Shortbread, and Chewy Chocolate Bars have home-baked appeal. For an extra special gift, present the treats with a redware-look pottery bowl or plate. Our simple painting techniques give ordinary clay pottery the look of antique redware, which was favored by the Pennsylvania Dutch settlers. Commonly used during the 1700s and 1800s, redware is now a collector's item.

Cookies From 'Round the World

Choose one or all of these international cookies to delight the cookie lovers on your gift list: *(from left)* Mexican Bizcochitos have a mild licorice flavor, Belgian Nut Cookies are filled with chocolate and raspberry jam, and Madeleines from France are flavored with Grand Marnier liqueur.

BELGIAN NUT COOKIES

¾ cup butter, softened
⅓ cup granulated sugar
1½ cups all-purpose flour
1½ cups ground toasted almonds
1 teaspoon vanilla extract
⅛ teaspoon salt
1 cup semisweet chocolate chips
½ cup raspberry jam

In a large mixing bowl, cream butter and sugar. Add flour, almonds, vanilla, and salt, stirring just until mixture is combined and forms a dough. Divide dough in half and wrap each half in plastic wrap. Refrigerate 1 hour.

Preheat oven to 350 degrees. Roll out dough to ⅛-inch thickness between two sheets of waxed paper. Remove top sheet of waxed paper. Using a 2½-inch long fluted tart mold or cookie cutter, cut out dough. Place cookies on lightly greased baking sheet. Bake 10 to 12 minutes or until lightly browned around edges. Cool cookies on baking sheet.

In the top of a double boiler over low heat, melt chocolate chips. Reserving ¼ cup of melted chocolate, spread a thin layer of chocolate on one-half of the cookies. Spread the remaining half of the cookies with a thin layer of raspberry jam. With one chocolate side and one raspberry side together, place two cookies together. Place cookies on waxed paper-lined baking sheet. Drizzle tops of cookies with reserved chocolate. Place cookies in refrigerator to set. Store cookies in airtight container in cool, dry place.
Yield: about 2 dozen cookies

BIZCOCHITOS

1 cup butter or margarine, softened
1 cup granulated sugar, divided
1 egg yolk
1 tablespoon milk
2½ cups all-purpose flour
4½ teaspoons ground cinnamon, divided
2 teaspoons anise seed
½ cup white wine

In a large mixing bowl, cream butter, ½ cup sugar, egg yolk, and milk. In another bowl, combine flour, 1½ teaspoons cinnamon, and anise seed. Add flour mixture to creamed mixture, stirring until combined. Stir in wine. Wrap dough in plastic wrap and chill at least 2 hours.

Preheat oven to 350 degrees. On a lightly floured surface, use a floured rolling pin to roll out dough to ⅛-inch thickness. Cut into desired shapes using a 2-inch cookie cutter. Transfer cookies to lightly greased baking sheets and bake 10 to 12 minutes or until edges are very lightly browned.

In a small bowl, combine remaining ½ cup sugar and remaining 3 teaspoons of cinnamon. Coat warm cookies with sugar mixture. Store in airtight container.
Yield: about 8 dozen cookies

MADELEINES

2 eggs
⅛ teaspoon salt
½ cup granulated sugar
½ cup all-purpose flour
½ cup butter, melted and cooled
Grand Marnier liqueur

Preheat oven to 400 degrees. In a large mixing bowl, combine eggs and salt. Gradually beat in sugar until mixture is thick and lightens in color (about 5 minutes). Fold flour into egg mixture a few tablespoons at a time. Fold in butter a few tablespoons at a time. Spoon 1 tablespoon of batter into each shell of a greased and floured Madeleine pan. Bake 8 to 10 minutes or until a cake springs back when lightly touched. Immediately remove from molds and cool on wire racks. Sprinkle Madeleines with liqueur.
Yield: about 18 Madeleines

Variation: To make chocolate Madeleines, reduce flour to ⅓ cup and combine flour with 3 tablespoons cocoa. Proceed with recipe as directed.

Teatime Treats

Your friends won't wait for teatime to try these treats: *(clockwise from top right)* Our Orange Chocolate Chip Scones are scrumptious versions of traditional teatime fare. Delicious served with biscuits or over cake, Old-Fashioned Pears with Ginger also makes a wonderful sweet sauce for meats. For a taste of the unusual, Kiwi Jam is tart and sweet with a flavor similar to strawberries.

ORANGE CHOCOLATE CHIP SCONES

2 cups all-purpose flour
¼ cup granulated sugar
2 teaspoons baking powder
1 teaspoon salt
½ cup butter or margarine, cut into pieces
2 eggs, lightly beaten
3 tablespoons orange juice
1 teaspoon vanilla extract
1 teaspoon grated orange peel
½ cup semisweet chocolate chips
½ cup coarsely chopped toasted pecans
1 egg yolk
1 teaspoon water
1 tablespoon granulated sugar

Preheat oven to 350 degrees. Lightly grease a 9-inch circle in the center of a baking sheet.

In a medium mixing bowl, combine the flour, ¼ cup sugar, baking powder, and salt. Using a pastry blender or two knives, cut the butter into the flour mixture until mixture resembles coarse meal. Make a well in the center of the dry ingredients and add eggs, orange juice, vanilla, and orange peel. Stir just until dry ingredients are moistened. Stir in chocolate chips and pecans.

Pat the dough into a 9-inch circle in the center of the baking sheet. Combine egg yolk and water and brush over dough. Sprinkle with 1 tablespoon sugar. Using a serrated knife, cut dough into eight wedges, but do not separate. Bake 20 to 25 minutes or until a toothpick inserted in center comes out clean. Cool on wire rack. Store in airtight container. Serve warm or at room temperature.
Yield: 8 scones

KIWI JAM

9 kiwis
6 cups granulated sugar
6 ounces liquid pectin
Green food coloring, optional

Wash and sterilize canning jars, lids, and bands. Peel and crush kiwis. In a large heavy saucepan, combine crushed fruit and sugar. Stir well. Bring mixture to a rolling boil over high heat, stirring constantly. Stir in liquid pectin. Return mixture to a rolling boil, stirring constantly, and boil 1 minute. Remove from heat. Skim foam from top of mixture with a large metal spoon. If desired, stir in a few drops of food coloring to intensify color. Fill sterilized jars to within ¼-inch of tops. Wipe jar rims. Cover jars with lids and bands. Invert jars for 5 minutes, then turn jars upright.
Yield: about 6 cups of jam

OLD-FASHIONED PEARS WITH GINGER

14 medium pears, cored, pared, and cut into thin slices
4 cups granulated sugar
1 lemon
1 tablespoon chopped crystallized ginger

In a Dutch oven over medium-low heat, combine pears and sugar. Stirring occasionally, cook until sugar is melted and forms a thick syrup (about 1 hour). Continue simmering gently until fruit begins to turn translucent, stirring occasionally. Add grated rind and juice of lemon to pears. Stir in ginger and continue cooking 15 minutes more. Store in airtight containers in refrigerator.
Yield: about 9 cups of pears

Christmas Cakes

These coffee cakes are a delectable way to spread Christmas cheer: *(clockwise from top)* The Poppy Seed Cake has a light lemony glaze that complements its buttery flavor, and extra-moist Cranberry Coffee Cake has a filling of tangy cranberry sauce. Our Christmas bread cloth makes a pretty wrapper for almond-topped Danish Pastries; the delicate flaky layers give them bakery-fresh flavor.

POPPY SEED CAKE

CAKE
- ½ cup poppy seed
- ⅓ cup milk
- 1 cup butter or margarine, softened
- 1½ cups granulated sugar
- 2 teaspoons grated lemon peel
- 1½ teaspoons lemon extract
- 1 teaspoon vanilla extract
- 4 eggs
- 2¼ cups all-purpose flour
- 1½ teaspoons baking powder
- ½ teaspoon salt
- ½ cup sour cream

GLAZE
- ½ cup confectioners sugar
- ¼ cup lemon juice

Soak poppy seed in milk 1 hour.

Preheat oven to 350 degrees. For cake, cream butter, sugar, lemon peel, and extracts in a large mixing bowl. Beat in eggs one at a time, beating well after each addition. Drain poppy seed; stir poppy seed into mixture.

In another bowl, combine flour, baking powder, and salt. Add flour mixture to creamed mixture, alternating with sour cream. Pour into a greased and floured 9¼ x 5¼ x 2½-inch loaf pan. Bake 45 to 50 minutes or until a toothpick inserted in center of cake comes out clean.

For glaze, combine ingredients, blending until smooth. Pour over warm cake in pan. Allow cake to cool completely before removing from pan.
Yield: 10 to 12 servings

DANISH PASTRIES

CAKE
- 1½ cups butter, softened and divided
- 3 cups all-purpose flour, divided
- ⅛ teaspoon salt
- ¼ cup cold water
- 1 cup milk
- ¼ cup granulated sugar
- 1 teaspoon almond extract
- 3 eggs

GLAZE
- 1½ cups confectioners sugar
- 2 tablespoons butter, softened
- 2 teaspoons vanilla extract
- 1 tablespoon milk

TOPPING
- 1 cup sliced almonds, toasted
- 2 tablespoons confectioners sugar

Preheat oven to 350 degrees. For cake, use a pastry blender or two knives to cut 1 cup butter into 2 cups of flour in a medium mixing bowl. Mixture should resemble coarse meal. Stir in salt and water to make a dough. Divide the dough into eight equal portions. Pat out each portion of dough into a 3 x 4-inch oval on an ungreased baking sheet. Refrigerate until ready to use.

In a large, heavy saucepan, combine remaining ½ cup butter and milk over medium heat. Bring to a boil. Add the remaining 1 cup of flour, sugar, and almond extract. Quickly stir until mixture forms a ball; remove from heat. By hand, beat in eggs one at a time until well blended. Spread dough thickly and evenly over chilled ovals. Bake 40 to 45 minutes until puffy and golden.

For glaze, combine confectioners sugar with butter in a small bowl; stir until well blended. Stir in vanilla and milk until mixture is smooth.

For topping, mix almonds with confectioners sugar in a small bowl.

Spread glaze evenly over warm pastries. Sprinkle each pastry with topping. Serve warm or at room temperature.
Yield: 8 pastries

Place on fold of fabric

CRANBERRY COFFEE CAKE

CAKE
- ½ cup butter or margarine, softened
- 1½ cups granulated sugar
- 2 eggs
- 1½ teaspoons almond extract
- 1 teaspoon vanilla extract
- 2 cups all-purpose flour
- 1 teaspoon baking powder
- 1 teaspoon baking soda
- 1 teaspoon salt
- 1 cup sour cream
- 1 cup whole-berry cranberry sauce

GLAZE
- 1 cup confectioners sugar
- 3 tablespoons milk
- ½ teaspoon almond extract

Preheat oven to 350 degrees. For cake, cream butter and sugar in a large bowl. Beat in eggs and extracts until well blended. In another bowl, combine flour, baking powder, baking soda, and salt. Add flour mixture to creamed mixture, alternating with sour cream. Pour half of batter into a greased 9-inch tube pan. Spoon cranberry sauce over top of batter. Top with remaining batter. Bake 55 to 60 minutes or until a toothpick inserted in center of cake comes out clean. Cool in pan 10 minutes.

For glaze, combine ingredients in a small bowl, blending well. Remove warm cake from pan and drizzle with glaze.
Yield: 14 to 16 servings

CHRISTMAS BREAD CLOTH

You will need two coordinating 18" squares of fabric, thread to match fabric, and tracing paper.

1. Use pattern and follow **Transferring Patterns**, page 156. With right sides together, fold one fabric square in half. Place pattern on fold where indicated by pattern and cut out. Repeat for remaining fabric square.
2. With right sides together and leaving an opening for turning, sew pieces together using a ¼" seam allowance. Clip curves and cut corners diagonally. Turn right side out and press; sew final closure by hand.

Cajun Dinner

Give a taste of New Orleans this Christmas with our spicy Red Beans and Rice Dinner. This traditional Cajun meal will satisfy the heartiest appetite! To present the dinner, tuck a jar of dried red beans, a bundle of special seasoning mix, and a bag of rice inside a small crate. We used a calligraphy pen to label the ingredients and to add a humorous message. Don't forget to include the recipe!

RED BEANS AND RICE DINNER

SEASONING MIXTURE
- 1 tablespoon dried bell pepper flakes
- 1 tablespoon dried minced onion
- ½ teaspoon dried minced garlic
- 2 teaspoons seasoned salt
- 1 bay leaf
- 1 teaspoon granulated sugar
- ¼ teaspoon cayenne pepper
- ½ teaspoon celery seed
- 1 teaspoon ground cumin
- ¼ teaspoon crushed red pepper

- 2 cups (about 1 pound) dried red beans
- 1 cup uncooked long grain white rice

In a small bowl, combine seasoning ingredients. Place in a small, sealable plastic bag.

Fill a pint canning jar with red beans. Fill a sealable plastic bag with rice. Include the recipe for Red Beans and Rice (recipe follows). Instructions follow for jar lid, rice bag, and seasoning bag.

RED BEANS AND RICE
- 2 cups red beans
- 1 ham bone
    - Seasoning mixture
- 1 cup uncooked rice
- 2 cups water
- 1 teaspoon salt
- 1 pound spicy smoked sausage, sliced
    - Salt and freshly ground pepper to taste

Wash beans. Place beans in a Dutch oven; cover with water and soak overnight.

The following day, add ham bone and seasoning mixture. If necessary, add additional water to cover the beans. Cook, partially covered over medium-low heat 3 to 4 hours.

About 30 minutes before serving, combine rice, water, and salt in a saucepan and bring to a boil. Reduce heat to low. Cover pan and cook 30 minutes without lifting lid.

About 20 minutes before serving, add sausage, salt, and pepper to beans. Serve over rice.

Yield: 4 to 6 servings

BEAN CRATE

For bean jar lid, you will need one regular canning jar lid and circle of osnaburg fabric and fleece batting same size as flat piece of jar lid.

For rice bag, you will need one 5½" x 14" piece of osnaburg fabric.

For seasoning bag, you will need one 9" dia. circle of fabric with pinked edges and bay leaf.

You will also need a 5" x 9" wooden crate, black felt-tip calligraphy pen with fine point, fabric glue, raffia, and excelsior.

Note: Refer to photo for style and placement of words.

1. For jar lid, use pen to write "Red Beans" in center of fabric circle. Glue batting to flat piece of lid; glue fabric to batting. Glue lid inside screw ring.

2. For rice bag, fold all edges of fabric under ½" and glue. With wrong sides together and matching short edges, fold bag in half; glue side edges together. Allow to dry. Use pen to write "and Rice" in center of bag and to draw border around words. Place plastic bag of rice in fabric bag. Referring to photo, tie each corner of bag with raffia; knot and trim ends.

3. For seasoning bag, center plastic bag of seasonings on wrong side of fabric circle. Use raffia to tie fabric around plastic bag and to tie bay leaf to bag.

4. Use pen to write "Don't spill the beans" on one side of crate. Tie raffia in a bow around jar. Place excelsior, jar, rice bag, and seasoning bag in crate.

Surprise a friend with a miniature feather tree filled with delicious Sugar Cookie Ornaments. Reminiscent of the days when most tree decorations were cookies or candies, this tree makes a charming gift. We cut our cookies in the shapes of antique Victorian glass ornaments and decorated them with colorful icing and candy accents.

SUGAR COOKIE ORNAMENTS

¾ cup confectioners sugar
½ cup butter or margarine, softened
1 egg yolk
1 teaspoon vanilla extract
½ teaspoon almond extract
1¼ cups all-purpose flour
½ teaspoon baking soda
¼ teaspoon cream of tartar
⅛ teaspoon salt
Purchased tubes of decorating icing
Candy sprinkles and dragées
Nylon line (to hang cookies)

In a large mixing bowl, combine sugar, butter, egg yolk, and extracts, beating until fluffy. In another bowl, combine flour, baking soda, cream of tartar, and salt. Stir flour mixture into butter mixture. Wrap dough in plastic wrap. Chill at least 2 hours.

Preheat oven to 350 degrees. On a floured surface, use a floured rolling pin to roll out dough to ⅛-inch thickness. Using patterns given or miniature cookie cutters, cut out dough. (To use patterns, trace over patterns with tracing paper. Cut out patterns and use a sharp knife to cut out dough around patterns.) Transfer cookies to a lightly greased baking sheet. Bake 5 to 7 minutes or until very lightly browned. Use a toothpick to make a hole for hanger in top of each warm cookie. Transfer cookies to wire rack to cool. Referring to photo, decorate cookies with icing, candy sprinkles, and dragées. Use nylon line to hang cookies from tree.

Yield: about 5 dozen cookies

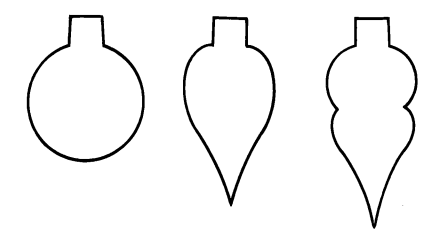

South of the Border Snacks

Spice up someone's holiday with a Mexican fiesta! Our selection of easy-to-make snacks includes hot and spicy Nacho Cheese Snack Mix *(clockwise from top left)*, Zesty Tomato Juice, Mexican Chocolate Brownies with a hint of cinnamon, and Spicy Jalapeño Spread. To add even more South of the Border flavor to your gift, present it with colorful stenciled accessories or a handmade snake decoration.

MEXICAN CHOCOLATE BROWNIES

1	cup cocoa
¾	cup butter or margarine, melted
1¼	cups all-purpose flour
½	teaspoon salt
3	cups granulated sugar
7	eggs, lightly beaten
1	tablespoon vanilla extract
2½	teaspoons ground cinnamon
1	teaspoon freshly ground pepper

Preheat oven to 350 degrees. In a small bowl, combine cocoa with butter, stirring until smooth. In a large mixing bowl, combine flour, salt, and sugar. Stir in cocoa mixture. Blend in eggs, vanilla, cinnamon, and pepper. Pour into a lightly greased 13 x 9 x 2-inch baking pan and bake 35 to 40 minutes or until center is set.
Yield: about 24 brownies

ZESTY TOMATO JUICE

1	can (48 ounces) tomato juice
¼	cup Worcestershire sauce
2	tablespoons juice from canned or bottled jalapeño peppers
1½	teaspoons hot pepper sauce
½	teaspoon onion juice
½	cup lemon juice

Combine all ingredients and stir well. Store in refrigerator.
Yield: about 6 servings

NACHO CHEESE SNACK MIX

6	cups rice cereal squares
4	cups Tidbits® cheese crackers
2	cups small pretzels
2	cups mixed nuts
½	cup butter, melted
1	tablespoon Worcestershire sauce
1	package (1.5 ounces) nacho cheese sauce mix
2	teaspoons chili powder
¼	teaspoon cayenne pepper

Preheat oven to 250 degrees. In a large, shallow baking pan, combine first four ingredients.
In a small bowl, combine remaining ingredients. Drizzle butter mixture over cereal mixture, stirring well. Bake 30 minutes, stirring every 10 minutes. Spread on waxed paper to cool. Store in airtight container.
Yield: 14 cups of snack mix

SPICY JALAPEÑO SPREAD

4	cups grated sharp Cheddar cheese
1	medium onion, finely chopped
2	cloves garlic, minced
6	jalapeño peppers, chopped
1	cup mayonnaise
½	cup chopped green onion
1	teaspoon garlic salt

In a large mixing bowl, combine all ingredients. Stir until well blended. Refrigerate overnight to allow flavors to blend before serving.
Yield: about 4½ cups of spread

STENCILED MOTIFS

You will need desired items to stencil (we used clay flower pots, napkins, place mat, table runner, and colored paper); acrylic paint; stencil brushes; sheet of Mylar® or clear, flexible plastic; craft knife or electric stencil cutter; black permanent felt-tip pen with fine point; removable tape; cardboard; and matte clear acrylic spray.

Note: Refer to photo for colors and placement of designs.
1. (Note: If necessary, use removable tape to mask areas on stencil next to areas being painted.) Follow Steps 2 and 3 of Apple Kitchen Accents, page 93, to stencil designs on items.
2. For clay flower pots, spray stenciled area with two coats of acrylic spray, allowing to dry between coats. Containers should be hand washed.
3. For fabric items, heat-set paint by pressing over design area with a hot, dry iron.

SNAKE DECORATIONS

You will need Sculpey modeling compound, acrylic paint, paintbrushes, and matte clear acrylic spray.

1. Use modeling compound to make snakes; bake following manufacturer's instructions.
2. Referring to photo, paint snakes and allow to dry. Spray with acrylic spray; allow to dry.

GIFTS FROM THE KITCHEN

Sweet Temptations

Candy is always a welcome holiday gift, and this sweet selection contains old-fashioned confections made with modern ease! Our collection includes delicious Peppermint-Orange Patties *(clockwise from top left)* and soft, chewy Gumdrops with a crystallized sugar coating. Our Never-Fail Divinity always turns out right because we substitute marshmallow cream for egg whites! Hard Candy Santas and Lollipops are favorite candies, and Rum-Raisin Fudge is spiked with rum-marinated raisins.

HARD CANDY SANTAS AND LOLLIPOPS

     2 cups granulated sugar
     1 cup water
    ⅔ cup light corn syrup
     1 teaspoon oil-based flavoring for candy
         making
    ½ to 1 teaspoon candy coloring
         Purchased lollipop sticks

In a large saucepan, combine sugar, water, and corn syrup over medium-high heat. Without stirring, cook to hard crack stage (300 degrees on a candy thermometer). Remove from heat and stir in flavoring and coloring.

For Santas, use balls of aluminum foil to prop oiled two-piece metal candy molds upright on a baking sheet. Pour mixture into molds. When mixture is hard, but not thoroughly cooled, remove candies from molds.

For molded lollipops, pour mixture into oiled metal lollipop molds. Quickly insert lollipop sticks into indentions before mixture hardens. When mixture is hard, but not thoroughly cooled, remove lollipops from molds.

For round lollipops, pour mixture into 3- to 4-inch diameter circles on an oiled baking sheet. Quickly insert lollipop sticks into circles before mixture hardens. When lollipops are thoroughly cooled, remove from baking sheet.
Yield: about four 3-inch tall Santas, fifteen 1½-inch molded lollipops, or ten round lollipops

NEVER-FAIL DIVINITY

    1½ cups granulated sugar
     ½ cup water
     2 tablespoons light corn syrup
     ⅛ teaspoon salt
     1 jar (7 ounces) marshmallow cream
    1½ teaspoons vanilla extract
     1 cup chopped pecans

In a large saucepan, combine sugar, water, corn syrup, and salt. Cook over medium-high heat to hard ball stage (250 degrees on a candy thermometer). Place marshmallow cream in a large mixing bowl. Beating constantly, gradually add syrup to marshmallow cream. Beat until mixture is stiff and forms peaks. Beat in vanilla and pecans. Quickly drop by heaping teaspoonfuls onto waxed paper. Store in an airtight container.
Yield: about 2 dozen candies

PEPPERMINT-ORANGE PATTIES

     7 cups confectioners sugar
     ½ cup butter, softened
     1 can (14 ounces) sweetened
         condensed milk
    1½ teaspoons orange extract
     ½ teaspoon peppermint extract
     2 cups semisweet chocolate chips
     ⅓ bar paraffin

In a large mixing bowl, combine first five ingredients. Blend until smooth. Cover and refrigerate mixture overnight.

Form mixture into 1-inch balls and flatten slightly with palm of hand to make patty shapes. Refrigerate patties 1 hour.

In the top of a double boiler over medium-low heat, melt chocolate chips with paraffin. Dip patties into chocolate mixture and place on wire rack over waxed paper to set. Store in airtight container.
Yield: about 14 dozen candies

Variation: To make Peppermint Drops, eliminate orange extract and increase peppermint extract to 1 teaspoon. Proceed as directed. Form mixture into 1-inch balls, but do not flatten into patty shapes. Continue with recipe as directed.

RUM-RAISIN FUDGE

     1 cup raisins
     ½ cup dark rum
    2½ cups granulated sugar
     ½ cup butter or margarine
     1 cup evaporated milk
     1 jar (7 ounces) marshmallow cream
     2 cups semisweet chocolate chips
     ½ cup chopped pecans
     1 teaspoon rum extract

In a small bowl, combine raisins and rum. Marinate overnight.

In a large, heavy saucepan, combine sugar, butter, and milk. Cook over medium heat, stirring constantly until mixture reaches soft ball stage (238 degrees on a candy thermometer, about 5 minutes). Remove from heat. Stir in marshmallow cream, chocolate chips, pecans, extract, and raisin mixture. Spread mixture into a lightly greased 10 x 8 x 2-inch baking pan. Cool and cut into squares.
Yield: about 48 pieces of fudge

GUMDROPS

     4 tablespoons unflavored gelatin
     1 cup cold water
    1½ cups boiling water
     4 cups granulated sugar
     ½ teaspoon desired flavoring: lemon
         extract, orange extract, peppermint
         extract, etc.
     3 to 4 drops desired food coloring
         Granulated sugar

In a large saucepan, soften gelatin in cold water 5 minutes. Stir in boiling water until gelatin is dissolved. Stir in sugar and bring mixture to a boil over medium-high heat. Boil 25 minutes, stirring frequently. Pour mixture into two 8 x 8-inch pans. To each pan add ½ teaspoon desired flavoring and desired food color (or do not add color for clear gumdrops). Stir until combined. Refrigerate pans overnight. Using a knife dipped in hot water, cut gelatin mixture into 1-inch cubes. Roll in granulated sugar until well coated. Place gumdrops on a sheet of waxed paper and allow to sit at room temperature two days to crystallize. Store in airtight containers.
Yield: about 10 dozen candies

GENERAL INSTRUCTIONS

TRANSFERRING PATTERNS

When entire pattern is shown, place a piece of tracing paper over pattern and trace pattern, marking all placement symbols and openings. Cut out traced pattern.
When one-half of pattern is shown, fold tracing paper in half and place folded edge along dashed line of pattern. Trace pattern, marking all placement symbols and openings. Cut out traced pattern; open pattern and lay it flat.

SEWING SHAPES

Center pattern on wrong side of one piece of fabric and use a fabric marking pencil to draw around pattern. If indicated on pattern, mark opening for turning. **DO NOT CUT OUT SHAPE.** With right sides facing and leaving an opening for turning, carefully sew fabric pieces together **directly on pencil line.** Leaving a ¼" seam allowance, cut out shape. Clip seam allowance at curves and corners. Turn shape right side out. Use the rounded end of a small crochet hook to completely turn small areas. If pattern has facial features or detail lines, use fabric marking pencil to lightly mark placement of features or lines.

FABRIC BAGS

1. To determine width of fabric needed, add ½" to finished width of bag; to determine length of fabric needed, double the finished height of bag and add 1½". Cut fabric the determined width and length.
2. With right sides together and matching short edges, fold fabric in half; finger press folded edge (bottom of bag). Using a ¼" seam allowance and thread to match fabric, sew sides of fabric together.
3. Fold top edge of bag ¼" to wrong side; press. Fold ½" to wrong side again; press. Stitch in place.
4. For bottom corners, match each side seam to fold line at bottom of bag; sew across each corner 1" from end **(Fig. 1).** Turn bag right side out.

Fig. 1

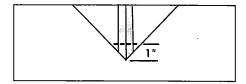

5. For casing, make a small vertical cut through one layer of fabric between top of bag and stitched line. Thread desired ribbon through casing.

CROSS STITCH

COUNTED CROSS STITCH

Work one Cross Stitch to correspond to each colored square on the chart. For horizontal rows, work stitches in two journeys **(Fig. 1).** For vertical rows, complete each stitch as shown in **Fig. 2.** When working over two fabric threads, work Cross Stitch as shown in **Fig. 3.** When the chart shows a Backstitch crossing a colored square **(Fig. 4),** a Cross Stitch **(Figs. 1, 2,** or **3)** should be worked first; then the Backstitch **(Fig. 8)** should be worked on top of the Cross Stitch.

Fig. 1

Fig. 2

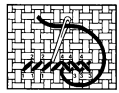

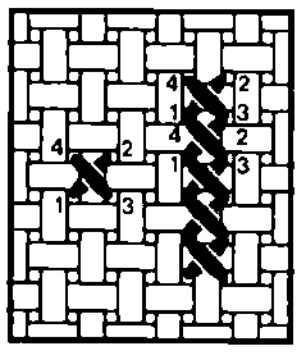

Fig. 3

Fig. 4

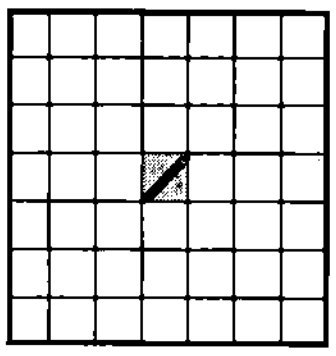

QUARTER STITCHES (¼X and ¾X)

Quarter Stitches are denoted by triangular shapes of color on the chart and on the color key. For One-Quarter Stitch (¼X), come up at 1 **(Fig. 5);** then split fabric thread to go down at 2. **Fig. 6** shows this technique when working over two fabric threads. When stitches 1 − 4 are worked in the same color **(Fig. 7),** the resulting stitch is called a Three-Quarter Stitch (¾X).

Fig. 5

Fig. 6

Fig. 7

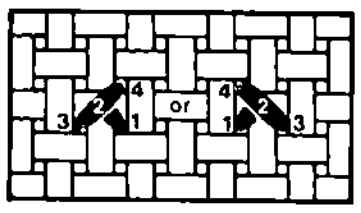

BACKSTITCH

For outline detail, Backstitch (shown on chart and on color key by black or colored straight lines) should be worked after the design has been completed **(Fig. 8).**

Fig. 8

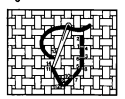

FRENCH KNOT

Bring needle up at 1. Wrap thread once around needle and insert needle at 2, holding end of thread with non-stitching fingers **(Fig. 9).** Tighten knot; then pull needle through fabric, holding thread until it must be released. For a larger knot, use more strands; wrap only once.

Fig. 9

EMBROIDERY STITCH DIAGRAMS

SATIN STITCH

Referring to **Fig. 1**, come up at odd numbers and go down at even numbers with the stitches touching but not overlapping.

Fig. 1

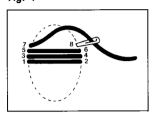

RUNNING STITCH

Referring to **Fig. 2**, make a series of straight stitches with stitch length equal to the space between stitches.

Fig. 2

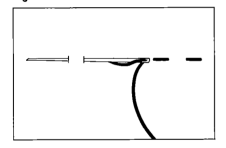

KNITTING

KNITTING

Hold the needle with the stitches in your left hand and the empty needle in your right hand. With the yarn in back of the needles, insert the right needle into the front of the stitch closest to the tip of the left needle from left to right. Bring the yarn beneath the right needle and between the needles from back to front (**Fig. 1**). Bring the right needle, with the loop of yarn, toward you and through the stitch (**Fig. 2**); slip the old stitch off the left needle.

Fig. 1

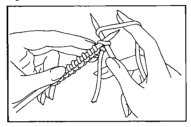

Fig. 2

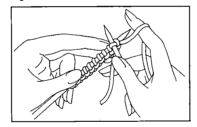

PURLING

Hold the needle with the stitches in your left hand and the empty needle in your right hand. With the yarn in front of the needles, insert the right needle into the front of the stitch from right to left. Bring the yarn between the needles from right to left and around the right needle (**Fig. 3**). Move the right needle, with the loop of yarn, through the stitch and away from you (**Fig. 4**); slip the old stitch off the left needle.

Fig. 3

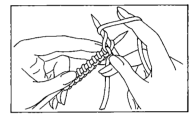

Fig. 4

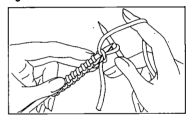

CROCHET

WORKING INTO THE CHAIN

When working into the beginning chain of a crochet project, insert hook **into the ridge** at back of each chain (**Fig. 1**).

Fig. 1

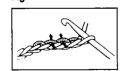

WORKING INTO ROWS

When working into rows of a crochet project, insert hook **under** the V of each stitch (**Fig. 2**). Be sure to pick up both loops.

Fig. 2

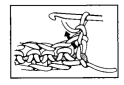

DOUBLE CROCHET

To begin a double crochet, wind yarn once over hook, bringing yarn from back over top of hook. Insert hook into ridge of chain or under V of stitch. Hook yarn and draw through. There should now be three loops on hook (**Fig. 3**). Hook yarn again and draw through the first two loops on hook (**Fig. 4**). Two loops should remain on hook. Hook yarn again and draw through remaining two loops (**Fig. 5**). One double crochet is now complete.

Fig. 3

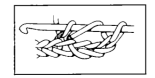

Fig. 4

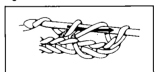

Fig. 5

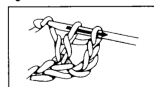

CREDITS

We want to extend a warm thank you to the generous people who allowed us to photograph our projects in their homes.

The Night Before Christmas: Tom and Christine McRae

An English Cottage Christmas: Jerry and Linda Wardlaw

A Sweet Noel: James and Joan Adams

A Splendid Holiday: Senator Douglas and Elizabeth Brandon

The Birds of Christmas: Larry and Becki Vassar

We especially thank the Department of Arkansas Heritage for allowing us to photograph our **Old Times Not Forgotten** collection in the Arkansas Territorial Restoration.

We're grateful to the businesses and private individuals who contributed some of the accessories shown in our photographs.

- The Antique Mall of North Little Rock, Arkansas: Selected pieces of stoneware featured in the **Old Times Not Forgotten** collection.
- Bob's Candies, Inc., of Albany, Georgia: Candy canes, page 10.
- Cock of the Walk Restaurant of Maumelle, Arkansas: Cast iron skillet, tin plate, and tin cup, page 39.
- Deanna Gann of Sterling, Illinois: Driftwood Santas, pages 140 and 142.
- Dorothy Fortner's Country Store of North Little Rock, Arkansas: Black top hat, page 114.
- Fifth Season of Little Rock, Arkansas: Tea set, page 25; Wedgwood "Ulander Ruby" dinnerware, flatware, and Dickens' Village cottages and figurines, pages 112, 114, and 116.
- Garrett's Stuff of North Little Rock, Arkansas: Spicebox, page 116.
- Geo. W. Millar & Co. of New York, New York: Brown perforated paper, page 24.
- Mrs. William Kenner: Decorated clock, pages 9 and 10.
- Linda Lindquist Baldwin of Joplin, Missouri: Hand-sculptured papier mâché Santas, page 132.
- Nelda Newby: Antique doll, page 128.
- Rowe Pottery Works of Cambridge, Wisconsin: Crocks, bears, and Santas, page 134; selected pieces of stoneware featured in the **Old Times Not Forgotten** collection.

- Mrs. Becky Thompson: Antique marble pouch, page 124; antique doll, page 130.
- Vaillancourt Folk Art of Sutton, Massachusetts: Santa, page 136.
- Mr. and Mrs. Jerome Yetmar: Antique clocks, pages 8, 9, and 10.

To Magna IV Engravers of Little Rock, Arkansas, we say thank you for the superb color reproduction and excellent pre-press preparation.

We want to especially thank photographers Ken West, Larry Pennington, and Mark Mathews of Peerless Photography, Little Rock, Arkansas, for their time, patience, and excellent work.

We extend a sincere thank you to all the people who assisted in making and testing the projects in this book: Andrea Ahlen, Jancy Baker, Jean Black, Jennie Black, Margaret Bredlow, Janet Boyeskie, Scarlett Burroughs, Lynn Conner, Trudi Drinkwater, Lori Dumont, Kathy Elrod, Nannette Easterling, Donna Hill, Sharon Holt, Sandra Honaker, Helen Hood, Karen Jackson, Edwina Jones, Jody Julian, Sherron Kilpatrick, Phyllis Lundy, Sherry Merritt, Judy Millard, Linda Pemberton, Dave Ann Pennington, Sandy Pique, Marcia Phillips, Mary Anna Phinney, Tracy Rhein, Catherine Spann, Ashlee Strickland, Susan Sullivan, and Veronica Vanaman.

Instructions for the following accessories are available in Leisure Arts publications:

- Afghan, pages 23 and 24: *Leisure Arts The Magazine*, July/August 1987.
- Wool Roving Sheep Ornaments, page 118: *The Spirit of Christmas, Book Two*.
- Prairie Doll, page 130: Leisure Arts Leaflet #1057, *Strings and Things*.
- Cross-stitched Santas, page 136: Leisure Arts Leaflet #743, *Christmas Gentlemen*.
- Cross-stitched Santa, page 140: Leisure Arts Leaflet #730, *And Miles to Go Before I Sleep*.

A TREASURY OF ANTIQUE SANTAS TO STITCH

Join us as we remember the many images of Santa Claus. Our new book, *Santa Remembered*, features 22 portraits of the old gentleman adapted for cross stitch from turn-of-the-century postcards. The 96-page treasury includes full-page reproductions of the postcards, exquisite photographs of the needlework, and easy-to-follow color charts.

To review *Santa Remembered* free in your home for 21 days, call the toll-free number on this page or write to Leisure Arts, P.O. Box 359218, Palm Coast, FL 32135-9218 . If you like our book, pay just $18.95 (in U.S. funds) plus $1.95 postage and handling. If not completely delighted, you may return the book within 21 days and owe nothing. If you keep it, we will automatically send you, on approval, future books in this annual series of beautiful Christmas designs. You are in no way obligated to buy any future annuals, and you may cancel at any time just by notifying us. Your book will arrive in October 1989 or 6-8 weeks after order is received. Limited time offer.

CALL TOLL FREE 1-800-423-1780 (in Florida, 1-800-858-0095)

SANTA REMEMBERED

YOURS FREE FOR 21 DAYS

ALSO AVAILABLE AT YOUR LOCAL NEEDLECRAFT SHOP